THE WORLD IS MY PARISH

Edited by
Timothy R. Eberhardt &
Sarah H. Lancaster

The World Is My Parish

Glad Tidings of Salvation in an Age of Crisis

Abingdon Press
Nashville

THE WORLD IS MY PARISH:
GLAD TIDINGS OF SALVATION IN AN AGE OF CRISIS

Library of Congress Control Number has been requested.

ISBN: 9781791041915

Chapters four and eight are also being published in the volume *Decolonizing Methodism*, edited by Upolu Vaai (Pasifika Communities University Press).

The cover for *The World Is My Parish* is a white background with black lettering for the title with an image of the globe and abstract sun and nature patterns in dark blues and yellows.

MANUFACTURED IN THE UNITED STATES OF AMERICA

CONTENTS

INTRODUCTION

Timothy Reinhold Eberhart

The theme for the Fifteenth Oxford Institute of Methodist Theological Studies—"The World Is My Parish: Glad Tidings of Salvation in an Age of Crisis"—was proposed by Institute Committee members long before Methodist-Wesleyan scholars and church leaders from around the world gathered at Keble College, Oxford, in August of 2024. The core premises, first shared with potential participants over five years in advance to spur reflection, research, and dialogue in preparation for the seven-day Institute, were: (1) that the current age is marked by a host of interconnected global crises; (2) that the Wesleyan-Methodist traditions contain distinctive theological convictions about the nature of sin and salvation, alongside practical resources related to the pursuit of holy living, which can help us better understand and respond to the crises of our time; and (3) that the aim of articulating a uniquely Wesleyan-Methodist public theology for today holds great promise for the broader church and world.[1]

Although those who decided upon the theme and articulated its premises could not have known what would unfold in the intervening years, the marks of the age—and signs of what was to come—have been apparent for some time: widening economic and social inequality through the ongoing consolidation of wealth and political influence among the ruling class; systemic racism and related forms of bigotry, oppression, and violence; the collapse of earth systems and broad yet unequal impact of climate destabilization political corruption, misogyny, discrimination against LGBTQ persons; and other manifestations of social violence, psychological distress, and civic instability. As many of the essays in this volume make clear, the reality is that the varied causes of the multiple crises of the present age have deep, centuries-long roots, and their disparate impacts have been unfolding for just as long, even as the burdens of those impacts have fallen disproportionately across particular communities and geographies over that time. In that sense, there was nothing especially prescient about a decision, made in spring 2019, to focus on the political, economic, ecological, cultural, and psychological crises of the present age. The crises of modernity have been unfolding—in one way or another, for some more than others—for generations.

What is perhaps new in recent years, however, is the globally *entwined* and increasingly *ubiquitous* nature of these crises and the rapid intensification of their mutually reinforcing eruptions. "Synchronous failure" is the name given by a team of social scientists, economists, and earth systems scientists to describe how multiple socio-ecological stressors now interact and amplify across interconnected systems at a global scale unprecedented in human history. In previous ages, the causes and impacts of any given crisis—economic, environmental, even civilizational—while potentially catastrophic for those impacted, generally unfolded within a relatively limited spatial and temporal scope. The causes and impacts of today's crises, however, interact at a global, planetary scale, such that multiple crises, of any type or scale, now spread and intensify across diverse economic, political, social, and environmental systems worldwide. A mortgage and banking crisis fueled by economic greed in one region, for example, erupts at the same time as climate-induced food production failures in another, alongside spiking oil prices, all of which contribute to civil wars and political unrest across multiple societies, and then to the mass migration of displaced populations, which triggers the re-emergence of overtly white supremacist and fascist political movements around the world. Inter-systemic crisis, poly-crisis, and meta-crisis are related technical terms, capturing the dominant reality of an age marked by ongoing climate-induced biodiversity loss, continual economic boom and bust cycles, mental health deterioration, misinformation and disinformation campaigns, emboldened bigotries, re-emergent authoritarian regimes, the collapse or dismantling of public infrastructure and services, the rapid spread of infectious diseases, and more. The broad pattern—experienced acutely and nearly universally these last few years—is one in which different stressors interact within a globally entwined system to generate system-wide failures, whereby multiple interconnected elements end up failing simultaneously and amplifying destructive impacts across increasingly expanded spatial and temporal scales.

The range of public theological, biblical, historical, moral, and pastoral questions confronting those of us stewarding the Wesleyan-Methodist traditions amidst the instability, uncertainty, and sufferings of the present are undoubtedly varied and complex. How does Scripture both resource and challenge us to interpret and respond to these crises? What precedents and resources exist in the early Wesleyan movement and later Methodist traditions to help guide and instruct us today? How might the doctrines of soteriology and holiness, including understandings and practices of atonement, inform broader public efforts to dismantle the intersecting realities of racism, sexism, and classism? What is the mission of the church and how are we to teach, proclaim, worship, and witness to the good news of Jesus Christ amidst the disruptions of a rapidly changing climate? These and related questions, which were the focus of deep engagement among participants in the Fifteenth Institute, will remain active and urgent for the present generation of Wesleyan-Methodist scholars, teachers, and leaders for some time to come—and likely for those of the coming generations to follow as well.

What became abundantly clear during our week of conferral is that the Wesleyan-Methodist traditions have much to offer the church and world amidst this precarious and opportune age. The reasons we might identify are many. In part, one can point to historical factors. Among the major protestant traditions, Wesleyan-Methodism's emergence in the eighteenth century, in the aftermath of and through the influence of the Lutheran, Reformed, Radical, and Anglican reformations, meant that the Wesleys and early Methodists gave birth to a movement of revival and reform at a time in which many of the dominant trends of our time were just ascending, even if in nascent form. The rise of capitalism in its industrial phase took place over the course of John Wesley's life, with its uniquely modern characteristics of capital accumulation, the factory system of manufacturing and the division of labor, massive investments in new forms of machinery and technology, intensified social and political disruptions caused by the displacement of peoples through ongoing land enclosures, and the spread of the capitalist mode of production worldwide. Relatedly, colonial expansion by European powers, driven by resource acquisition and profit maximization, continued to accelerate during the eighteenth century and expanded across the Americas, Africa, Asia, and Oceania, at the same time that anti-colonial people's movements of resistance and independence also accelerated across these same geographies. The uniquely modern conceptions of race and the attendant logics and practices of racism, including chattel slavery, were developed alongside capitalist, colonial expansion, with pseudo-scientific classifications of racial hierarchies used to justify conquest, theft, dehumanization, and exploitation. Proto-feminist figures and movements were ascendant, as were early criticisms of the impact of modern industry on human well-being, animal welfare, and the health of the natural world. Each of these historical trends deeply shaped the Wesleys and early Methodists, and although their attempts to understand and engage them are by no means beyond criticism—which was equally apparent at the Institute—the very existence of their attempted engagement provides our tradition with a range of theological, moral, and practical resources surprisingly still relevant and instructive for us today.

Relatedly, the distinctive theological emphases of the Wesleyan-Methodist tradition concerning the nature of sin and salvation remain both critically and constructively generative in an age in which the manifestations of sin and evil are so diverse and the need for salvation so comprehensive. The depth and breadth of Wesleyan soteriology is particularly significant. For Wesley, salvation is not reducible to any single sphere of existence, compartmentalized within a certain spiritual part of the human person, confined to some isolatable aspect of religious experience separate from the whole of life, delayed until the future, applicable only to individuals and not also institutions and society, or limited only to humans and not the whole of the created world. Instead, the "holistic" nature of Wesley's soteriology entails the affirmation that the breadth and depth of God's healing, forgiving, liberating, empowering, and transforming power for salvation extends to every sphere and aspect of human, creaturely, material, institutional, cultural, political, economic, ecological, and temporal existence. In an age of poly-crisis, marked by ongoing threats to life's flourishing within and across each of these spheres and more, the Wesleyan-Methodist tradition is robustly equipped to speak, practice, and offer the good news of God's saving power for all people and places in ways that are as comprehensive as the crises we face. Especially in a time marked by heightened levels of anxiety, despair, and ultimately nihilism, this particular theological charism of our tradition—the affective, spiritual, rational, and practical assurance that God is capable of bringing about not only new life but also a whole new creation in spite and in the face of sin, folly, wickedness, and death—may be one of the most important gifts we can offer the broader church and world today.

What the holistic soteriology of our tradition implies, moreover, is the need for ongoing, inter-systemic analyses of and inter-connected responses to the varied dynamics and forces undermining creation's flourishing today. In a time of inter-systemic crisis, it is not sufficient to attend as a tradition only to single-issue analyses, reductively focused on a simple root cause of or response to the many, entwined injustices, oppressions, and sufferings facing people and the planet today. Instead, what is needed is an approach that, in the Methodist-Wesleyan tradition, we might call *inter-connectionalism*, or a way of integrating intersectional analyses with connectional responses. Such an approach unites: (1) *multiple critical analyses* to understand the particular histories, legacies, and ongoing dynamics, for example, of capitalist exploitation, colonial violence, systemic racism, misogynistic and heterosexist oppressions, ableist exclusions, environmental degradations and injustices, and related forms of systemic harm that denigrate the inherent dignity and goodness of any person, living creature, or place; (2) *inter-systemic analyses* capable of clarifying how each form of systemic harm impacts, is influenced by, and amplifies the damaging consequences of the other forms and how such harms intersect in particular configurations within certain individuals, communities, and geographies; and (3) *inter-connected responses* that integrate a plurality of theoretical, theological, moral, practical, and organizational resources in order to effectively and holistically address the many entwined crises that are erupting and reverberating at a global scale. The history of Methodist-Wesleyan engagements over the last several hundred years across a wide swath of moral concerns and commitments, including the marshalling of resources in recent years around each of the systemic harms named above, makes the transformative potential of our tradition to engage in and model such *inter-connectional* approaches immense.

Finally, the Wesleyan-Methodist tradition continues to have much to offer the broader church and world today out of the wealth of its practical, organizational wisdoms and structures. On the one hand, at the local, communal level, we can point to the ongoing vitality of the early Methodist small group structures meant to foster social holiness via classes, bands, meetings, and more. As Frederick Herzog understood, drawing on this aspect of our tradition, the freeing of individuals and communities from the intersecting ties that bind us to multiple forms of violence today requires both right teaching or instruction (*didache*) and the kind of character formation that can only occur through supportive, accountable community (*koinonia*). "The 'solutions to such vast socioanthropological dilemmas,' as John Wesley rightly sensed," Herzog wrote, "can never come in sheer theory, but will come only, if at all, in bands and groups of people who *communally* seek to embody a new way of life." The promise—and in many cases material necessity—of such groups of mutual support, aid, and transformation in order to "spread scriptural holiness across the land" amidst the many sociopolitical, economic, and environmental challenges ahead cannot be overstated.

On the other hand, the global nature of today's inter-systemic crises requires globally informed perspectives and globally coordinated partnerships aligned in concert toward global, planetary redemption. Here, the importance of *didache* and *koinonia* are added to the *oikoumene* (the inhabited earth, the whole world). The global nature of the Methodist-Wesleyan traditions, with growing vitality in Africa, the Philippines, Latin America, Oceania, and beyond, is a crucial strength in this regard, with still untapped possibilities for broader collaborations, solidarities, and mutual transformations. Precisely because the global dynamics of exploitation, extraction, oppression, and theft central to modernity's escalating crises have disproportionately impacted the global South, the intellectual, spiritual, praxiological wisdoms gained from Wesleyan-Methodist leaders and communities across these regions about how to navigate the realities of poly-crisis in order to sustain life out of love for God and neighbor will become increasingly valuable to those in other regions now facing similar challenges.

These particular marks of the Methodist-Wesleyan traditions—historically emergent alongside many of modernity's dominant crises, theologically resourced with a holistic soteriology, ethically equipped for interconnectional analyses and responses, and praxiologically oriented toward both local formation and global collaboration—provide a rich starting point for the development of a distinctively Methodist-Wesleyan public theology for today. Each of these, and more, were creatively articulated and diversely embodied at the Fifteenth Institute, which was the most racially, ethnically, and geographically diverse institute yet.

Within the Institute working groups, organized by academic or professional disciplines, participants took up a wide range of present-day crises with unflinching honesty: ecological devastation and runaway climate change; Christian nationalism; racism and white supremacy; technological isolation; extreme social polarization; theological, ecclesial, and academic complicity in systems of domination; despair and anxiety about the future; emotional exhaustion; the fracturing of once-stable communities; the decline of civic institutions; and even the possibilities of civilizational collapse. In the face of these crises, many of the groups acknowledged how our tradition and its institutions, including the academic disciplines, have been complicit in the crises we face by undergirding the logics and practices of domination, calling us therefore to ongoing examination, confession, mourning, repentance, and repair. Others identified the importance of hearing and naming the particular histories, dynamics, and impacts of each crisis, looking for interconnections between them but avoiding attempts to rank them in hierarchies of perceived significance. Instead, across the groups, the principles and practices of humility, deep honesty, accountable truth-telling, vulnerability, the allowance of diverse perspectives, and patient listening were named as crucial to meaningful and constructive engagement in the spirit of genuine Methodist conferencing.

Despite the challenging and complex nature of the theme, a range of constructive proposals emerged from the working groups. These included the importance of centering the voices, perspectives, agencies, and practical wisdoms of those most burdened by today's inter-systemic crises; connecting the gifts of scholarship with the contextual needs of local churches and communities; fostering scriptural interpretations, theological teachings, and practical ministerial resources that provide "glad tidings of salvation" in ways that will be heard in particular social contexts; recognizing that any given crisis will be experienced and understood differently depending on one's social location, context, and interpretive frameworks; insisting that the Wesleyan message of salvation is for all, including for the renewal of creation; affirming the transformative potential of education across our Methodist institutions to bring about critical awareness amidst differences, global solidarities, and liberative transformation; and recognizing the power of hymnody, liturgy, prayer, preaching, and worship as means of comfort, discomfort, lament, healing, and transformation.

Finally, a range of questions were raised throughout the week, which warrant continued reflection and engagement. How might the work of the Institute better speak to and connect with local congregations? What is the role of our Methodist-Wesleyan institutions, including those of higher education, in this time of poly-crisis? When should we seek to redeem the particular language, symbols, and marks of our traditions, and when ought we to leave them behind? How are we to engage the realities of the world through transformative participation while maintaining prophetic distance? How do we move from analysis and conversation to embodied action, institutional change, and social transformation?

In addition to the diverse engagements that emerged from the working groups over the course of the Oxford Institute, daily plenary addresses explored the possibilities and challenges of Methodist-Wesleyan public theological contributions to the church and world in an age of crisis around a set of focused areas, including political economy, race/racism, and ecological degradation. Each of the chapters in this volume were given as lectures or panel presentations around these topics, while a few focused more broadly on the general theme.

In chapter 1, Tom Greggs explores the relationship between declining church membership in Western societies and rising levels of societal despair brought on by the cascading crises of the twenty-first century, including financial crashes, failed wars, extreme polarization, and nationalism. Rather than focusing on institutional preservation in "an economy of scarcity," he calls Methodists to center instead on Wesley's concept of "the one thing needful," which is the restoration of God's image in humans through sanctification understood as humanization. Viewing Methodism as a renewal movement within the church, analogous to the role of monastic movements within Catholicism, he calls for the reactivation of the church's prophetic vocation today, enabling critical distance outside of clerical hierarchies and institutional power structures to speak the truth with boldness. Relatedly, by attending to the church's primary mission of fostering ongoing sanctification, or deepening participation in Christ's perfect humanity, Methodists will be freed, he argues, to focus on the well-being of all, including especially the vulnerable and marginalized, as a proleptic realization of our eschatological hope.

In chapter 2, Blanches de Paula turns to John Wesley's "theology of affection" in response to the crises erupting throughout Latin America and the Caribbean, highlighting how practices of reconciliation, care for all creation, and community-centered spirituality nurture hope amidst the realities of environmental degradation, economic inequality, mental health deterioration, and political extremism. Each of these crises, she argues, represent failures of relationship and social solidarity. Wesley's fundamentally relational theology, in which love for God and neighbor are inseparable, centers the significance of affective changes among those being renewed in God's image, manifesting in compassion, patience, care for the marginalized, as well as social and political efforts to address systemic injustices. In doing so, Methodist communities embody the "good news of joy" through ministries of reconciliation, environmental stewardship, social unity, and pastoral care toward affective healing.

Richard A. Davis argues in chapter 3 that contemporary discussions of Methodist social ethics must grapple with the fundamental tension between neoliberal capitalist ideology and core Wesleyan theological commitments related to the nature of divine grace. He contends that neoliberal capitalism advances an ethics of desert that legitimates extreme wealth inequality by asserting that billionaires have earned their fortunes through merit while the impoverished deserve their condition. But for Wesley, he argues, salvation derives from grace rather than works, which means the wealthy possess no inherent right to hoard resources but ought to steward their resources by distributing them to those in need. Relatedly, the poor merit assistance simply through their humanity as bearers of God's image. Today, this means striving for the implementation of merit-based rather than desert-based frameworks for social assistance, Davis concludes, wherein society extends help grounded in human dignity and need rather than judgments about whether individuals have "earned" support, thereby reflecting the theological conviction that divine grace operates independently of human desert.

Joerg Rieger contends in chapter 4 that Methodist-Wesleyans today must reconceptualize the current epoch not as the "Anthropocene," as many have done, which diffusely blames all humanity for planetary crises, but as the "Capitalocene," where specific concentrations of wealth and power bear responsibility. The Anthropocene framework, he argues, problematically treats all human beings as equally culpable and thereby centers our responses around individual behavior. Identifying our age as the "Capitalocene" rightly names systemic exploitation of people and planet for elite profit as the core problem. He notes that John Wesley astutely analyzed the nascent capitalist structures emergent in his time, recognizing the dynamics of manufactured scarcity, critiquing the luxuries of the rich, and condemning the interconnected systems of the British mercantile subjugation of India and the slave trade. In beginning with a systemic rather than an individualistic analysis of today's crises, Rieger invites us to reframe the meaning of Wesleyan sanctification in ways that might transform exploitation relationships at their roots, pointing to emerging alternatives like worker cooperatives that democratize profit and decision-making.

In chapter 5, Tamara Lewis explores John Wesley's critique of Enlightenment racial constructs and his enduring relevance to contemporary anti-racism efforts. Wesley's position on slavery, she shows, underwent a significant transformation throughout his life, evolving from initial ambivalence toward vocal abolitionism. As she describes, Wesley recognized that the transatlantic slave trade operated through constructions of race that established a caste system based solely on physical characteristics. Wesley employed a range of critical models to challenge this framework, which included refuting claims of African inferiority, disseminating accurate accounts of sophisticated West and Central African civilizations, rejecting racist biblical interpretations through his theology of prevenient grace, defending natural rights as universal, and promoting racial inclusion within Methodist societies. Lewis concludes by naming the reality that Enlightenment assumptions about race continue to permeate modern consciousness, asking what will be required to realize their abolition.

Helmut Renders, in chapter 6, offers a comparable analysis of John Wesley's views in his pamphlet *Thoughts on Slavery*, examining both his anti-racist contributions and problematic reproduction of racist assumptions. Wesley's anti-racist models, he argues, include presenting positive narratives of West African societies, inverting European civilizational superiority, prioritizing neighbor-love passages over texts tolerating slavery, collaborating across religious boundaries, and recognizing Christianity's complicity with slavery. At the same time, Renders stresses the importance of identifying Wesley's many failures, including patronizing references to "poor Africans," the disqualification of African traditional religions as "idolatry," and paternalistic abolitionism that centers European rather than African voices. Renders concludes that contemporary Methodist-Wesleyan churches must engage contemporary hermeneutics rooted in the perspectives of those experiencing racism, acknowledge ongoing complicity within racist cultures, and embrace humility by recognizing that even well-intentioned anti-racist work can reproduce assumptions it seeks to dismantle.

In chapter 7, Dong Hyeon Jeong gives an account of realities facing international students in United States United Methodist theological institutions through a reparative justice lens. Drawing on his own experiences as an international student across various United Methodist institutions, Jeong examines how international student recruitment has roots in Cold War politics and is entangled with global whiteness that imposes hegemonic normality, as well as capitalist logics that commodify students as revenue sources. He argues that approaches to "hospitality" often mask hostility and that expectations of academic "rigor" often demand colonial performance of the "model minority." At the same time, he notes that while international students who seek Western institutional authority often risk repeating neo-colonial patterns upon returning to home geographies, our theological institutions nevertheless can provide safe havens for persecuted individuals and communities. Jeong ultimately insists that Methodism constitutes a living entity accountable for undoing present racism, advocating institutional approaches that center co-creation and sustainable co-flourishing.

Catherine Keller argues in chapter 8 that John Wesley's concepts of stewardship, salvation, and soul must be "recycled" and reinterpreted for contemporary Methodist environmental engagement rather than abandoned. Despite widespread ecotheological criticism that "stewardship" reinforces anthropocentric dominion and hierarchical separation from nature, she proposes reclaiming the term because Wesley's economically rooted usage directly addresses neoliberal capitalism driving climate change, radically distinguishing stewards from debtors by insisting nothing is "properly our own" and rejecting private property on principle. In addition, Wesley's soteriology includes nonhuman animals possessing souls who ultimately participate in salvation's "general deliverance," with a range of practical implications. Most radically, Wesley teaches we should "see the Creator in the glass of every creature" and warns that viewing anything "as separate from

God" constitutes "a kind of practical atheism," describing God's "intimate presence" as "in a true sense, the soul of the universe." This interconnected theological framework, she contends, provides depth for Methodist environmental engagement while offering bridges to diverse publics including young environmentalists, mystically inclined seekers, and "spiritual not religious" individuals seeking solidarity.

In chapter 9, Daniel Shin examines declining religious affiliation among American millennials and proposes reimagining church communities as "affective assemblages" capable of addressing personal, social, and planetary crises through embodied practices rather than doctrine-centered approaches. He argues that religious institutions function as "emotive institutions" where feelings are shaped communally through routines and rituals rather than solely through beliefs and thus critiques cognitive-linguistic approaches privileging texts and rational consciousness while eclipsing embodied experience. This framework suggests the promise of creating "bloom spaces" aligned with Wesleyan pietist spiritualities emphasizing small groups, experimental innovations, and experience-oriented sacramental practice. Local churches, he suggests, can function as affective assemblages where divine love circulates through polyphonic music, rituals, and storytelling. Rather than treating "nones" as evangelistic targets, therefore, churches might create spaces for mutual discovery in an "affectively suffused cosmos."

Finally, in chapter 10, Claudia Lombardo suggests that Methodist educational institutions should respond to digital transformation and contemporary economic challenges, arguing that education must offer hope and tools for building alternative futures rather than mere adaptation. She describes a world radically altered by technology characterized by constant connectivity dissolving temporal and spatial boundaries, cultural convergences transforming consumers into content producers, and digital capitalism commodifying immaterial aspects of life including human relationships. Digital culture creates new subjectivities where identity shifts from internalized self-reflection to performative self-presentation through social media, becoming "alter-directed" rather than "intro-directed." Simultaneously, workplace restructuring through automation and remote work produces multiple "expulsions," including individuals, communities, and companies systematically pushed from socioeconomic order by predatory policy and market forces. In this context, she proposes, Methodist institutions must reinvent themselves by providing language and tools to help people interpret and rewrite their world. Education in this way might function as inherently ethical and political practice to educate for transformation rather than adaptation, build alliances with change agents, practice Wesleyan spirituality through mercy and justice, and form leaders committed to peace, solidarity, and inclusion.

The need for ongoing, collaborative, and constructive discernment among Methodist-Wesleyan scholars, pastors, and church leaders about the unique contributions of our traditions to both local and global efforts for justice, reconciliation, and repair amidst the crises of our time will remain long after the publication of this volume. As new crises—and new opportunities—arise in the coming years from which to proclaim the glad tidings of salvation, the witness of the Fifteenth Oxford Institute of Methodist Theological Studies offers encouragement that these traditions are very much yet alive.

Notes to the Introduction

1. The Oxford Institute of Methodist Theological Studies, an affiliate of the World Methodist Council, has gathered scholars and church leaders in the Methodist-Wesleyan traditions, typically once every five years in Oxford, England, since 1958. The aim is "to foster and support disciplined theological study among professional scholars and scholarly ministers and laypersons within the Methodist and Wesleyan traditions around the globe, with a goal of undergirding and enriching the ministry of these traditions in their global settings." In addition to shared plenary sessions, worship, and meal gatherings, participants engage one another in diverse working groups through paper presentations and dialogue oriented around a chosen Institute theme. Although this volume only contains chapters developed from the plenary presentations at the Fifteenth Institute, many of the working group papers are available on the Oxford Institute of Methodist Theological studies website, http://oxford-institute.org/. Archives containing the themes, attendants, working groups, and papers of all prior fourteen Institutes can also be found on the website.

2. Homer-Dixon, T. B. Walker, R. Biggs, A.-S. Crépin, C. Folke, E. F. Lambin, G. D. Peterson, J. Rockström, M. Scheffer, W. Steffen, and M. Troell. 2015. "Syn-

chronous failure: the emerging causal architecture of global crisis," *Ecology and Society* 20(3): 6. http://dx.doi.org/10.5751/ES-07681-200306.

3. See Randy Maddox, "Reclaiming Holistic Salvation: A Continuing Wesleyan Agenda," in *Holy Imagination: Thinking About Social Holiness*, ed. Nathan Crawford, Jonathan Dodrill, and David Wilson (Lexington, KY: Emeth Press, 2015).

4. Frederick Herzog, "Full Communion Training," in *Theology from the Belly of the Whale: A Frederick Herzog Reader*, ed. Joerg Reiger (Harrisburg, PA: Trinity Press, 1999), 282–83.

[illegible] failures: the emerging causal architecture of global crisis," *Ecology and Society* 26(4) [illegible], http://dx.doi.org/10.5751/ES-0[illegible]-[illegible]0506.

3. See Randy Madden, "Reclaiming Holistic [illegible]: A Continuing [illegible]," in *[illegible]*, ed. Jonathan [illegible] and [illegible] (Chicago: [illegible], 2019).

4. [illegible] "Truth Commissions [illegible]," in *[illegible] of the [illegible]*, ed. [illegible] (Harrisburg, PA: [illegible] Press, 19[illegible]), [illegible]–83.

1. THE PROPHETIC VOCATION OF THE CHURCH

Speaking and Living the "One Thing Needful"

Tom Greggs

There is a wonderful sermon of John Wesley's entitled "The One Thing Needful." This is a sermon which takes seriously, in a different modality, the kinds of concerns about hierarchies of goods that we find considered in the likes of Augustine and Aquinas.[1] In the sermon, Wesley reflects on the story of Martha and Mary (Luke 10:38-42). Martha and Mary are both joined by Jesus, and while Martha busies herself, Mary sits and learns from Jesus. Annoyed with her sister, Martha asks Jesus to intervene and chastise her sister for not helping. To this, Jesus replies: "Martha, Martha, you are worried and distracted by many things; there is need of only one thing" (vv. 41-42). Wesley conducts a thought experiment to ask what someone who knew nothing about us would think is our "one thing needful" or the core of our lives if that person watched us all day. Clearly, the point he wants to make is that often our lives do not reflect the reality that they are supposed to be lived fully and completely for Jesus Christ in seeking the renewal of our broken and fallen humanity. Wesley writes:

> Could we suppose an intelligent being, entirely a stranger to the state of this world and its inhabitants, to take a view of their various enterprises and employments, and thence conjecture the end of their existence, he could surely conclude that these creatures were designed to be busied about many things. While he observed not only the infinite difference of the ends which different men were pursuing, but how vast a multitude of objects were successively pursued by almost every different person, he might fairly infer that for all these things were the sons [and daughters] of men [and women] placed upon the earth, even to gratify their several desires with sensual pleasure, or riches, or honour, or power.[2]

We need, asserts Wesley, to consider how we live our lives in relation to the ultimate good which we espouse in terms of *renewing our fallen nature*, and not busy ourselves with the many disparate things and their capacity to dissipate our energies. This does not mean that the one needful thing is expressed in a uniform way: there are many ways it can and should be expressed depending on our circumstances. This "one thing" is one "in which, 'tis true, many things are comprised."[3] But all these endeavours should point to the *restoration of the image of God in humanity.*

I am unsure that there could be a more relevant message to today's church in the world. At a time when we are consumed with division and falling numbers, with crumbling church buildings which seem to highlight the edifice complex with which all ecclesiasticals seem to live, when the discourse between liberal and conservative wings of our church seems only to involve throwing grenades at each other and binarize one another through cancelation, the call back to the one needful thing could not be more clarion or necessary.

For a denomination founded by someone who considered that all the world was his parish, the global situation of diminished hope makes this message even more pressing. I went to university here in the late 1990s, and have just had my twenty-fifth anniversary in a college just down the road. Thinking back to that time at university, at least in the Western World, the new millennium was anticipated with such hope. The Iron Curtain had fallen. The Cold War had ended. The Berlin Wall was down. Apartheid had ceased. The internet was in its nascence and offered such possibility; though all I could access was a very early version of the BBC, it still excited me a great deal. Democracy and a social (perhaps even moral) form of capitalism seemed to be the global consensus. Globalism seemed our future. Education levels were rising. Universities were opening up to people who could never have anticipated college education just a couple of decades before. Quality of life was on a clear upward trajectory which seemed never-ending. Such was the newly perceived global norm that Francis Fukuyama could assert *The End of History and the Last Man,* transforming political science and historical study in that book. The (perhaps naïve) sense was that the world had arrived at a shared late capitalist, democratic, global reality. Hope abounded—at least in the context of the West.

The new millennium itself has not fulfilled these anticipations. In fact, the opposite has been true. Indicatively:

- 9/11 presented the world with a new divisive, global reality;
- the financial crash of 2008 has led to a decline in living standards;
- the Afghan war ended in a return of the Taliban;
- the global context presents more of a challenge to advanced western, capitalist democracy than has been the case since the 1930s;
- the Covid-19 pandemic brought the world to a halt and showed the limits of medical advancements;
- globalism has given rise to a variety of protectionist nationalisms;
- global economies have been replaced by Glo-cal economies;
- life expectancy has not increased in several major Western Countries;
- South Africa's hopefulness of a rainbow nation has not been as fulfilled as we hoped;
- the internet has led to algorithmically controlled life that creates binarized divides;

- technology is at the point of AI surpassing human intelligence;
- so-called post-modern paradigms have led to fractures in culture as truth becomes a contested reality, especially around identity; and
- the environmental crisis has captured society with a frightening apocalypticism.

This situation has led to widespread despair. This despair has been captured in other academic discourses, perhaps most notably in Nobel Economics Laureate Angus Deaton and Anne Case's bestseller *Deaths of Despair and the Future of Capitalism*.[4] What has not been sufficiently captured has been that all the while hope declined, so too did religious adherence in the West, especially in relation to the mainline Christian denominations—and most especially Methodists. "Nones," those who do not identify themselves with any religion in surveys, are now the biggest category of people in the US while Western Europe is more secular still. In the UK, Methodists are, I believe, the only denomination losing membership at a rate faster than the Church of Scotland. This is a statistical fact which worries me greatly since I preach most weeks at either a Church of Scotland or a Methodist Church, perhaps the only person to do so, so I fear I am the linking cause. But what I worry about more is that in church life (nationally and internationally), sometimes it feels as though I am observing while the deckchairs are rearranged on the sinking *Titanic* as the fiddlers play on.

I want, therefore, in this paper to begin to sketch what it might mean to recover the prophetic vocation of the church in this context. Rather than the focus we so often have in church and denominational life on preservation and continuity in an economy of scarcity, let us recover the focus on transformation and change from an economy of divine abundance.

Wesley states:

> Our one great business is to rase out of our souls the likeness of our destroyer, and to be born again, to be formed anew after the likeness of our Creator. It is our one concern to shake off this servile yoke and to regain our

> native freedom; to throw off every chain, every passion and desire that does not suit an angelic nature. The one work we have to do is to return from the gates of death to perfect soundness; to have our diseases cured, our wounds healed, and our uncleanness done away.[5]

What fascinates me, here, is that for Wesley this was not merely spiritual; *for Wesley, there is no merely spiritual.* The spiritual became meaningful as it worked itself out in time and space, in a life which is holy *for a purpose.* After all, Wesley wrote a tract on medicine and against slavery. And, if anyone knows anything about Wesley outside of our churches and traditions, it is that he coined the term: "cleanliness is next to godliness." Freedom from chains, cured diseases, healed wounds and uncleanness removed are no mere rhetorical allusions of a preacher in Wesley's terms: the renewal of human nature is material as well as spiritual; to be otherwise would be to be dualist.

In resisting, or attempting to, the constant temptation to dualism which we have, I want to do four things:

1. Consider the tradition of prophetic calling in which I believe Methodism stands in a way which parallels monastic communities for the Roman Catholic church.
2. Consider the one thing needful in the life of the church and its priorities.
3. Consider the task of the sanctification as humanization.
4. Consider in conclusion and briefly what this might mean for political discourse and the church.

Each of these will of necessity have to be brief in the time we have allotted. I want to fly some kites and hope you will think along with me about some of these issues. My work tends to be focused on ecclesiology within systematic theology, so I exist at the crossroads of different disciplines and discourses; but, perhaps more significantly, it is difficult in this institute to forget I am also one of Mr. Wesley's preachers.

The Prophetic Vocation of the Church

The Methodist Church was born in a prophetic vision of how to change society for the better. As a renewal movement within the life of the church catholic, its impact is far beyond its own denominational and connexional walls. Not only is its spirituality felt throughout evangelical Christianity (though not always in ways Mr. Wesley would have approved), Methodism likely prevented revolution in Britain. It provided here denominational impetus for the ending of the global slave trade; it was foundational to the trade unions movement; it improved literacy; it established free children's education; it rescued people from addiction; and it is said that there is more of Methodism than of Marxism in the British Labour Party. The strangely warmed heart of Aldersgate Street did not rest on his pietistic laurels in its interior life but engaged with the transformation of souls and the transformation of society. The two could never be separated. Wesley understood the evangelistic calling to be a prophetic calling, and writes:

> So, the Great High Priest of our profession sent apostles and evangelists to proclaim glad tidings to all the world, and then pastors, preachers, and teachers to build up in the faith the congregations that should be found. But I do not find that ever the office of an evangelist was the same as that of a pastor, frequently called a bishop.[6]

For Wesley, there remains a truly prophetic calling; and this calling involves not only the preaching of a spiritual gospel of lowliness and holy desire and love of God but also of a material transformation in love of neighbor, doing good, and suffering persecution for Christ's sake (the *for Christ's sake* here being key).[7]

Of course, as Wesley realized, this prophetic identity of the church is something which we find in the very origins of Christianity—not least in relation to the life of Christ. Time does not allow a thoroughgoing discussion of this, but in succession from John the Baptist and in analogy with Moses (forty days in the wilderness compared to forty years, coming out of Egypt, etc.), Jesus is the Great Prophet—the one who is the personification of Isaiah 61:1-3 (NRSVue):

The spirit of the Lord God is upon me
    because the Lord has anointed me;
he has sent me to bring good news to the oppressed,
    to bind up the brokenhearted,
to proclaim liberty to the captives
    and release to the prisoners,
to proclaim the year of the Lord's favor
    and the day of vengeance of our God,
    to comfort all who mourn,
to provide for those who mourn in Zion—
    to give them a garland instead of ashes,
the oil of gladness instead of mourning,
    the mantle of praise instead of a faint spirit.

In the early church, this prophetic office seems to have continued, and Wesley claims in his sermon "Prophets and Priests," it was distinct as an order of ministry until the Constantinian-ization of the church where administration rolled the pastoral and the prophetic offices of the church together in the priesthood. According to Wesley, in the (and I quote) "evil hour" in which Constantine called himself a Christian, these offices of prophet and evangelist on one side and priest and pastor on the other became one. One should note that just for a High Church Anglican Tory to evoke the Constantinian fall thesis is radical and prophetic enough! And he speaks in his twelfth sermon on the Sermon on the Mount of the fact there are false prophets who administer the sacraments.[8] (On an aside, it is clear he sees his own appointing of Local Preachers, of whom I am one, as a recovery of the prophetic role of teacher).

But there is, of course, a long tradition of prophetic influence on the church after Constantine. It is perhaps best to think of monastic movements in this way in relation to the broader church, and of monasteries as in some sense a precursor to Methodism in terms of a prophetic vocation ordered to renewal. Wesley, after all, imagined Methodism as a church renewal movement, not the establishment of another ecclesial denomination with all its bureaucratic and technocratic power struggles. His was a dominantly lay movement, something we often forget also shaped the monastic religious communities. Once again in "Prophets and Priests," Wesley makes this clear, seeing the preachers he appointed as continuity of the prophetic office without the priestly. The monastic movements were thought of similarly. And it is perhaps of little surprise to us that redemptorist movements also began in the eighteenth century attempting to engage with the Roman Catholic Church in the same way that the Methodists were attempting to renew the Church of England; Wesley, by the way, thought the Church of Scotland was pretty good. . . . Perhaps it has lost its Wesleyan prophetic edge now as well.

But it must also surely not be lost on us academics that the precursors to the modern university were also the monasteries as places of radical learning and enquiry into the truth. From the sixth century onwards, there was a commitment to learning, the preservation and cultivation of knowledge, preserving (in a way which is perhaps shocking in context) both religious and "pagan" texts.[9] The life of the monastery often put it at odds with—sometimes even marginalized from—the clerical hierarchies of the church. They were in many ways places of vast social advancement in comparison to the communities within which they existed. Monasteries were, for example, places where the section of society who were denied access to education and clerical service could learn and serve: the place of women in the monastic movement was a challenging and prophetic statement to the church and society at large. Early Methodism's increased role for women who were able to preach and teach also presents us with some parallels here. The position monasteries fulfilled and their demarcated modalities of authority from the clerical power structures determined that abbots and abbesses (and their monks, friars, and nuns) exercised a different kind of authority to that of "secular" bishops and priests; and clashes and struggles over authority inevitably ensued.[10] I wonder if one might think of Bishop Butler and Wesley in a similar way, with not dissimilar dynamics playing out in the Church of England in the eighteenth century.

While monasteries were prophetic witnesses to the world (a theme which continues to be important for the church),[11] they were and are (perhaps more importantly) also a prophetic witness to the church as well. Prophets in the Hebrew Bible often spoke out against the priesthood—not because of a rejection of God and the cult but because of a desire to reform and make better the priesthood and the cult (see, for example, Malachi 1:6–2:9 and Hosea 4–7). Indeed, one of the oracles spoken against the priests in Hosea involves the lack of teaching the people are receiving from the priests: "My people are destroyed for lack of knowledge!" (Hos 4:6). Jesus's clearing of the temple and speaking against the temple belongs in this prophetic tradition, as does his very identity as an outsider to the priestly caste. From outside the priestly hierarchies, the prophet tells forth to those hierarchies, calling them back from their waywardness to the ways of God and God's ways with the world. Wesley's own ministry may well reflect that same kind of approach to the priestly caste of his own day; he is hardly glowing about his brother Anglican priests.

It is tempting for us when thinking of Wesley's position not to focus on his preaching to the ne'er-do-wells and in public but to consider what we might think of as a failing in not becoming a bishop and change the Church of England. Surely that is the kind of effect we would rather he had had? Uncomfortable with that prophetic origin, it seems so often that that is the way we behave. Whether it has been Jabez Bunting or contemporary discussions with the Church of England, have we not tried to find a way of finding our way inside to structures and acceptability—perhaps as those who have lost their prophetic charism and vocation? And, of course, Wesley's immense organizational power prepared fertile soil for the kinds of institutionalization we so often orient ourselves toward. As one senior Methodist colleague once said to me about Methodist faith and order: the problem is, it's all order and no faith! While the monastery and the prophet exist outside the usual orders, hierarchies, and clerical structures, that position often brings with it the potential awkwardness of being an outsider, and certainly in the UK we feel that acutely. As such, we can try to cover for it. As a non-Anglican, all kinds of doors are closed to us. The temptation to establishment is always there; and isn't that so often what happened in monastic communities as well—or at least the Reformation has us believe that. But there are also the great benefits of being free from clericalism or establishment and its dependence if only we recognize the particular charism we have in the life of the church—a charism to be a renewing and reforming prophetic movement.

For Local Preachers (trained and licensed preachers who do not have the pastoral charge of churches but work in the world for money), so important in British Methodism that still the majority of services will be taken by Preachers and not Presbyters, there is, for example, a financial, economic, and structural degree of independence afforded to speak, unencumbered by dependence upon the church for employment, salary, pension, and even housing. This position gives these preachers the privilege of great freedom. With that freedom comes the possibility—or better, responsibility—of speaking truth borne from deep experience, life, and thinking to churches and their structures. This is a role which has always been needed throughout the history of Israel and the church. It is the prophetic vocation.

Perspective and Focus: Reordering the Church's Priorities

But what might it mean for us as a prophetic church to be centered on Wesley's call to the "One Needful Thing" within the life of the church catholic? What might this prophetic calling look like for us in terms of our theology and church? What is the theological account of this vocation which we might offer? Now, here, we should realise that there is a complexity. There is, of course, an innate tension in speaking about living in a tradition of the prophetic. Isn't the prophetic anti-traditional and de-institutionalized? Isn't it sporadic? Isn't it momentary and forward-looking? Well, perhaps.

But I would want to argue that the prophetic vocation of the church lies first and foremost in an encounter with God which involves listening. This vocation is grounded in the deep calling to listen. The prophets, after all, did not speak in their own authority but only as they heard the voice of God. Clearly, we need to listen in our context differently from those who first received the lively oracles of God. But listening is the first condition of the prophetic vocation: after all, a theologian who does not and has not studied has nothing at hand with which to teach. For Christians committed to the life of the church, this listening comes in searching Scripture and tradition using the critical apparatus of reason (and the reflections that exist on reason which we might call philosophy), all in the context of the lived complexities of life which we experience. These interact in dynamic ways. And for us as Methodists, the distinctive emphasis we have particularly is that the faith by which we believe is also a point of data for the faith that we believe. We need to listen to experiences as well.

But key to the interaction between the data points of our theology is that there is always a constant dynamic of listening and then speaking which is ongoing in a manner which resembles a spiral—learning and speaking and learning some more and speaking differently. In this, there will no doubt be a desire to be true to the apostolic traditions of Christianity without believing these to be static monoliths. The living Word of God is always and continually heard and received before it is proclaimed. Repeated and faithful prayerful attentiveness to the illumined reception of the Word of God through Scripture, tradition, and reason in the contexts of contemporary life is the basis for any teaching office and the proclamation of the Gospel that flows from it. Spirituality and prayerfulness are the foundations for teaching within which critical exercise of intellectual faculties and hard and focused work and research must take place.

Hearing and listening involve attentive listening to the voices of the past as well as the church in the present. But that listening might also involve hearing unexpected figures from outside the usual walls that we build around the church. Christians have always been influenced by wise cultural thinkers outside the more usual canon of doctors of the church. Where would Christianity be without Plato or Aristotle? And the significance in the modern era of figures like Feuerbach and Nietzsche should never be underestimated.[12] But, if we are to speak prophetically and perhaps outside the parameters of the church's usual power structures, there is a responsibility to know what that church is and what reparative resources might be available to it from its tradition and from life at large to bring it back to a focus on God and God's ways with the world.

But what of the prophetic component of this? Well, this is, after all, what the prophets did: they knew the promises of God and knew the contemporary condition of the covenant people of God. To think in a more directly theological register, it is worth noting that at the start of the most significant events in the history of Israel (the flight from Egypt and the giving of the Law), God reveals Godself in new and exciting ways both through the burning bush and through the events of liberation which God superintends. In this event, God reminds Moses of the past activity, faithfulness, and teaching of God: "I am the God of your father, the God of Abraham, the God of Isaac, and the God of Jacob" (Exod 3:6 NRSVue). We, of course, would wish to add—and of Sarah, Rebbekah, and Rachel! The conformity to the tradition—even as it is about to change and is about to reveal a new name and new events—is vital. There is something there in that tradition which is centered and centering: we grow where we are planted; we speak to those we are placed with. This involves listening. But this listening is a particular kind of listening for which the university setting might be particularly well placed. Rowan Williams makes this point well:

> The loyal and uncritical repetition of formulae is seen to be inadequate as a means of securing continuity at anything more than a formal level; Scripture and tradition require to be read in a way that brings out their strangeness, their non-obvious and non-contemporary qualities, in order that they may be read both freshly and truthfully from one generation to another. They need to be made more *difficult* before we can actually grasp their simplicities. Otherwise, we read with eyes not our own and think them through with minds not our own; the 'deposit of faith' does not really come into contact with *ourselves*.[13]

These kinds of free engagements with the heritage and authority of the church are difficult. How many preachers and thinkers have been removed from their pulpits for going against the received "wisdom" of repeated theological certainties and claims? But reflecting on the church's past, there is a need to engage in a *"ressourcement*, rather than simple innovation or simple repetition."[14] This is a prophetic reception of tradition which sees tradition as alive and living to be *received*—not a monolith to be accepted or else fracked.

However, this critical self-reflection does not only involve the past. We need also to think with a degree of critical distance from the contexts and realities, however fast they are changing and however demanding this might be, in the here and now. To follow the same biblical line of thinking, Exodus 3:12 has God reassure Moses of God's *presence with* him and the people: "I will be with you," says God. Crucial to the monumental event of the freeing of the Hebrews from slavery is the presence of the living God with them. In this, God leads the people and reminds them of God's presence through the pillars of cloud and fire (Exod 13). The reality of the God who is with us is something we need to be reminded of time and time again. Indeed, the return to God is, for our age and generation, the one needful thing above all. At a time when there has been considerable diminishment in the West of the church's power, authority, and influence, there has been a temptation to look to means to reset that trend. Although it is now rather an old account, there remains much worth in the sensitive description of this process by David Martin. He describes this as "the collapsing of a social frame around which the vines of faith have traditionally been twisted."[15] According to Martin, the secular process is fourfold (but not unified or singular): first, the decreased power, wealth, influence, range of control, and prestige of ecclesiastical institutions; second, the decreased frequency, number, intensity, and perceived efficacy of religious rituals, customs, and practices; third, a movement in the intellectual sphere toward the rationalistic, empirical, and sceptical; and fourth, a shift in attitude toward the reverential, charismatic, and noumenal.[16] In response to these realities (and the realities of people being "spiritual" but not "religious" or believing but not belonging),[17] the responses of churches and their leaders have involved a diffusion of energies into all kinds of different endeavors. Michael Jinkins has helpfully described this dissipation of activities and energies as "the hyperactivity of panic." He goes on to unpack this thus: "This manifests itself in clutching for any and every programmatic solution and structural reorganization in the desperate hope that survival is just another project or organizational chart away."[18] In a time of monumental change for the church, made more pronounced by the Covid-19 pandemic, the temptation to dissipate energies and to engage in ecclesiological naturalism or atheism is tempting. However, we need calmly to remember the aliveness of the living God who is with the church at all times, accompanying it through all that is happening in the world.

This return to God will mean a reassessment of the values we place on different enterprises. There is a need for the church to consider its hierarchy of goods: to consider its one thing needful. In the current climate, the dissipation of energy leads ministers to focus on everything from being a school governor to creating five-year management plans. There are even MBA degrees focused on management and leadership in church contexts.[19] Outdated buildings and dwindling congregations (meaning dwindling finances and human resources) have meant that church ministry is often focused on fire-fighting and responsive engagement with "pressing" matters. Core issues have become secondary, and secondary issues have become core.[20] But without the spiritual food with which to feed congregations and the world, without a sense of the God who is with us, without sitting with and dwelling with Christ (to return to the Martha imagery), the church will have nothing to offer. Strategies and forms are meaningless without content. Refocusing on the life of God who is present to God's church—discovering more about God and God's ways—is the task of the church. To return again to the image of God in the Exodus: the church needs to focus on the direction and presence of God (in the pillars of cloud and fire) and not wander aimlessly, looking for our own direction. This one thing needful needs to call us back prophetically to who we are called to be.

Indeed, the image of the pillars of cloud and fire are also helpful ones to consider the prophetic task not just of telling forth but of foretelling or at least seeing ahead and anticipating—the role of guiding the church into its future: God is the God who is always ahead of us, leading us, in front of us, resting with us for a while and leading us onward. Most of what I have thus far said concerns the prophet in terms of a critical turn in the present. But as well as there being a past sense to the revelation of God (Exod 3:6) and a present sense to the revelation of God (3:13), the name God offers Godself indicates something of the ongoing and future revelation of God. This "futurity" of God is something which the church must never forget. When God reveals God's name, there are two aspects to the name which are important. The first is the aspect of the name that points to God's constancy and transcendence. This is felt in most of our translations that follow the Septuagint's translation of the Hebrew to *ego eimi ho ōn* (I am the being), which is rendered in the Latin of the Vulgate *ego sum qui sum* (I am who I am). The Hebrew, however, does not just point to this transcendent, ahistorical nature of God. There is also something more dynamic captured by the name—more historical, more active. The Hebrew, *eyeher asher eyeher*, can also mean "I will be who I will be"; "I will cause to be what I cause to be"; as well as "I am who I am"; and any combination, perhaps, thereof.[21] What is key to take from this is that there is a future and a causative element to the nature of God; indeed, we see that in the history which is about to take place, as God does something monumental, history shaping, and new in the book of Exodus. These two aspects of the divine life are contained within the divine eternality of God which Boethius describes as *interminabilis vitae tota simul et perfecta possessio* ("the simultaneous and complete [or perfect] possession of infinite [or unending] life").[22] Time is a passing and changing form of eternity—the eternity which is already perfect in the creature's future. As Alpha and Omega, God is already perfectly in God's post-temporal eternity who God is perfectly in God's co-temporal eternity.[23] It is the creature who moves toward God's future.

Our prophetic calling as the church involves in the present discerning the direction in which God's future is leading. It is worth considering where the church would be were it to have ignored the role of discerning the reception of the deposit of faith in a particular generation—to have failed to seek the gracious illumination of God's Spirit in receiving God's Word. Perhaps we would be burning heretics, churching women, or crusading against those who are members of other religions? What will be the issues that people in hundreds of years' time look back upon that seem barbaric appropriations of the Gospel that we have engaged in and perpetuated? Tradition needs to become a living ecology rather than immutable stone tablets. As Macquarrie argues, "Tradition . . . can become dead and mechanical, so that all growth and healthy development are inhibited." Our job is to interpret tradition and "interpretation need to be done over and over again."[24] That is the prophetic point about the past: God is constant and constantly ahead of us calling us back to God's future.

Sanctification as Humanization

It might seem now that we have left Methodism and Wesley long behind. But I want in this penultimate section to say something brief about themes I've written much about—sanctification and humanization and their social dynamics. Here, I must be even more telegrammatic than I have even been thus far; but I have spilt a lot of ink already on these themes.

Wesley's interest in the Greek fathers is of course a theme much discussed: his theology is in some ways an eighteenth-century repristination (almost resoucement!) in Protestantism of theosis. We are holy sanctified and therefore "changed from glory into glory," sharing in God's heavenly life. But I wonder in our age of dehumanization whether the traditional language of theosis is helpful. Furthermore, when we consider the dependence of this idea on the demarcations of the processions and missions, it is in the mission of the eternal Son's sharing of God's life with us as Jesus Christ that we are conjoined in theosis. There is no ontological change in us; we simply participate in God's eternal life. I wonder whether this is a place where our interpretation needs to be done over and over again.

In my own work, I have suggested that it might be better for us to take the line of saying that sanctification is a sharing in the true humanity of Christ—a humanity we do not yet possess in our fallen and broken nature. Now, I could give a series of lectures on this. But let me say this briefly: the fall myth rests on the idea of humans desiring to be like God (isn't that what the serpent says?); to save us from that, God becomes human to reveal to us the humanity God always desired for us—a humanity deeply, intimately resting on love of God and love of others in creation. In other words, we want to be god; God wants us to be human and becomes human for that purpose. While I know very precise and thoughtful accounts of theosis capture this reality of being fully dependent on God, I wonder if today humanization is a better term than theosis. While everyone knows the misquoted "the glory of God is the human fully alive" from Irenaeus, his point rather is: *Gloria enim Dei vivens homo*—God's glory is a living person, and in context for Irenaeus, this person is clearly Jesus Christ. It is not that we become "god" but that God becomes human.

What I think this means is that sanctification is first and foremost a story of the humanity of Jesus, and our relationship to that humanity as it humanizes us. It is a story of who Jesus is for and what Jesus does for all humanity.[25] This all is important—not just for those of us who can still recite the four alls! In Christ are the all who participate in is humanity *de iure* through sharing in his humanity and the changed situation for humans it brings. And in Christ are those many who participate de facto in his humanity through the active life of the sanctified. It is only, therefore, as part of that all and many that each of us (as individuals or communities) shares in Christ's humanity, that each of us is sanctified in Christ. Crucially, here, sanctification in Christ is a reminder of the grace which is given to us freely, and the givenness of the other helps remind us of this. As in the story of the ungrateful servant, the other (symbolized in the debtor) who owes ten denarii should become the locus in which we are able to be reminded of the unmerited nature of grace and also become the object for the sharing of the grace in which we have participated. The given other should in our relationship to them help us to take the sanctified form of the life of grace in the likeness of the God who God's humanity in Jesus Christ has been perfectly gracious to us. Karl Barth points powerfully to the role of the other in sanctification in Christ in the horizontal sphere of existence:

> The knowledge of the man Jesus includes the knowledge and enclosure of our own and every other human existence in His. There are, therefore, no saints (and saints are those who know the man Jesus) to whose participation in the sanctity of this One there does not also belong a knowledge of the all-embracing character of His existence in its comprehension not only of themselves but also of the children of the world.[26]

To know oneself sanctified in the humanity of Christ is to know the "all-embracing" character with its effects not only on the individual, or only on the church, but also on the world. This emphasis on the unique and singular sanctification of Christ is also an emphasis simultaneously on the universality of sanctification. The foundation in Christ of all humanity is the basis for the one who knows her sanctification in Christ, and serves as means of recalling the undeserved and unmerited gracious and merciful nature of sanctification in Christ. As such, it is a means of aiding the Christian to take the form of the One sanctified in his life *for the other in which his true sanctity rests.* Christ is, after all, the One who is so sanctified that he can eat with prostitutes and tax-collectors and sinners: His sanctification is one which is what I would term in my writings abductive and socio-poesitic; his is the sanctification of the priest *on behalf of God and the human other.* As a result of this work of Christ, just as the human does not need to justify themself so they also does not need to sanctify themself. Their sanctification consists in their participation in Christ's sanctification—in his sanctification *for them.*[27]

But any account of this sanctification in Christ requires an account as well of the active form of this sanctification in which the believer grows in space-time in sanctified grace (albeit not in any progressivist sense, necessarily). The opening of 1 Corinthians holds both of these aspects together—the singular and objective with the temporal and subjective:

> To the church of God that is in Corinth, to those who are sanctified in Christ Jesus, called to be saints, together with all those who in every place call on the name of our Lord Jesus Christ, both their Lord and ours:
>
> Grace to you and peace from God our Father and the Lord Jesus Christ.
>
> I give thanks to my God always for you because of the grace of God that has been given you in Christ Jesus, for in every way you have been enriched in him, in speech and knowledge of every kind—just as the testimony of Christ has been strengthened among you—so that you are not lacking in any gift as you wait for the revealing of our Lord Jesus Christ. He will also strengthen you to the end, so that you may be blameless on the day of our Lord Jesus Christ. God is faithful, by whom you were called into the partnership of his Son, Jesus Christ our Lord. (1 Cor 1:2-9 NRSVue)

Paul, here, addresses the church in Corinth (the saints) who are sanctified (vv. 2-3). This condition is an objective reality: they are sanctified in that the grace of God has been given to them (v. 4). But along these unconditional and *de iure* statements follows a run of statements by Paul which imply growth, enrichment, and strengthening in order that the believer might be "blameless on the day of our Lord Jesus Christ" (v. 8). This growth rests in the faithfulness of God (v. 9), but that faithfulness has a terminus in the created spatio-temporal reality in which inevitably the reaching of sanctification involves active participation in grace and the growth that comes with it.[28] In other words, in the context of the anticipation of the *eschaton*, there is in creation the outworking of the singular and unique event of the life, death, and resurrection of Jesus Christ in the lives of the believers as they participate actively in that sanctified life as his sanctified body: "Sanctification takes place as God fashions a people as holy people."[29]

The means of accounting for this growth, the "reaching" of this sanctification to the sphere of the spatio-temporal for those who participate actively within Christ's humanity is through an account of the work of the Holy Spirit. This sanctification in which all humans participate in Christ *de iure* is also that which in the believer by an event of the act of the Holy Spirit of God may participate *de facto*: they, too, may be actively sanctified and may live within the sanctification of Jesus Christ as a genuine participant who shares actively in the spatio-temporal reality of creaturely life in all its quotidian givenness in God's sanctifying grace through participating actively in Christ's humanity. The Spirit breathes breath into the human: to be spirit-filled is to be fully human.

Crucially, this same Spirit is, according to Jesus in John's Gospel, the One who leads us into all truth—the very futurity of God as I pointed to in the previous section. But the effect of this is not only eschatological but is known and felt and realized proleptically and in anticipation in the present in the difference in the believer from what she "used to be" (1 Cor 6:11a). This work in the present, in the time of the church, is a work of the Spirit: by an event of the act of the Spirit, the believer is freed to participate *actively* in Christ, to move within God's gracious movement.

There is an ongoing history in space-time to the unique and singular act of Christ's sanctifying work: this history is that of the event of the act of God's Spirit in space-time in which as the *Holy* Spirit, in His constancy and faithfulness, the Spirit constitutes us as ever more fully human in time as those who share actively and intensely in the same Spirit who rested perfectly and fully on the human Jesus in his perfect holiness.

But where does this all relate to the one thing needful? And what are the global political realities to this in which we consider the whole world our parish? I had wanted to say something political and about church and politics. . . .

Conclusion: One Thing Needful for Church and Politics

The key point I want to bring everything back to on my long theological detour is this: for Wesley, the one thing needful is the restoration of the image of God in humanity. This is the focus of all our endeavours and activities. Sanctification as humanization might be a way of trying to capture that one needful thing. But rather than any idea that the restoration is one which is retroactive, the argument I have made about the nature of God as the one who is eternally ahead of us—who will be who God will be—determines that that restoration is to the humanity which God desires us all *to grow into*. In other words, we are not yet fully human because we have not yet grown into the full humanity which lies ahead of us as we grow into the future of the God whose image is restored to us.[30] Our humanity can be enhanced.

The potential universality of this claim is something we need to emphasize in a world of binarized differences at war with itself. Of course, that very universality includes and arises from all particularities: humanity does not exist *in abstracto* but only in relation to the particular and unique humans which make up our species. (On an aside, the specificity of the spatio-temporality of the particular person of Jesus is very important here). In seeking to restore the image of God in creation, we need to focus on the ongoing task of listening and learning the deposit of faith which will always be before us in the God who is the unending end of all things.[31] Such an inbreaking from the future is one which also captures the fact of the prophetic calling. This prophetic calling is one which involves both a Yahwistic *ethic* (as with the Deuteronomist) and a Yahwistic *eschatology* (which is expressed in apocalyptic materials) all at once. These two, indeed, are conjoined in our witness to the world. In the words of Brueggemann:

> "widow, orphan, alien" are ciphers for those most vulnerable and powerless and marginated in a patriarchal society, who are without legal recourse or economic leverage. . . . Their destiny is linked to the destiny of the whole community. Thus, the Mosaic ethic, as practiced by prophetic mediation, is broadly based covenantal-communitarianism, in which justice and righteousness assure that individual good is a subset of communal well-being.[32]

Focusing on the futurity of God's life into which we are being led is a way of unpacking what is meant by speaking about the work of the Spirit as Jesus does in John.

> I still have many things to say to you, but you cannot bear them now. When the Spirit of truth comes, he will guide you into all the truth, for he will not speak on his own but will speak whatever he hears, and he will declare to you the things that are to come. (John 16:12-13 NRSVue)

The work of Christ is one which involves teachings which are ahead of us and into which the Spirit will lead us. They are teachings which the Spirit who works in the contingencies of the present leads us into—truths which are the eternal and unchangeable truths of God into which we are being led. These truths are not limited to the truths of faith, but since faith is the means by which Christians understand all things in the world, and since the Spirit is present to all of creation, these truths are unlimited. Christians are not called to repeat their traditions *ad nauseam* but to engage in truth-seeking in all the world. Daniel Hardy helpfully argues that the church's mission is one which involves seeking to understand all of creation in relation to the identity of God:

> Against their "inversion" as forms of purely human consciousness and action, . . . culture, pragmatics and theology must struggle to uncover their transcendent origin, sustenance and goal. The possibility which they have for the realization of the "transcendental notes" of unity, truth, goodness and beauty . . . must be uncovered.
>
> Such a struggle will raise basic issues of faith in their most acute form. These are the issues of the very *identity of God* and the *character of God's life in the world*, and how they are constitutive for the *world and human life*. Such issues go deeply into the nature and action of God—into the features of the life of God, and how this life is so rich and abundant as to be the source, sustenance and completion of the world—its nature, history, societies, human rationality and behaviour, expressions of meaning, and religions—and in turn how they are raised to their full stature by being re-orientated to the worthship of God [since all worth is God's]. These are the dimensions of the task in which religious education, religious institutions and university theology must combine their efforts today.[33]

To be guided into all truth is to understand all of creation in relation to God and God's ways. As the Cappadocian Fathers have told us, this journey into the truth of God is one which is eternal to correspond to the unending depths of God.

Such a vision is innately political. It values the world and all human life in its distinct realities; it seeks to *listen* and only to speak from that listening. It believes that the best is ahead of us, and we are likely to find it precisely in the places where boundaries are crossed, where humanity is upheld and enhanced. And it has a condition by which to understand failing not as an end in itself but in light of a wider hope of restoration: after all, isn't that the reality and message of most prophets?

As a church we have become captive to culture—reflecting the pessimism, dismay, binarized dehumanization, cancellation, and technocratic bureaucracy of the society within which we live. What would it mean for us to take seriously "the one thing needful"? Might in that we find "the more excellent way" in the business of our lives—ecclesial and secular? That sermon of Wesley is where I would turn next to work out the consequences of this paper.

But perhaps we might be wise to end as Wesley did himself, pointing out in this overwhelming challenge: "Best of all, God is with us!" Or, as

I might argue, the God who is eternally ahead of us, drawing us and all creation into God's future: Best of all, this God, the God who is supremely alive, this God is with us, restoring God's image to us and all creation.

Notes to Chapter 1

1. Augustine, "Of the Morals of the Catholic Church," in *Augustine: The Writings Against the Manichaeans and Against the Donatists*, ed. Philip Schaff (T&T Clark), 14, accessed 18 September 2024, https://ccel.org/ccel/schaff/npnf104/npnf104.i.html.

2. The original language in Wesley has been preserved with sad acknowledgment of its gender exclusivity. The words used by John Wesley have been reproduced exactly as they appear in *The Bicentennial Edition of the Works of John Wesley*. John Wesley Sermon 146, §preface 1, in "The One Thing Needful" in Sermons IV, ed. Albert C. Outler, *The Bicentennial Edition of the Works of John Wesley* (hereafter *Works*), vol. 4 (Nashville: Abingdon Press, 1987), 4:352.

3. Wesley, Sermon 146, "The One Thing Needful," §I.1 in *Works* 4:353.

4. Anne Case and Angus Deaton, *Deaths of Despair and the Future of Capitalism* (Princeton University Press, 2020).

5. Wesley, Sermon 146, "The One Thing Needful" §I.5, in *Works* 4:355.

6. Wesley, Sermon 121, 4, 77. "Prophets and Priests" §7 in *Works* 4:77.

7. Wesley, Sermon 32, "Upon Our Lord's Sermon on the Mount, Discourse the Twelfth" §I.7 in *Works* 1:678.

8. Wesley, Sermon 32, "Upon Our Lord's Sermon on the Mount" §II.8 in *Works* 1:682–83. Cf. For Wesley the greatest wound Christianity received was struck in the fourth century by Constantine the Great, when he called himself a Christian, and poured in a flood of riches, honours, and power upon the Christians; more especially on the clergy. Then, not the golden but the iron age of the church commenced. See Sermon 61, "The Mystery of Iniquity" §27 in *Works* 2:462–63.

9. Lester K. Little, "Monasticism and Western Society: From Marginality to the Establishment and Back," *Memoirs of the American Academy in Rome* 47 (2002): 90, https://doi.org/10.2307/4238793.

10. See for example Barbara H. Rosenwein, Thomas Head, and Sharon Farmer, 'Monks and Their Enemies: A Comparative Approach', *Speculum* 66, no. 4 (1991): 764–96, https://doi.org/10.2307/2864632.

11. John Paul II, "Vita Consecrata," 25 March 1996, https://www.vatican.va/content/john-paul-ii/en/apost_exhortations/documents/hf_jp-ii_exh_25031996_vita-consecrata.html.

12. For example, in Karl Barth's introductory essay to the English translation of Feuerbach's *The Essence of Christianity*, Barth states that "the attitude of the anti-theologian Feuerbach was more theological than that of many theologians," and that "the content of his anti-theology may have such a significant bearing on the problematic features of modern theology . . . that decisive theological material might escape us if we refused to hear him." See Ludwig Feuerbach, *The Essence of Christianity*, trans. George Eliot (Harper & Row, 1957), xxx and x respectively.

13. Rowan Williams, *Arius: Heresy and Tradition* (SCM Press, 2001), 236.

14. Rowan Williams, *Why Study the Past? The Quest for the Historical Church* (William B Eerdmans Publishing Co, 2018), 96–97.

15. Williams, *Why Study the Past?*, 239.

16. David Martin, *The Religious and the Secular: Studies in Secularization* (Routledge & Kegan Paul, 1969), 48–54.

17. Grace Davie, *The Sociology of Religion: A Critical Agenda* (SAGE Publications Ltd, 2012).

18. Michael Jinkins, *The Church Faces Death: Ecclesiology in a Post-Modern Context* (Oxford University Press, 1999), 9.

19. https://gtfeducation.org/home/masters-programs/master-of-business-administration-in-pastoral-planning-and-church-management-m-b-a/. There is also a mini-MBA for Deans and Bishops of the Church of England: https://www.churchofengland.org/sites/default/files/2017-12/gs_2026_-_nurturing_and_discerning_senior_leaders.pdf.

20. Around a decade ago, I was contacted by a Methodist district in the north of England and asked if I would lead a Bible study on the Greek text of Mark's Gospel for the district. Since I am not a New Testament scholar (though I have taught Greek previously) and I was already preaching most weeks (and more) on top of my job at the university, I declined, asking if one of the ministers in the district might be able to offer this instead. The response I received shocked me: I was told that they had already asked the ministers in the district, and tried to identify one to do so, but none felt qualified to deal with a gospel in Greek. I was appalled by this, and so offered to teach Koine Greek to them instead, so they could offer it to the people. I was told that this was not a priority for those in ministry—not a priority for those who preached week in and week out on these texts. The concern I had was not about Greek (I'm Protestant enough to believe God speaks through the vernacular!); but is instead about priorities. There are all kinds of things that those who spend their full time working for the church do and have time to do.

21. See, for example, H. C. Brichto, *The Names of God* (Oxford University Press, 1998), 24; and B. W. Anderson, *The Living World of the Old Testament* 4th Edition (Longman, 1993), 62–63.

22. Boethius, de Consolatione Philosophiae, prose VI. This eternity is one which includes the perfect possession of time all at once (with its order and movement) but without the passing mutability of created time:

> What we should rightly call eternal is that which grasps and possesses wholly and simultaneously the fullness of unending life, which lacks naught of the future, and has lost naught of the fleeting past; and as such an existence must be ever present in itself to control and aid itself, and also must keep present with itself the infinity of changing time. Boethius, de Consolatione philosophiae ed. Wilhelm Weinberger (Vienna: Akademie der Wissenschaften in Wein, 1934).

23. Karl Barth, *Church Dogmatics*, 4 vols. (T&T Clark, 1956–1975), II/1, 630–40. *CD* hereafter.

24 John Macquarrie, *Principles of Christian Theology* (SCM Press, 2003), 11.

25. It is Christ's perfectly obedient humanity which is that which (as perfect and Great High Priest) is offered to God for the sanctification of all humanity. Paul is emphatic about this: "[God] is the source of your life in Christ Jesus, who became for us wisdom from God, and righteousness and sanctification and redemption" (1 Cor 1:30). According to John's Gospel, Jesus is himself the One whom the Father has sanctified (John 10:36). Sanctification is, therefore, effected objectively for humanity in Christ. However, the uniqueness and singularity of this sanctification of the One human Jesus does not remove the effect of sanctification for humanity. Christ's holiness is a holiness for the other—the holiness of the one who is the perfect high priest and the perfect oblation: "this One [Jesus Christ] is no more holy in isolation than the holy God." *CD* IV/2, 515.

26. *CD* IV/2, 519–20.

27. Wolfhart Pannenberg, *Systematic Theology*, trans. Geoffrey W. Bromiley (Eerdmans, 2009), 406.

28. For more on this passage, see: Craig S. Keener, ed., 'Commentary on 1 Corinthians', in *1–2 Corinthians, New Cambridge Bible Commentary* (Cambridge University Press, 2005), 20–142, https://doi.org/10.1017/CBO9780511802980.003.

29. *CD* IV/2, 511. Barth continues: "The sanctification of man, his conversion to God, is, like his justification, a transformation, a new determination, which has taken place de jure for the world and therefore for all men. De facto, however, it is not known by all men, just as justification has not de facto been grasped and acknowledged and known and confessed by all men, but only those who are awakened to faith. . . . It is the witness of the love with which God has loved the world. What has come to it de facto has come to all men de iure."

30. Another way to say this might be to say that the radical position is the conservative position and vice versa. We are restored in the future to the eternal determination we were eternally destined to by the God who will be who God will be.

31. Or in a different idiom, in the words of Barth: "The main concern of the ongoing of the history of the prophecy of Jesus Christ which fills our time is with non-Christians. . . . . It is for their sake that it must go forward, that Jesus Christ as the living Word of God is still on the way to-day. Their conversion from ignorance to knowledge, from unbelief to faith, form bondage to freedom, from night to day, is the goal of His prophetic work so far as it has a temporal goal." *CD* IV/3, 364.

32. Brueggemann, *Theology of the Old Testament: Testimony, Dispute, Advocacy* (Fortress, 1997), 645.

33. Daniel W. Hardy, *God's Ways with the World: Thinking and Practising Christian Faith* (T & T Clark, 1996), 310.

Bibliography

Augustine, "Of the Morals of the Catholic Church," A Select Library of the Nicene and Post-Nicene Fathers of the Christian Church, vol. 4, *Augustine: The Writings Against the Manichaeans and Against the Donatists,* ed. Philip Schaff. T&T Clark. Accessed 18 September 2024, https://ccel.org/ccel/schaff/npnf104/npnf104.i.html.

Barth, Karl. *Church Dogmatics,* 4 vols. T&T Clark, 1956–1975. II/1. CD hereafter. CD IV/2, 515. CD IV/2, CD IV/3, 364.

Boethius, *de Consolatione Philosophiae*, prose VI. This eternity is one which includes the perfect possession of time all at once (with its order and movement) but without the passing mutability of created time:

> What we should rightly call eternal is that which grasps and possesses wholly and simultaneously the fullness of unending life, which lacks naught of the future, and has lost naught of the fleeting past; and as such an existence must be ever present in itself to control and aid itself, and also must keep present with itself the infinity of changing time.

Brichto, H. C. *The Names of God.* Oxford University, 1998; and B. W. Anderson, *The Living World of the Old Testament*, 4th edn. Longman, 1993.

Brueggemann, Walter. *Theology of the Old Testament: Testimony, Dispute, Advocacy.* Fortress Press, 1997.

Case, Anne and Deaton, Angus. *Deaths of Despair and the Future of Capitalism.* Princeton University Press, 2020.

Grace Davie, *The Sociology of Religion: A Critical Agenda.* SAGE Publications Ltd, 2012.

Hardy, Daniel W. *God's Ways with the World: Thinking and Practicing Christian Faith.* T & T Clark, 1996.

Jinkins, Michael. *The Church Faces Death: Ecclesiology in a Post-Modern Context.* Oxford University Press, 1999.

John Paul II, 'Vita Consecrata', 25 March 1996, https://www.vatican.va/content/john-paul-ii/en/apost_exhortations/documents/hf_jp-ii_exh_25031996_vita-consecrata.html.

Keener, Craig S., ed. 'Commentary on 1 Corinthians' in *1–2 Corinthians. New Cambridge Bible Commentary.* Cambridge University Press, 2005.

Little, Lester K. "Monasticism and Western Society: From Marginality to the Establishment and Back," in *Memoirs of the American Academy in Rome* 47, 2002.

Macquarrie, John. *Principles of Christian Theology.* SCM Press, 2003.

Martin, David. *The Religious and the Secular: Studies in Secularization.* Routledge & Kegan Paul, 1969.

Rosenwein, Barbara H., Head, Thomas and Farmer, Sharon. "Monks and Their Enemies: A Comparative Approach," *Speculum* 66, no. 4 (1991).

Wesley, John. *Sermons.* Edited Albert C. Outler. Vol. 1–4 of *The Bicentennial Edition of the Works of John Wesley.* Abingdon Press, 1984-1987.

Williams, Rowan. *Arius: Heresy and Tradition.* SCM Press, 2001.

———. *Why Study the Past? The Quest for the Historical Church.* William B Eerdmans Publishing Co, 2018.

2. GOOD NEWS OF JOY

Salvation, Creation, and Affection as an Expression of God's Care in the World

Blanches de Paula

Introduction

First, I would like to thank all of you for the invitation extended to me, as a person born in Latin America, to share some reflections on the good news in the face of a world in crisis. My perspective is from Practical Theology. I cannot fail to mention those from whom I learned my initial knowledge of Wesleyan Theology: professors like Rui de Souza Josgrilberg, José Carlos de Souza, Claudio Ribeiro, Bishop Paulo Ayres Mattos (in memory), as well as Helmut Renders and Martin Barcala, with whom I had the privilege of sharing reflections during Wesleyan Weeks at FaTeo, a School of Theology in São Bernardo do Campo, where we were faculty until December 17, 2023.

I began my broader Wesleyan studies after joining the Wesleyan Studies Center in 2022. Since then, I have grown increasingly interested in research on affection, creation, salvation, mourning, and death. My friend Helmut Renders is coordinating a proposal to create an Arminian Wesleyan Association in Brazil. This is good news! However, I still consider myself a beginner in Wesleyan studies. For a long time, I have heard about the Oxford Institute, but I never thought I would visit Oxford, much less participate in such a distinguished meeting as one of the Latin American and Caribbean voices.

This year's theme, "'The world is my parish': Glad Tidings of Salvation in a Time of Crisis," is thought-provoking and addresses the theme of crisis and a path to salvation that is rooted in the values of the Gospel. I believe all of us here, as well as those within the Methodist movement spread across the world, have much to say about this.

I would like us to reflect on what *good news* means in our century. Good news touches on our affections and grievances. Good news is not synonymous with the absence of suffering but rather the presence of dignity, solidarity, and justice in the face of the losses we experience. Thus, the good news that comes from the Gospel does not always bring comfort; it can even generate new crises because it defends poor people, children, women, Black people, refugees, vulnerable and invisible people, and others. Crises arise because the Gospel can confront the totalitarian powers of the world that create measureless inequalities and injustices. Seeds of hope are present in the theologies that are based on the justice of the Kingdom of God. Thus, I believe that dialogue with facets of God's good news, such as creation and salvation, from a Wesleyan perspective, expands our senses, hopes, and God's care in the world.

Crisis as a Challenge for the Twenty-First Century

It's not difficult to list the crises of the present century. However, discerning ways to deal with these same crises has been a challenge for people who have chosen the Gospel as the way of life. In predominantly Christian Latin America and the Caribbean, we witness coup attempts, the kidnapping of the dignity of life, and growing alienation among people. For example, Bolsonarism in Brazil is one of the most dangerous and misguided interpretations of the Good News. Christians who follow the Good News as synonymous with the "Messiah Bolsonaro" base themselves on Dominion's Theology.[1] Dominion's Theology advocates that humans have dominion, not care, over creation. Moreover, this dominion extends over non-Christian people, in the case of Brazil. The absence of mature leadership that looks to life values is striking. Polarizations, not only political but also religious, spread throughout the world. It seems we live in a kind of polarization of existence.

There are ways to deal with crises such as hunger, environmental degradation, the growth of fundamentalism, narcissism, mental health deterioration, and the commodification of bodies that deny the Gospel and spread injustices. Unfortunately, this kind of solution cultivated by some political and religious leaders shames the Gospel. This situation provokes an immediate shock to John Wesley's preaching, which defended the world as our parish and a place where the values of the Gospel should be lived. John Wesley left us a legacy of reflection and testimony on human dignity, health, education, creation, and salvation as part of the Gospel's preaching, which later became hallmarks of Methodism.

Wesley's sermons, notes upon the New Testament, and diaries presented a path of Christian life marked by solidarity, community living, shared faith, and affections transformed by the encounter with Christ. In his sermon "The Almost Christian," for example, Wesley invites us to revisit the meaning of the Gospel in our relationships with God and with each other. Affection, being part of humans and animals, evokes bonds of acceptance and rejection.

On the one hand, affection here is an expression of how we can see others with love's eye. However, affection can also be expressed in situations or people's actions that do not affect us in a good way. We feel uncomfortable, sometimes angry, with revenge or desire. Generally, we call this disaffected because it doesn't have the desire for good things for others but for bad things.

Affection not only has a subjective dimension but also a communal and social dimension and is indispensable for continuing life. Affection is linked to being affected by something or moving toward something or someone. Thus, affection has both an internal and external dialogue, like the movement from inside to outside and from outside to inside. The development of affection requires dedication and constant reconsideration of oneself and others. Affection is what moves us to life and hope. In this sense, affection is also linked to an intersubjective bond and its social regulations.

Finally, affection is a reaction to emotions and the various ways of bonding with someone, which is not limited only to humans. In affectivity, we build paths for organizing life in the subjective sphere, family, work world, church, and society. In addition, in Wesley's theology, it seems that affection is linked with the values of the kingdom of God, which touches us in our way of having a relationship.

For example, during the Covid-19 pandemic, our affections were "tested" in various dimensions through the denial of reality and the re-signification of attachment to life and to each other. Another example is that loved ones were not able to be at the bedside of their dying loved ones. It seems that during the Covid-19 pandemic, the challenges of dealing with the world of affection were laid bare. Some affective relationships equalized, but many also dissolved. With the rising unemployment rate and economic crisis, we have exposed disaffections and acts of solidarity in the face of life's finitude. Themes such as losses, mourning, and death were experienced more publicly. The private and the public mixed.

From the turn of the twentieth to the twenty-first century, discussions about affection also involved the advancement of technology. For example, disaffections have erupted and sickened many people and relationships, for instance excessive internet use deprives people of human dialogue. Given this brief overview of crises, I believe Wesley's theology on creation and salvation can help us find paths of hope.

The Legacy of John Wesley

Salvation and Care

In John Wesley, salvation is linked to affection. In Wesley's sermons, affection appears to be a recurrent theme of his theology, as mentioned earlier. John Wesley deeply cultivated affection directed toward God and neighbor. That is, Wesley considered the affections dedicated to God, neighbor, and humanity as the foundation of Christian identity and new birth. It seems that Wesley develops, therefore, a theology of affection. We find examples of Wesley's theology of affection in his sermon "On Love." Also in "The Almost Christian," John Wesley addresses the love of God and a life dedicated to humanity as true or pure Christianity. Let's see one part from Wesley's sermon "On Love":

> "Love is patient," or long-suffering. If you love your neighbor for God's sake, you will put up with all their weaknesses: if they lack wisdom, you will be merciful, and not despise them. If they fall into error, you will gently strive to recover them, without any harshness or reproach: if they are overtaken by a fault, you will work to recover them, in the spirit of meekness. And, if perchance this cannot be done immediately, you must be patient with them; and wait for God, possibly, to bring them to the knowledge and love of the truth. In all provocations, whether of weakness or malice of men, you should show yourself a pattern of gentleness and meekness; and, however often they may be repeated, be not overcome with evil, but overcome evil with good. Let no man deceive you with vain words: whosoever is not thus long-suffering, has not love![2]

John Wesley describes fully Christian life as the love of God and a life dedicated to others. This relational life is a central theme in the process of sanctification. Through it, the Gospel becomes present in the world.

> First, the love of God. For thus says the Word: "Thou shalt love the Lord thy God with all thy heart, and with all thy soul, and with all thy mind, and with all thy strength." Such love fills the entire heart, amalgamates all affections (. . .)

The second thing implied in being altogether a Christian is the love of neighbor. For thus says the Lord in the following words: "Thou shalt love thy neighbor as thyself." If anyone asks, "Who is my neighbor?" we answer: every man in the world.[3]

For Wesley, cultivating affection was materialized in acts of compassion and defense of life, especially of those made invisible and considered unworthy of God's love by the religious mentality of the time. Therefore, his theology of grace is the basis for experiencing empathy, which is important to Christian values. Randy Maddox reminds us in his book *Responsible Grace: John Wesley's Practical Theology* that Wesley's anthropology was relational;[4] human beings find meaning in their relationships. Thus, Maddox reminds us of Wesley's theological conception of affection.

> To develop this point, it is important to recognize that Wesley was not using "will" to designate the human faculty of rational self-determination, as is typical in current usage; rather, he equated will with affections. These affections are not simply passive "feelings" for Wesley; they are motivating dispositions of the person. In their ideal expression, they integrate the rational and emotional dimensions of human life into a holistic inclination toward particular choices or actions. Thus, the primary example of an affection for Wesley is love of God and neighbor.[5]

It seems that Wesley addresses the theme of affection from two dimensions: (1) looking at the human being and (2) looking at all of God's creation. From this perspective, Wesley highlights the virtues we must cultivate from the new birth and Christian identity, which needs to be revisited. That is, for the testimony of being Christian, it is necessary to review the affections and how they are implemented, especially in cultivating gestures of peace, dignity, justice, mercy, and compassion. In this sense, Walter Klaiber reminds us that "being a Christian does not consist in an existence restricted to the private sphere, but links what is most personal and intimate with what is communal, social, and global."[6]

Creation and Care: A Necessary Dialogue for the Meaning of Life

Creation, as God's care, is not unknown to us. Moreover, our intention is not to fall into an anachronism by reading Wesley's theology through the lens of a different era in which it was constructed, as José Carlos de Souza cautions. The intentionality is to recognize that John Wesley included the theme of creation in his theology, which helps us read him in light of our own time. We highlight the sermon "The New Creation."

> But the most glorious of all will be the change which then will take place on the poor, sinful, and miserable children of men. These had fallen, in many respects, from a great height to the lowest depth, relative to any other part of creation. But they will "hear a great voice from heaven, saying: Behold, the tabernacle of God with men. God will dwell with them. They will be God's people, and God himself will be with them." Consequently, a state of purity and happiness will arise, far superior to what Adam enjoyed in paradise. How beautifully and affectionately this is described by the apostle: "And God will wipe away every tear from their eyes; there shall be no more death, nor sorrow, nor crying. There shall be no more pain, for the former things have passed away" (Rev. 21:3-4).[7]

In line with Wesley's thought, Theodore Runyon reminds us that the Wesleyan perspective gives new meaning to people's life stories. God's creation is perceived in its entirety. In Wesley, there is a proposal of care that does not exclude nature and nonhuman animals.

> For Wesley, therefore, sanctifying faith cannot, in any way, be divorced from caring for the environment. To see things truly, to be "pure in heart," is to see ourselves again "as part of the family of nature," to overcome the ignorance and indifference that have made us strangers to what sustains us, and to joyfully embrace the spiritual and physical disciplines and necessary sacrifices not only to protect the earth but to maintain the covenant with generations yet unborn. For "Social holiness" today includes not only our association with the current inhabitants of planet Earth. There can be no holiness today that is not social holiness shaped by this task, nor can there be a spirituality that is not nurtured and animated by the Creator Spirit.[8]

Social holiness is a frequent theme in Wesleyan theology. Social holiness is directly linked to the practical theology lived by Wesley, as also advocated by Helmut Renders.

As Wesley presents in his theology, creation announces God and God's care. One dimension of God's nature is to create and care. It is interesting to note that theologians such as Leonardo Boff, Claudio Ribeiro, and Jürgen Moltmann have included the same principle in their eco-theology. Therefore, caring for the world is linked to what is now called planetary health. That is an interconnection of health from the intersectionality between human beings, nature, and social, political, economic, and ethnic dimensions. Furthermore, the New Creation is also linked to the New Birth.

> First—Why do we need to be born again? What is the foundation of the doctrine of the new birth? Its foundation goes as far back and as deep as the creation of the world. In the biblical description of this event, we read: "And God," the Triune God, "said: let us make man [and woman] in our image, according to our likeness." "So God created man [and woman] in His image, in the image of God He created him" (Gen. 1:26-27); not merely in His natural image, a portrait of His immortality; a spiritual being, endowed with understanding, freedom of will, and various affections; not merely in His political image, the governor of this lower world, having "dominion over the fish of the sea and all the earth"; but primarily in His moral image, which, according to the apostle, is "righteousness and true holiness" (Eph 4:24). According to this image, man was made. "God is love": consequently, man, at his creation, was filled with love, which was the sole motivation for all his dispositions, thoughts, words, and actions. God is full of justice, mercy, and truth: so was man when he came out of the hands of his Creator.[9]

The new birth also relates to affections, to the bonds that human beings establish with God and simultaneously with one another. In other words, Wesley links love for God to justice. "Dominion" in Wesley's biblical interpretation is not synonymous with the superiority of one created being over another. God gave humans the responsibility to care, as previously mentioned.

We are experiencing unprecedented environmental suffering. In 2002, the theme of Wesleyan Week in Brazil was Environment and Mission: The Ecological Responsibility of the Churches. On this occasion, the texts presented were based on Wesley's theology in dialogue with the environment, especially in the context of the Amazonia. Thus, themes such as salvation, social holiness, grace, and the Amazonian issue were on the event's agenda. At that time, meetings like this strengthened Wesley's missionary theme: "The world is my parish." Twenty-two years later, we reaffirm that the ecological issue, as in Wesley's thought, must be a permanent agenda in our reflection and praxis.

Very close to us, there are certainly people being affected by the degradation of nature caused by humans. Unfortunately, we are experiencing an environmental grief of broad impact. There is a growing number of environmental refugees. This category is not restricted only to the relationship between humans and the environment but also to relationships among human beings. "The 'environmental refugee' is a migrant in a situation of environmental vulnerability, which may or may not be combined with other forms of vulnerability (social, economic, political)."[10] The poor are the most affected by exclusions of any kind of environment. Environmental grief evokes the vocation to care proclaimed by God from the beginning of creation. The well-known expression: "A new Heaven and a new Earth" has been constantly promoted in the Christian tradition, including by Wesley, who encourages us to revisit the foundations of our faith and care as part of the sanctification process. John Wesley left us a legacy, from the reading of his time, of the depth and seriousness of biblical hermeneutics and a spirituality that included existential, economic, and social crises and sought to respond to the crises of his time.

Researchers like Léo Pessini (2015), a Catholic theologian, argued that the proliferation of the globalization of indifference is one of the causes of environmental illness. Indifference is traumatic grief. As Bjung Chul Han, a South Korean philosopher, states in his book, *The Burnout Society*, we are living through unprecedented exhaustion, especially in the world of work. This is not to mention the impacts of artificial intelligence on the labor market and the world of affection.

The situations described above were not present in John Wesley's time. However, Wesley lived with the impact of the Industrial Revolution, slavery, and profound social inequalities that were considered social sins in Wesley's theology. But we remember that Wesley made a reading of his time and sought to offer answers from his biblical hermeneutics, theological reflection, and pastoral praxis.

It is important to remember that Wesley's thought inspires us to rethink actions in our life contexts. I recall the Social Creed of the Methodist Church in Brazil:

> The items of Social Welfare (health, security, education, etc.) are guaranteed rights to every citizen. Human beings must manage the earth and its resources, which God has entrusted to them, according to the Lord's criteria.

> One of the ways to effectively act in the transformation of society is participation in the drafting of fair public policies.[11]

In this same document, we find the recognition and defense of human rights as an expression of justice and peace in the world and in keeping with the Gospel. It is vital to remember the hospitality of God who welcomed the mourners of the earth: orphans, widows, and foreigners.

Given this brief reflection on creation, the question arises: How can Methodism be good news in the face of the environmental crisis we are experiencing in our world? The environment or the whole environment, as Leonardo Boff says, has roots that involve not only the survival of all of us but also the hermeneutics that point to our place in God's creation.[12] In light of this, we can also ask: how can Methodism contribute to affections that are based on justice and dignity? How does the new creation, proclaimed by Wesley, need to be revisited in our churches? In the next section, we present some themes that are necessary to seek hope and joy in a world in crisis.

Final Considerations—Good News of Joy in World in Crisis

We started to discuss the crises in the world and the connection between salvation, creation, and affection. We can realize that this connection has a deep connection with the Gospel's proposal that is life. And now our challenge is to offer some ways to deal with them in our context.

To begin with, we can ask: why the good news of joy? A way to answer this question can be found in John Wesley's Sermon 24, "On the Sermon on the Mount" (Matt 5:3-16), where we find a well-known phrase that states, "Christianity is essentially a social religion, and to turn it into a solitary religion is to destroy it."

In Latin American Protestantism, practical theology was directly influenced by missionaries, especially at the end of the eighteenth and nineteenth centuries. But at that time, intercultural diversity, precarious economic situations, indigenous and African heritage, racism, and colonialism had not yet been included in the main themes of theology received in Latin American lands. We can say that these are still topics that have little room for dialogue in many Protestant expressions on the continent. When we speak of dialogue, we consider starting from Latin American theological thinking that includes social, economic, and political agendas.

I identify with Joerg Rieger's reading of grace under pressure. His reading is very relevant given the agenda that insists on remaining in Latin America, the Caribbean, and other parts of the world, such as poverty and social inequality.

> Since the days of John Wesley, Methodism has been most alive, creative, and productive when it has dealt with situations of pressure. When Methodism has placed itself directly in the pressures of everyday life, new experiences of grace have materialized, new encounters with God have occurred and both the church and the world have been transformed.[13]

In the face of pressure, grace can generate solidarity. In this sense, we reaffirm that the Gospel evokes the importance of human beings reconciling with their affections—affections linked to God, oneself, others, animals, and nature. Since the turn of the twentieth to the twenty-first century, affections have been involved in an acceleration of the bonding process among people and a decrease in the time of in-person dedication in relationships. The human condition goes through deep suffering in affections, whether at the individual, family, collective, or environmental level, and the joy of living has been significantly affected. One example is the rising suicide rate in the American continent in the present century.

With inspiration from Wesley's theology, we reaffirm that our task is also to promote the ministry of reconciliation in a divided world, where so many discontents have echoed and created wars, separations, and despair. Affective coexistence among us is essential so that we can experience salvation as a space of health and shalom. As Filipe Maia states: "Yes, the other opens the doors to my salvation. In the world between us, there is salvation, and outside of it, there is no salvation. In the encounter, there is salvation, of which we sing and poetize like Jesus: today there was salvation in this house."[14]

This reconciliation with the Gospel's affectivity, based on the values of the kingdom of God, is linked to a new beginning, mercy, forgiveness, and a new path to a new creation. As we have mentioned, Wesley's understanding of the new creation and salvation is a significant contribution of John Wesley to a theology of affection in our days. Reconciling with God requires horizontality, that is, the other! By entrusting us with the ministry of reconciliation, we realize that the experience of reconciliation with God makes us seek reconciliation with others, as we have already stated. Thus, God calls us to exercise the ministry of reconciliation as a possibility of changes in the lives of many people and in our society. Reconciliation also evokes the relationship between justice, forgiveness, and an anti-narcissistic life (2 Cor 2:5-11). The challenge is to go beyond what is seen in some current scenarios, in which revenge, insensitivity, and the loss of meaning in life have governed the lives of many people (2 Cor 5:14-15).

In the face of the crisis of spirituality that we are experiencing amid theological polarizations in Latin America, unity is also a foundation of the Gospel that must be nurtured. Thus, another highlight of the good news is the strength of unity. In Wesley's sermon "The Catholic Spirit," we remember that this is good news that constantly questions our intolerant decisions and positions. It is the prophetic voice that denounces polarizations and announces unity in diversity.

Our communities must continue to cultivate hope as a space of care and healing for personal, family, social, political, and economic life. Amid immense inequalities, pastoral care that promotes affection allied with social holiness is essential for people's well-being. I remember the reflection of Ailton Krenak, a Brazilian Indigenous leader:

> When, sometimes, they talk to me about imagining another possible world, it is in the sense of reordering relationships and spaces, of new understandings of how we can relate to what is considered nature as if we were not part of nature.[15]

I believe that if John Wesley visited Latin America today, he would seek a dialogue with Latin American theologies, even though he was raised in a colonizing context. Who knows, he might help us adopt a decolonial pastoral praxis that responds to the cries of the people of America—that is, to assume the ground of life in which the Gospel is expressed prophetically and hopefully. We believe that we can dream and proclaim the joy of living in the light of the Gospel and learn with children how to receive the kingdom of God day by day.

Notes to Chapter 2

1. For more about Dominion's theology, see: https://www.ihu.unisinos.br/categorias/637556-o-panico-sobre-a-teologia-do-dominio-e-a-cegueira-sobre-a-ganancia-laica.

2. John Wesley, "On Love" II.8, https://wesley.nnu.edu/john-wesley/the-sermons-of-john-wesley-1872-edition/sermon-139-on-love/.

3. John Wesley, "The Almost Christian" II.1–2, https://wesley.nnu.edu/john-wesley/the-sermons-of-john-wesley-1872-edition/sermon-2-the-almost-christian/.

4. Randy L Maddox, *Responsible Grace: John Wesley's Practical Theology* (Kingswood Books, 1994), 69. In translation: *Graça responsável: a teologia prática de John Wesley.* Tradução de Elizangela Aparecida Soares (São Bernardo do Campo, SP: EDITEO: Universidade Metodista, 2019), 133.

5. Maddox, *Responsible Grace*, 134.

6. Walter Klaiber and Manfred Marquardt, *Viver a Graça de Deus: Um Compêndio de Teologia Metodista* (São Bernardo do Campo. Editeo, 1999).

7. Wesley, 2006, Sermon 64, §18.

8. Theodore Runyon, *A nova criação: teologia de João Wesley hoje. Tradução de Cristina Paixao Lopes* (Editeo, 2002), 258.

9. Wesley, 2006, Sermon 45, §1.

10. Carolina de Abreu Batista Claro, *A proteção dos "Refugiados Ambientais" no Direito Internacional* (Tese de Doutorado Universidade de São Paulo, 2015), 79.

11. https://www.metodista.org.br/credo-social-da-igreja-metodista-nossas-bases-biblicas/

12. Leonardo Boff, *Saber Cuidar*, 19.

13. Joerg Reiger, *Graça sob pressão: negociando o coração das tradições metodista. Tradução de Felipe Maia* (Editeo, 2012), 21.

14. Felipe F. Ribeiro Maia, *Fora da relação não há salvação. Um ensaio de uma teologia da salvação relacional a partir de M. Buber e J. Moltmann* (Revista Caminhando, v. 13, n. 22, jul-dez 2008), 75.

15. Ailton Krenak, *Ideias para adiar o fim do mundo / Ailton Krenak.* 1ª ed. (Companhia das Letras, 2019), 32.

Bibliography

Bíblia de estudo Almeida. Tradução de Joao Ferreira de Almeida. Barueri: Sociedade Bífblica do Brasil, 2006.

Boff, L. *Saber Cuidar: Ética do humano—compaixão pela terra.* Petrópolis:Vozes, 2003.

Bortolleto Filho, Fernando (org.). *Dicionário Brasileiro de Teologia.* São Paulo, SP: ASTE, 2008.

claro, Carolina de Abreu Batista. *A proteção dos "Refugiados Ambientais" no Direito Internacional.* São Paulo. Tese de Doutorado Universidade de São Paulo, 2015.

Colegio Episcopal da Igreja Metodista. *Carta pastoral do Colégio Episcopal da Igreja Metodista: discípulas e discípulos nos caminhos da missão cuidam do meio ambiente.* São Paulo: Angular Editora, 2019. 37 p.

Klaiber, Walter e Marquardt, Manfred. *Viver a Graça de Deus: Um Compêndio de Teologia Metodista.* São Bernardo do Campo. EDITEO, 1999.

Krenak, Ailton. *Ideias para adiar o fim do mundo* / Ailton Krenak. 1ª ed. – São. Paulo: Companhia das Letras, 2019. Tal. Bibliografia. ISBN 978-85-359-3241-6.

Heitzenrater, Richard P. *Wesley e o povo chamado metodista.* São Bernardo do Campo: EDITEO, São Paulo: Editora Cedro,2006. 366 p.

Maddox, Randy L. *Graça responsável: a teologia prática de John Wesley.* Tradução de Elizangela Aparecida Soares. São Bernardo do Campo, SP: EDITEO : Universidade Metodista, 2019.

Maia, Filipe F. Ribeiro. *I da relação não há salvação.* Um ensaio de uma teologia da salvação relacional a partir de M. Buber e J. Moltmann . São Bernardo do Campo. Revista Caminhando v. 13, n. 22, jul-dez 2008.

Miguez Bonino, José. *Luta pela vida e evangelização: a tradição metodista na teologia latino-americana.* São Paulo, SP : Paulinas, 1985.

Rieger, Joerg. *Graça sob pressão: negociando o coração das tradições metodista.* Tradução de Felipe Maia. São Bernardo do Campo: Editeo, 2012. 104 p.

Runyon, Theodore. *A nova criação: teologia de João Wesley hoje.* Tradução de Cristina Paixao Lopes. São Bernardo do Campo: Editeo, 2002.

https://brasil.un.org/pt-br/sdgs / accesssed 13 July 2024

https://edisciplinas.usp.br/pluginfile.php/5727070/mod_resource/con tent/1/ideias-para-adiar-o-fim-do-mundo-1-34.pdf accesssed 13July 2024.

https://www.maisrelevante.com.br/2023/05/10-nova-criacao-john-wesley.html. Accessed 13 July 2024

https://wesley.nnu.edu/john-wesley/the-sermons-of-john-wesley- 1872-edition/sermon-139-on-love/ accesssed 13 July 2024

http://www.eventosfateo.com.br/sermoes/ accesssed August 2020

3. THE GRACE OF METHODIST SOCIAL ETHICS AND THE "JUST DESERTS" OF NEOLIBERAL CAPITALISM

Richard A. Davis

Introduction

During the 2024 general election campaign in the United Kingdom, I twice heard the Conservative candidate for Cambridge promise to work for "hard-working families." When he said this at the election hustings at the Wesley Methodist Church in Cambridge, the heckler in me wanted to yell: "What about lazy families?" I wisely resisted this temptation, because he was cleverly playing into a common notion of an ethics of desert—some people deserve more help than others, with hard work a widely perceived basis for deserving help from the government. Lazy families, one must surmise, do not deserve government assistance. At the other end of the scale, it is billionaires who deserve their money—they even "earned" it. And if we work hard enough, we can be billionaires too (or so the story goes).

We live in an unequal world, where the rich get richer and the poor get poorer. The statistics are well known and keep getting more dramatically unequal. In January 2024 the international charity Oxfam reported on the new state of global inequality by sharing this information:

> The world's five richest men have more than doubled their fortunes from $405 billion (£321 billion) to $869 billion (£688 billion) since 2020, while the wealth of the poorest 60 per cent—almost five billion people—has fallen. . . . If current trends continue, the world will have its first trillionaire within a decade but poverty won't be eradicated for another 229 years.[1]

Oxfam goes on to suggest that a wealth tax can help overcome this, "Just imagine what £22 billion a year invested in public services and infrastructure could pay for; improving the lives of every one of us who live in the UK and providing our elderly, young and vulnerable with the care and support they need and deserve." The Oxfam report implies that the billionaires do not deserve their fantastic wealth. Billionaires may claim that they earned their money justly and therefore they deserve their wealth. Some philosophers argue that the outcomes of free-market capitalism are just and therefore deserved.[2] Other philosophers disagree, arguing that no one deserves to be a billionaire.[3] Theologians, by contrast, have generally been quiet on this notion of desert in relation to distributive justice, something that needs addressing if they are to contribute to a fair society that can afford to eradicate poverty. This paper will attempt to untangle the interconnected concepts of justice, desert, and neo-liberalism and show how underpinning desert claims is an implicit theology which offers a point of entry for Methodist social ethics to make claims about what people really deserve.

What do humans deserve? At the root of the crises our unequal world faces are issues of distributive justice. The argument of this paper is that there is a tension between Methodist theologies of mercy and grace, which say that God gives us what we do not deserve and does not give us what we do deserve, and neoliberal capitalism, which teaches that people deserve what they get and get what they deserve. While neoliberalism does not necessarily claim that the market produces justice, it does offer a justificatory framework which naturalizes inequality. As a result, some people appear to think that they deserve to enjoy fantastic wealth while people go homeless. By contrast, Methodists sing of God's love and grace they do not deserve. The United Methodist Church defines *grace* as "the undeserved, unmerited, and loving action of God in human existence through the ever-present Holy Spirit."[4] As sinners we do not deserve grace, but God gives it freely anyway. Getting what we do not deserve might seem unjust, but God's grace and love is greater than any human conception of justice. Yet, even among Methodists, this grace does not necessarily translate into our social ethics. From this background, this paper will engage with the neoliberal social theology of former British Methodist Prime Minister Margaret Thatcher. This paper examines Thatcherite neoliberalism from the perspective of Methodist theology and finds an alternative in its teachings of grace and mercy that can offer a useful response to neoliberalism. The basis for this is built on the notion of desert and its relation to justice. The ethics of desert justify inequality and a reification of the notion of desert based on market outcomes. By contrast, the Methodist emphasis on unmerited grace provides a basis for equality and a challenge to the neoliberal notion of just deserts.

Neoliberalism as a Cosmic Reality

This paper sees the social context in which we live as a neoliberal one, with neoliberalism offering a worldview or social imaginary that operates with an understanding of the nature of human beings and our good life that drives our political economy. "Neoliberalism" is a contested concept and defies simple definition.[5] It is commonly defined by several characteristics. Take, for example, these two statements:

> Perhaps the best way to conceptualize neoliberalism is to think of it as four intertwined manifestations: (1) an ideology; (2) a mode of governance; (3) a policy package; (4) a particular form of capitalism.[6]
>
> Neoliberalism is a philosophy in which the existence and operation of a market are valued in themselves, separately from any previous relationship with the production of goods and services, and without any attempt to jus-

> tify them in terms of their effect on the production of goods and services; and where the operation of a market or market-like structure is seen as an ethic in itself, capable of acting as a guide for all human action, and substituting for all previously existing ethical beliefs.[7]

These definitions reveal the nature of neoliberalism as a comprehensive ideology and ethics that governs and manages society and human interactions. It valorizes market processes and outcomes as just and deserved.[8] Neoliberalism, I suggest, reinforces an ethic of desert in which the market distributes incomes and wealth according to desert. This in turn creates a plutocratic hierarchy where the rich rule and the poor become an underclass unable to compete in the marketplace.

In their 2024 book, published just in time to be bought and read before the July 2024 UK general election, George Monbiot and Peter Hutchison write that neoliberalism has become naturalized, allowing the free market to sort the winners and losers and, in turn, justify their position as that which they deserve; hardworking entrepreneurs deserve their wealth, and the "feckless, weak and incompetent" deserve their poverty.[9] Of all the complexities of neoliberal capitalism, this paper will focus on the feature of desert, and specifically on how neoliberalism justifies and implements the idea that people get what they deserve and deserve what they get, whether it's multiple mansions or homelessness.

Margaret Thatcher heralded the beginning of the New Right or neoliberal program in the UK. Even before her election in 1979 she actively promoted this ideology, aligning it with her version of Methodism. Thatcher was the last Prime Minister of the UK to be overtly a Christian and to bring social theology into the centre of her approach to political economy. This proved controversial with right and left alike. One speech she made to the Young Conservatives in 1977 included this infamous sentence: "Our religion teaches us that every human being is unique and must play his part in working out his own salvation."[10] This theological confusion may have come from her father's doctrine of personal responsibility for one's well-being, which was transposed into individual responsibility for one's salvation.[11] As one letter writer put it in *The Times*, based on her speech she appears to be more a Pelagian protestant than a Lutheran.[12]

Yet Margaret Thatcher was famously a Methodist, albeit a Methodist of a particular stripe, heavily influenced by her Methodist lay preacher father. Consistent with definitions of neoliberalism as an ideology, she once famously said that her aim was to radically change the nation: "Economics are the method; the object is to change the heart and soul."[13]

Her neoliberal economics was based in part on John Wesley's sermon on "The Use of Money" and its summary: "Make all you can; save all you can; give all you can." She promoted the notion of everyone making all they could, she advocated that the government save all the taxpayer money that it could,[14] but failed when it came to promoting charitable giving (as did Wesley in his own time). With regret she said: "I cut taxes and I thought that we would get a giving society and we haven't."[15] She appeared to believe in the goodness of humanity and that Wesley's "give all you can" would automatically flow from the getting and the saving. In summary, Thatcher brought about "new economic consensus" but without the "boundaries on individual freedom" that her Methodist upbringing has taught.[16] A favorite saying of hers from Wesley was taken from his sermon on "The Use of Money": "The fault does not lie in the money, but in them that use it,"[17] suggesting that money is not corrupting.

Thatcher also claimed that she took from Wesley an ethics of desert, suggesting that he "inculcated the work ethic, and duty. You worked hard, you got on by the result of your own efforts: then, as you prospered, it was your duty to help others to prosper also."[18] She claimed to have located the essence of Methodism in the parable of the talents (Matt 25:14-30), which she interpreted as, "You have a duty to make what you can out of your talents, and to assist others."[19] In brief, Thatcher's mantra of individual responsibility came with an ethic of desert: one got deservedly richer or poorer depending on one's individual competitiveness in the marketplace.

The Ethics of Desert (and Merit)

Writings on the ethics of desert tend to take two forms; there is philosophical ethics with ethical theory, with various positions on the ethics of desert in relation to justice, then there are the commonplace notions of the just world within the discipline of social psychology. This paper cannot do justice to all the debates within these disciplines or their interrelation. Suffice to say that I wish to discuss the world's billionaire crisis and the claims that billionaires deserve their status within the frames of Methodist theology and ethics.

In approaching the ethics of desert, I will draw on the writings of the theologically educated philosopher Louis Pojman. He describes how ingrained merit- and desert-based concepts of justice are in every culture, with examples from Greece, Rome, Buddhism, and Islam. He also finds these notions in scripture, summarized by Galatians 6:7 (NRSVue): "for you reap whatever you sow." He also cites Exodus 21:23-25 (NRSVA): "If any harm follows, then you shall give life for life, eye for eye, tooth for tooth, hand for hand, foot for foot, burn for burn, wound for wound, stripe for stripe." From the New Testament he also cites 2 Corinthians 9:6 (NRSVue): "The point is this: the one who sows sparingly will also reap sparingly, and the one who sows bountifully will also reap bountifully."[20]

In a long footnote Pojman expands on this theological analysis using the parable of the talents (Matt 25:14-30).[21] From this he gleaned four main lessons that support his thesis: (1) "The Stewardship Thesis," which teaches that our gifts are divinely bestowed to be used in service to God and the world; (2) "The Inegalitarian Thesis," which teaches the inequality of our gifts and results that flow from them; (3) "The Desert Thesis," which explains that "desert is the basis for rewards and punishment. We are responsible for what we do with our talents, and each person will be rewarded on how well he uses his talents"; and (4) "Desert is a Function of the Good Will," which means that what counts is effort, consisting "in how hard one worked to develop one's talents and contribute to society." Because the third servant exerted no effort toward increasing the one talent he was given, he had no merit and was deservedly rebuked by his master.[22] This conclusion is shared by Thatcher in her various uses of the parable in speeches and interviews.[23] Pojman claims this notion of desert as effort is shared by St Paul in 2 Corinthians 8:12 (ESV): " For if the readiness is there, it is acceptable according to what a person has, not according to what he does not have."

It is revealing that Pojman recognizes the lack of grace in the parable of the talents.[24] He reminds readers of St Paul's teaching in Ephesians 2:8-9 (NRSVue): "For by grace you have been saved through faith, and this is not your own doing; it is the gift of God—not the result of works, so that no one may boast." While Pojman recognizes that humans cannot be saved by works, for him there is still "work" involved, because God's forgiveness is "procured in part on the basis of our repentance, our intention to reform." Thus, God gives us more "more than we deserve" and "not give us less good than we deserve." But sinners still need to work by "the initial act of commitment and the subsequent acts of obedience to God which become the basis of meritocratic judgment."[25] For Pojman, "the overall thrust of the Old and New Testaments inclines towards identifying effort as the decisive criterion of merit, what I have called the paradigm notion of desert."[26] If it is works that is the basis for desert, in order to deserve justification, then we need to have works in order to be justified. This is not only a problem with Pojman's theology, but it is a problem for his ethics of desert which is partly based on this theology (and similar religious and philosophical ideals).

John Wesley would consider Pojman's soteriology justification by works. A point he addresses in several of his writings is that faith is *not* works. Wesley addressed this confusion directly in his short 1779 treatise "Thoughts on Salvation by Faith," when he admits that justification by faith is a conditional justification and is not justification by divine decree. Wesley cites "he that believeth shall be saved," making faith the condition of salvation and specifically a faith "which worketh by love."[27] In his sermon "The Lord Our Righteousness," he writes, "All believers are forgiven and accepted, not for the sake of anything in them, or of anything that ever was, that is, or ever can be done by them, but wholly and solely for the sake of what Christ hath done and suffered for them."[28] In support of this perspective, Wesley approvingly quotes the following from the Church's Homilies: "That we are justified by faith alone, is spoken to take away clearly all merit of our works, and wholly to ascribe the merit and deserving of our justification to Christ only."[29] This was a perennial theme in Wesley. Commenting on Philippians 2:13 ("For it is God which worketh in you both to will and to do of his good pleasure" [KJV]), he states that this verse,

> removes all imagination of merit from man, and gives God the whole glory of his own work. Otherwise, we might have had some room for boasting, as if it were our own desert, some goodness in us, or some good thing done by us, which first moved God to work. But this expression cuts off all such vain conceits, and clearly shows his motive to work lay wholly in himself—in his, own mere grace, in his unmerited mercy.[30]

It is not simply that we do not deserve salvation; according to Wesley, we actually do not get what we do deserve: condemnation. In the sermon "Justification by Faith" he writes: "Whereas we have transgressed the law of God, and thereby deserved the damnation of hell, God does not inflict on those who are justified the punishment which they had deserved."[31] Another sermon, "Salvation by Faith," reads: "For all our works, all our righteousness, which were before our believing, merited nothing of God but condemnation; so far were they from deserving faith, which therefore, whenever given, is not of works."[32] And finally, in "The Repentance of Believers," Wesley writes that the "*strict justice* of God" would condemn sinners to death. Sinners err by

> either thinking themselves condemned when they are not, or thinking they *deserve* to be acquitted. Nay, the truth lies between: they still *deserve*, strictly speaking only the damnation of hell. But what they deserve does not come upon them, because they "have an Advocate with the Father." His life, and death, and intercession still interpose between them and condemnation.[33]

These texts all show one thing: we do not deserve salvation; we deserve punishment. That the justified do not get what they deserve is central to Wesley's theology. But we must be careful here with the words Wesley uses and cites, because he does not distinguish between "merit" and "desert" in the way modern philosophers might. In fact, he explicitly wrote that he cannot tell the difference between them.[34] Nevertheless it is clear that Wesley did not believe in the necessity of desert for salvation and did not accept its validity in ethics either. This is a major difference with modern secular doctrines of desert.

In recent discussion there is often a distinction made between merit and desert. Louis Pojman notes that these words are frequently used as synonyms but can be differentiated.[35] "Merit," he writes, refers to a quality of someone that is praiseworthy or blameworthy. It is based on results and characteristics such as "basic intelligence, personality type, skin color, good looks, smiling eyes, good upbringing, and genetic endowments."[36] On the other hand, "desert" is about effort or intentions. Pojman puts this in this way: "Desert, on the other hand, is typically or paradigmatically connected with action, since it rests on what we voluntarily do or produce. It is typically connected with intention or effort."[37] We often say things like, "Spain deserved to win the football because they trained hard and gave 110 percent." Pojman draws on the parable of the good Samaritan to illustrate the point further: "The Good Samaritan deserved gratitude and benefit for helping the helpless, wounded Jew, which deserved to be reciprocated preinstitutionally, but he would have deserved praise even if his efforts failed."[38] But people don't *deserve* to win the EuroMillions lotto; people don't *deserve* to be poor when working several jobs.

Pojman summarizes the difference between desert and merit in this straightforward way: "Desert, then, is closely connected to effort and intention, whereas merit signifies positive qualities that call forth positive response." But then he continues in a curious theological way, drawing on commonplace notions of God's calculus of punishment and reward: "While God, knowing our inner motivations, rewards purely on the basis of desert, we fallible beings, being far less certain as to how to measure effort and intention, tend to reward merit, the actual contribution or positive results produced."[39] What basis is there for claiming that God rewards desert and not merit? Pojman does not elaborate; one supposes that he thinks that God rewards our intentions and efforts toward being good people. But is this really the case? That only God truly knows our true intentions is surely not enough to say that God looks only at intentions. God's intentions and characteristics of mercy and love surely also matter here as to how God judges us.

On the other hand, Pojman acknowledges that people reward merit—we do not reward intention and effort but results. We reward the fastest runner at the Olympics, not based on their hard work and efforts to win the 100-meter sprint, but on who crosses the finish line first. Pojman also uses the example of students meriting the top grades when they write excellent papers and exams. The reason scholars use blind peer review for papers is that they are supposed to reward merit and not desert.

Ideas of merit and desert do not live outside of worldviews or beliefs about the nature of the cosmos. In practice they are inextricably connected to views about the world, such as distributive justice and beliefs in a just world, and in our time neoliberal capitalism.

Just World Beliefs

Margaret Thatcher tried to reintroduce an ethics of personal responsibility against collectivism in the 1970s to 1990s. Aligned with this was an ethics and theology of desert, one that distorted Wesley's teaching. This neoliberalism, I argue, offers a new vision of a just world supported by an ethics of desert. Pojman argued in 1999 that the ethics of desert has waned as society began to reject religious explanations where God's justice would ultimately prevail, and was replaced with social scientific and philosophical explanations of people's situation which diminishes personal responsibility for outcomes.[40] Thatcher rejected social explanations of poverty and wealth, attributing people's relative positions to their own individual responsibility. And in practice she overcame what some people thought of as an obstacle to an ethics of desert—"distributing goods according to desert."[41] For neoliberals, like Thatcher, the market does that exceptionally well. In making the market free of state interference and therefore the arbiter of just outcomes, neoliberal market capitalism effectively replaced Christianity as a "just" cosmos.

Neoliberalism, according to English authors George Monbiot and Peter Hutchinson contend that the market, "if left to its own devices [will] determine who deserves to succeed and who does not. The talented and hard-working will prevail, whereas the feckless, weak, and incompetent will fail."[42] This creed then flips into providing a justification to the rich for their wealth to believe that they only have their wealth because of their "enterprise and virtue," allowing them to conveniently overlook the head start they have in the market due to "advantages of birth, education, inheritance, race and class."[43] Where a rich person genuinely believes this, they have fallen into the "self-attribution fallacy."[44] This is something John Wesley noticed in America among the newly rich merchants and tradesmen:

> The more riches they acquired, the more they were regarded by their neighbours as men of weight and importance: And they would naturally see themselves in at least as fair a light as their neighbours saw them. And, accordingly, as they rose in the world, they rose in their opinion of themselves. . . . So, the richer they grew, the more admiration they gained, and the more applause they received. Wealth then bringing in more applause, of course brought in more pride, till they really thought themselves as much wiser, as they were wealthier, than their neighbours.[45]

The market also delivers the opposite results. The poor are only poor, according to this way of thinking, because the market delivers them the market outcome they deserve. If one is poor, then one's skills are not valued highly by the market. It is the individual's fault for not upskilling, being poorly educated, and not working hard enough. In the market people get what they deserve; the market rewards the rich and punishes the poor. Neoliberalism has delivered this system of ordering society, replacing previous hierarchical orders, such as feudal or class-based ones. The only thing neoliberalism shares with these previous schemes is that the ordering now seems to be the only way things are and can be. Neoliberalism as an ideology of desert has naturalized economic inequality and it is now hard to imagine any alternative.

This all relates closely to social psychological debates over the just world thesis. This notion is related to commonplace ideas that we live in a world in which people, generally speaking, get what they deserve and deserve what they get. According to social psychologists, this is not an ontological claim about the nature of the cosmos as just, but is about how people make sense of the world. Melvin Lerner defines a "just world" as one in which people "get what they deserve."[46] Belief in a just world has been described as a "pervasive cognitive tendency,"[47] related to the idea that "things happen for a reason." Social psychologist Claudia Dalbert writes that "the just-world hypothesis states that people need to believe in a just world in which everyone gets what they deserve and deserves what they get. This belief enables them to deal with their social environment as though it were stable and orderly and thus serves important adaptive functions."[48] The adaptive function here is that belief in a just world allows one to adapt to an unjust unequal world by saying to oneself that a billionaire earned and therefore deserves their wealth, at the same time blaming the homeless person for their poverty because they haven't made enough effort to improve their situation.

Social psychologists have found that belief in a just world correlates with religious belief.[49] An updated review article by Carolyn L. Hafer and Robbie Sutton found that belief in a just world (BJW) correlates with both conservative ideology and religious belief, with the caveat being that "BJW is more strongly associated with specific facets of Protestant Work Ethic beliefs, such as the (nonreligious) belief that hard work leads to good outcomes."[50]

Religious teachings support BJW, as social psychologists Zick Rubin and Letitia Anne Peplau outline in their article "Who Believes in a Just World?" They say that "Belief in a just world may also be fostered by religions such as Judaism and Christianity which teach that although just rewards may not occur immediately, they are ultimately inevitable. In the Old Testament, from the original sin to the delivery of Daniel from the lions' den, the message that the wicked will be destroyed and the righteous will triumph is brought home over and over again."[51] They link these biblical ideas directly with the "Protestant Ethic" that "emphasizes the links between hard work, financial success, and spiritual salvation."[52] Based on the "justice" involved in these teachings, they "hypothesize . . . that children who grow up in 'religious' households are likely to develop a strong belief in a just world."[53] Believers in a just world are likely to attribute success and failure to the individual and desire to reinforce that belief as they make sense of the world by attributing desert to the lucky and also "deny the existence of suffering or to conclude that it is in fact deserved."[54]

By contrast, as Rubin and Peplau observe, "Others, like Job himself, may recognize more clearly that the world is often unjust. These people are more likely to attribute misfortunes to their social context or to the arbitrary workings of fate."[55] Any decline in the belief of fate, social explanations for injustice, "unseen magical or religious powers,"[56] such as God or providence, reinforces belief in a just world of desert.

Just world beliefs can be seen in scripture, reinforcing the view that religious people hold to just world beliefs. Rubin and Peplau begin their article by agreeing with Job's view of the world as unjust. When Job suffers the loss of all that he has, his friends' arguments in response were that Job deserved this suffering because God would not punish him if he were innocent. Job claimed his innocence and the injustice of the world, confounding his friends. The reader of the book of Job has the privilege of seeing behind the scenes of the story to see what is really going on. This tale can be used to highlight the prevalence of just world beliefs in Job's friends or the reality that not all suffering is deserved. In the end Job's fortunes are restored (Job 42:10). If this conclusion were a later editorial addition, perhaps it was so because readers could not tolerate the injustice of the world the story portrayed.

Here mention can be made to notions of ultimate justice and penultimate justice. Many religious believers believe that while injustice might be suffered in this world, ultimately things will be put right in the end (as with Job) or the next life. While evildoers might prosper in this world, in the next they will suffer, as illustrated in the parable of Lazarus (Luke 16:19-31). Such interpretations are comforting for those currently enduring injustices, who may place their hopes in ultimate justice for themselves and for their persecutors.

In addition to Job, there are other places in scripture where people express the view that those who suffer must have sinned and thus deserve their fate. In the gospel of Luke, Jesus replies that those crushed by the Tower of Siloam did not deserve their fate any more than anyone else (Luke 13:1-5). When asked whether a blind man deserved his disability due to sin, Jesus answered that he was innocent and did not deserve to be blind because of his or his parents' sins (John 9:1-3). The world in these cases does not appear to adhere to commonplace notions of justice.

Similarly, the biblical records contain many passages when people or entire cities do not get what they deserve. Once he completed his mission to Nineveh, Jonah seemed disappointed that God did not give the city the punishment that he thought it deserved (Jonah 4:1). He was convinced that it should be destroyed, yet God spared the city (Jonah 3:10). God's mercy triumphs over Jonah's understanding of desert-based justice. Some of the psalms appear to comfort those who witness the evil getting richer and the good getting poorer. Consider Psalm 37, which consoles those that see the wicked prosper and not get the punishment they deserve from God in a timely fashion. Psalm 94 implores God to deliver to the proud what they deserve. Psalm 28:4-5 implores God to deal justly with the evil as they deserve:

> Repay them according to their deeds
> and according to the wickedness of their devices.
> Reward them according to the work of their hands
> and pay them their just deserts.[57]

In the New Testament we have already seen Jesus saying that "laborers deserve their food" (Matt 10:10), which is a strange use of the term, for the "work" mentioned here is the apostles going on a mission trip, which to an agricultural audience would have hardly seemed the kind of hard day's work to deserve a meal at the end of the day. In Revelation 2:23 God declares, "I am the one who searches minds and hearts, and I will give to each of you as your works deserve." Given these citations, some have claimed that the Bible provides us with a paradigmatic ethics of desert.[58] Scripture, however, does not speak with one voice; there is alternative tradition, where people do not get what they deserve.

A perfect example of this mentality is illustrated in Jesus's parable of the workers in the vineyard (Matt 20:1-16). The workers who did a full day's work thought that they deserved more pay than those who worked a half day or even one hour. However, the eventual equal pay for unequal work might be interpreted in at least two ways here: first, everyone *deserves* the same daily rate because they were all equally willing to work all day, it not being their fault no one hired them (everyone who showed up for hire got the same); or, second, that everyone *merits* by virtue of their humanity to have a day's pay in order to feed their families.

These issues cannot be resolved or examined solely through scriptural interpretation. The notion of grace within theology makes the notion of desert problematic. Christians have believed that as sinners we deserve God's praise and reward for doing the right thing, and we deserve just punishment by God for our sins against God and our neighbour. Instead, Christians receive God's mercy and forgiveness. God's grace and mercy that allows us to receive what we do not deserve being everlasting life with Christ.

The Protestant Work Ethic and the Just World

Several recent secular authors have related the problems posed by inequality, neoliberalism, and the ethics of desert directly to theological ideas of the Protestant work ethic and God's justice. For example, Monbiot and Hutchinson, engaging directly with the ethics of desert and how both rich and poor are deemed to deserve their relative positions, write about how we are propagandized to believe this: "The doctrine has religious, quasi-Calvinist qualities: in the Kingdom of the Invisible Hand the deserving and the undeserving are revealed through the grace bestowed upon them by the god of money."[59] We are supposed to know that the rich deserve their riches because they are rich and clearly worked hard for their wealth. On the other hand, the poor must lack something, such as initiative or the wherewithal to improve themselves.

Philosopher Michael Sandel also uses Calvin in his analysis, but in a more rigorous and extended way, when, over several pages in his book *The Tyranny of Merit*, he expounds a brief history of the morals of merit.[60] Sandel identifies Christianity as having a "cosmic meritocracy," at least in some forms of Protestantism.[61] This is the idea that it is our merits before God as judge that will ultimately determine our fate. This is a major soteriological and eschatological claim about God's judgement, and one that translated itself into the Protestant work ethic, which in turn gave rise to the spirit of capitalism and meritocratic ways of thinking.[62] The result of this move to merit or desert, according to Sandel, has a dark side: "The more we view ourselves as self-made and self-sufficient, the less likely we are to care for the fate of those less fortunate than ourselves. If my success is my own doing, their failure must be their fault. This logic makes meritocracy corrosive of commonality."[63]

Margaret Thatcher was a strong believer in the protestant work ethic linked here with meritocratic neoliberalism. Rubin and Peplau write, "We would expect people with strong beliefs in a just world to be authoritarian, to be trusting, to be religious, to adhere to the Protestant Ethic, and (although we are less confident about it) to have a sense of internal or personal control of their reinforcements."[64] An earlier study confirmed "that those who strongly endorse the Protestant Ethic are negative in their attitudes toward the poor."[65] Many critics of Thatcher would subscribe to the notion that this summarizes her character.

These secular intellectuals have become amateur theologians in grappling with understanding neoliberalism. I read this as a sign that theology is at the root of our modern world. I also read this as a sign that better theology can improve our world. Given our mixed ethos of desert, can Wesley's theology speak into the common everyday ethics of desert where it is believed that billionaires deserve their wealth, and that the poor deserve their lot?

What would Wesley make of the belief in a just world? He certainly did not believe that outcomes were based on individual effort. In Wesley's time the doctrine of providence furnished a veil of mystery over the orders of society. He believed the "riches and poverty" are bestowed by "God's providential dispensations."[66] In his sermon "The Imperfection of Human Knowledge," Wesley said that we know little about "divine dispensations . . . to individuals," continuing that, "We know not . . . why one is born of rich or noble, the other of poor parents; why the father and mother of one are strong and healthy, those of another weak and diseased."[67] The social order was the product of mysterious forces, even divine providence that defies reason. In our time, however, providential explanations have been replaced by reasoned economic or sociological ones, which explain why people are born poor and remain poor. It is now possible to say that a billionaire deserves their wealth, which they earned, while condemning the greed which inspired their quest for wealth.

Far from condemning or blaming the poor, Wesley was concerned with preaching to the poor. He celebrated the fulfilment of Jesus's words in Matthew 11:4-5, that in his time, "And surely never in any age or nation, since the apostles, have those words been so eminently fulfilled, 'The poor have the gospel preached unto them,' as it is at this day."[68] Based on this, Theodore Jennings sees as Wesley's main focus of Christian ministry the "preaching of good news to the poor."[69] This, of course, raises the question of what precisely is the good news for the poor that must be preached? Do we know exactly *what* Wesley preached to the poor? One can imagine that today, in a meritocratic neoliberalism, many sermons are preached to the poor that they need to lift their game, work harder, get an education, give to the church, or whatever it takes to make an effort to deserve more and rise out of poverty.

Wesley resisted the notion that the poor themselves were to blame for their state. His examination of the issues in his tract "Thoughts on the Present Scarcity of Provisions" offers sociological reasons for poverty being the lack of work combined with the high prices of commodities and high taxation, all of which are outside the control of the poor.[70] Elsewhere Wesley also rejected claims that poor are to blame for their fate.[71] In a famous entry in his Journal he wrote: "So wickedly, devilishly false is that common objection 'They are poor only because they are idle.'"[72] John Wesley knew this first hand from knowing the poor and visiting them, commenting that, "One great reason why the rich, in general, have so little sympathy for the poor, is, because they so seldom visit them."[73] Wesley's socially embodied epistemology would not allow him to tolerate blaming the poor for their poverty. This approach would be valued by Rubin and Peplau, who link strong beliefs in a just world to having "relatively little personal experience with injustice."[74] This is one way in which Wesley's counsel to be alongside the poor can help us overcome adherence to unrealistic and even dangerous just world beliefs.[75] Rubin and Peplau also suggest that our narratives conveyed through education, media, and religion can be unhelpful in understanding the reality of injustice in this world. For the church, they suggest that clergy "might make less of stories like that of Lot's wife (who was turned into a pillar of salt for failing to follow God's orders [Genesis 19]) and more of the story of Job (whose suffering was undeserved)."[76] Sandel also values the lessons of Job, concluding that: "Faith in God means accepting the grandeur and mystery of creation, not expecting God to dispense rewards and punishments based on what each person merits or deserves."[77]

Implications for Rich and Poor in Methodist Social Ethics

I have shown that the biblical record, as the primary source of Methodist ethics, shows a mixed record in supporting an ethics of desert. Those urging an ethics of desert are frustrated by God and Jesus pointing out that in this world the evil prosper and that those suffering do not necessarily deserve their fate. I have tried to show that John Wesley did not support an ethics of the desert. It is, therefore, a distortion of the equivocal Christian tradition to say that it supports an ethics of desert.

Even though Wesley did not have an ethics of desert, he did believe that the poor merited help, and the rich did not deserve their wealth. Why does he believe that the poor merit help? This is because they are made in the image of God and in need of salvation:

A poor wretch cries to me for an alms: I look and see him covered with dirt and rags. But through these I see one that has an immortal spirit, made to know and love and dwell with God to eternity. I honor him for his Creator's sake. Lo, I see through all these rags that he is purpled over with the blood of Christ. I love him for the sake of his Redeemer.[78]

From 1785 the Strangers' Friend Society began charitable work among the poor with John Wesley's endorsement.[79] In the Manchester Strangers' Friend Society, relief was provided to the poor without inquiring into whether they were "deserving": "Weekly contributions were to be made, and no questions to be asked of those who needed help. Only the extent of their distress mattered."[80] In view of this, I was surprised to read two online sources that claimed help from the Strangers' Friend Societies was only available to the deserving poor.[81] Although given the pervasive nature of the just world thesis, Methodists were not immune from developing charities that applied notions of desert.

It is well known that John Wesley knew the poor, served the poor, and did many things to support them. It is also well argued that Wesley and later Methodists preached to the poor. Later Methodists have urged our contemporary churches that we need to adopt this ethos of care for the poor, in the face of the temptation of becoming a middle-class church which seeks to be upwardly mobile.[82] I agree with these theologians calling us back to the basics of our faith in scripture and John Wesley's teachings and example. Yet this is no longer enough; our new context demands that our analysis go deeper.

While we must continue fighting indifference to the plight of the poor, we must also contend with false theological teaching that justifies the plight of the poor and the immense wealth that is being stolen from them. As shown above, this is a theologically grounded political and economic doctrine of desert embedded within a neoliberal "just world" in which people get what they deserve and deserve what they get, justifying the ultra-rich in their wealth and blaming the poor for their poverty. Preaching glad tidings to the poor might be that they do not deserve to be poor. It is not necessarily their fault. Mirroring the salvation by God based on nothing we are or have done, good news to the poor is that they merit assistance from the government or charities or both, simply by virtue of being a human being made in the image of a redeeming God.

Rare among preachers and theologians, John Wesley had plenty to say about the rich. He would be shocked at the number of billionaires today. For Wesley one does not become rich by accident. The notion of deserving that much money would have been foreign to his thinking. One's relative position was the result of God's providence and if one was wealthy, one was merely a steward of God's bounty to be used for the alleviation of other's poverty. In his sermon "The Danger of Riches," Wesley states that God ordains the portion of the world's goods that we have, remains their "Proprietor," and "only lends them to us as Stewards; reserving the property of them to himself. And, indeed, he cannot possibly do otherwise, seeing they are the work of his hands; he is, and must be, the possessor of heaven and earth."[83] In another sermon on riches, Wesley also notes the sin of having one's heart set on riches, listing the way the rich gain their wealth "with or without labour; whether by trade, legacies, or any other way" and says that "unless thy charities increase in the same proportion; unless thou givest a full tenth of thy substance, of thy fixed and occasional income; thou dost undoubtedly set thy heart upon thy gold."[84] Wesley here is saying that the rich do not deserve to keep their surplus wealth (even if they labour for it) since it is not theirs to keep, but it must be given away for charitable purposes. To not do this and hoard wealth is to have one's heart set on wealth and fall into judgment. Wesley wrote further on this danger in his "Thoughts upon Methodism": "As riches increase, so will pride, anger, and love of the world in all its branches."[85] Wesley's solution was to lay up treasure in heaven by gaining, saving, and *giving* all one can.[86]

Wesley's more famous sermon on "The Use of Money," if read seriously, would condemn the ultra-rich for how they make their money, how they spend their money, and how they hoard their money. For example, Wesley condemns tax avoidance and evasion, which in his time was smugglers "robbing or defrauding the king of his lawful customs."[87] Wesley condemned the ostentatious display of wealth which the wealthy indulge in.[88] Another reason for condemning the rich in our context is that they do disproportionally more harm to our fragile climate than the poor.[89] Can someone deserve to live in such a way that is ecologically unsustainable, accelerates climate change, and makes the world a dangerous place?

In brief, then Wesley did not believe that the poor deserve to be poor, and the rich did not deserve their wealth. In this way he provides a counterpoint not only to Margaret Thatcher's distorted Methodism but also to the neoliberal ethics of desert that allows the billionaire to claim that their wealth is deserved while others are homeless and hungry in the streets.

Conclusion

In summary, I have argued that notions of desert are in tension with Methodist theology and ethics. The Bible can be used to support an ethics of desert, but only if some verses are cherry-picked and others ignored. Desert also falls foul of justification by works, since deservedness is based on actions or works intended, attempted, and enacted that are meritorious and earn the person reward or punishment in due measure. Methodist theology, by contrast, teaches that we get what we do not deserve: God's grace and mercy. As sinners we deserve only condemnation, but God's grace allows us to enjoy second chances and God's unmerited favour. Translated into social ethics, egalitarianism may mean people getting things that public opinion thinks they don't deserve, albeit public opinion shaped for a generation by the worldview of neoliberalism.

This ethics opposes the ideology of neoliberalism as a cosmic system that justifies, through its ethics of desert, both extreme wealth and abject poverty, and the inequalities this brings into economic, social, and political power. Neoliberalism allows us to valorize greed and wealth while saying that the poor deserve their fate. It distorts our souls by naturalizing inequalities based on greed and exploitation. We are encouraged to believe that everyone gets what they deserve and deserves what they get. If they are poor, they deserve to be poor because they are not making an effort; the rich are rich and deserve their wealth because they worked to obtain it. In this way neoliberalism with its ethics of desert is counter to Methodist ethics and theology and ought to be resisted as such.

In Wesley's theology we get what we do not deserve: salvation; and we do not get what we do deserve: damnation. John Wesley thought and lived out an ethics of merit—poor people should be assisted because they were poor. The poor did not need to demonstrate why they deserved help. This ethos flows from Wesley's theology of undeserved grace and mercy from God. God approaches us in prevenient grace because we merit his love and forgiveness by virtue of our fallen humanity, which we all share.

Notes to Chapter 3

1. "Wealth of Five Richest Men Doubles since 2020, as Wealth of Five Billion People Falls," *Oxfam* GB, 15 January 2024, https://www.oxfam.org.uk/mc/hffm8s/.

2. Lisa Herzog, *Inventing the Market: Smith, Hegel, and Political Theory* (Oxford University Press, 2013), 88–118, https://doi.org/10.1093/acprof:oso/9780199674176.001.0001.

3. Ingrid Robeyns, *Limitarianism: The Case Against Extreme Wealth* (Allen Lane, 2024).

4. United Methodist Church (USA), *The Book of Discipline of the United Methodist Church, 2016* (The United Methodist Publishing House, 2016), 51, https://find.library.duke.edu/catalog/DUKE008404106.

5. Taylor C. Boas and Jordan Gans-Morse, "Neoliberalism: From New Liberal Philosophy to Anti-Liberal Slogan," *Studies in Comparative International Development* 44, no. 2 (June 2009): 137–61, https://doi.org/10.1007/s12116-009-9040-5; Bruce Rogers-Vaughn, Caring for Souls in a Neoliberal Age (Palgrave Macmillan US, 2016), 36.

6. Manfred B. Steger and Ravi K. Roy, *Neoliberalism: A Very Short Introduction*, 2nd ed. (Oxford University Press, 2021), 12, https://doi.org/10.1093/actrade/9780198849674.001.0001.

7. Paul Treanor, "Neoliberalism: Origins, Theory, Definition," 20 May 2023, https://web.archive.org/web/20230520180529/http://web.inter.nl.net/users/Paul.Treanor/neoliberalism.html.

8. Margaret R. Somers, "Dedemocratizing Citizenship: How Neoliberalism Used Market Justice to Move from Welfare Queening to Authoritarianism in 25 Short Years," *Citizenship Studies* 26, no. 4–5 (2022): 661–74, https://doi.org/10.1080/13621025.2022.2091250.

9. George Monbiot and Peter Hutchison, *The Invisible Doctrine: The Secret History of Neoliberalism (& How It Came to Control Your Life)* (London: Allen Lane, 2023), 3.

10. Margaret Thatcher, "Speech to Greater London Young Conservatives (Iain Macleod Memorial Lecture—'Dimensions of Conservatism')," Margaret Thatcher Foundation, 4 July 1977, https://www.margaretthatcher.org/document/103411.

11. John Campbell, M*argaret Thatcher, Volume One: The Grocer's Daughter*, Pimlico 456 (Pimlico, 2001), 16.

12. C. A. W. Dale, "Letter to the Editor," *The Times*, 11 July 1977, 13, https://archive.org/details/NewsUK1977UKEnglish/Jul%2011%201977%2C%20The%20Times%2C%20%2360052%2C%20UK%20%28en%29/page/n12/mode/1up.

13. Margaret Thatcher and Ronald Butt, "Interview for Sunday Times," Margaret Thatcher Foundation, 1 May 1981, https://www.margaretthatcher.org/document/104475.

14. Eliza Filby, *God & Mrs Thatcher: The Battle for Britain's Soul* (Biteback Publishing, 2015), 143; other sources on Thatcher's faith include, Mark Vickers, *God in Number 10: The Personal Faith of the Prime Ministers, from Balfour to Blair* (Society for Promoting Christian Knowledge, 2022); Nick Spencer, "Margaret Thatcher (1979–90)," in *The Mighty and the Almighty: How Political Leaders Do God*, ed. Nick Spencer (Biteback Publishing, 2017), 1–10; Antonio E. Weiss, "The Religious Mind of Mrs Thatcher," Margaret Thatcher Foundation, 14 June 2011, https://www.margaretthatcher.org/document/112748.

15. Filby, *God & Mrs Thatcher*, 348.

16. Filby, *God & Mrs Thatcher*, 337, 348.

17. Margaret Thatcher, "Speech at Jagiellonian University in Krakow," Margaret Thatcher Foundation, 3 October 1991, https://www.margaretthatcher.org/document/108284; John Wesley, "The Use of Money," in The Works of John Wesley, Volume 2: Sermons, II, 34–70, ed. Albert C. Outler, The Bicentennial Edition of the Works of John Wesley (Abingdon Press, 1985), 268.

18. Margaret Thatcher and Bruce Anderson, "Interview for Sunday Telegraph,"Margaret Thatcher Foundation, 26 June 1987, https://www.margaretthatcher.org/document/106660.

19. Thatcher and Anderson, "Interview for Sunday Telegraph."

20. Louis P. Pojman, "Justice as Desert," *QUT Law Review* 1, no. 1 (1 August 2001): 98–99, https://doi.org/10.5204/qutlr.v1i1.64.

21. Pojman, "Justice as Desert," 99n29.

22. Pojman, "Justice as Desert," 99 n29.

23. See, for example, Margaret Thatcher, "Speech at St Lawrence Jewry," Margaret Thatcher Foundation, 4 March 1981, https://www.margaretthatcher.org/document/104587.

24. Pojman, "Justice as Desert," 100n29.

25. Pojman, "Justice as Desert," 100n29.

26. Pojman, "Justice as Desert," 99–100n29.

27. John Wesley, "Thoughts on Salvation by Faith," in *The Works of John Wesley, Volume 13: Doctrinal and Controversial Treatises II*, ed. Paul Wesley Chilcote and Kenneth J. Collins (Abingdon Press, 2013), 555.

28. John Wesley, "The Lord Our Righteousness," in *The Works of John Wesley, Volume 1: Sermons, I,* 1–33, ed. Albert C. Outler, The Bicentennial Edition of the Works of John Wesley (Abingdon Press, 1984), 455.

29. Wesley, "The Lord Our Righteousness," 456.

30. John Wesley, "On Working Out Our Own Salvation," in *The Works of John Wesley, Volume 3: Sermons, III,* 71–114, ed. Albert C. Outler, The Bicentennial Edition of the Works of John Wesley (Abingdon Press, 1986), 202.

31. John Wesley, "Justification by Faith," in *The Works of John Wesley, Volume 1: Sermons,* I, 1–33, ed. Albert C. Outler, The Bicentennial Edition of the Works of John Wesley (Abingdon Press, 1984), 188.

32.John Wesley, "Salvation by Faith," in *The Works of John Wesley, Volume 1: Sermons, I,* 1–33, ed. Albert C. Outler, The Bicentennial Edition of the Works of John Wesley (Abingdon Press, 1984), 126.

33. John Wesley, "The Repentance of Believers," in *The Works of John Wesley, Volume 1: Sermons I,* 1–33, ed. Albert C. Outler, The Bicentennial Edition of the Works of John Wesley (Abingdon Press, 1984), 344–45. Italics in original.

34. John Wesley, Letter: To the Rev. Charles Wesley, in *The Works of John Wesley, Volume 28: Letters IV: 1766–1773,* ed. Randy L. Maddox, The Bicentennial Edition of the Works of John Wesley (Abingdon Press, 2023), 406; also see John Wesley, "Circular Letter on 1770 Minutes," in *The Works of John Wesley, Volume 28: Letters IV: 1766–1773,* ed. Randy L. Maddox, The Bicentennial Edition of the Works of John Wesley (Abingdon Press, 2023), 397.

35. While not universally agreed upon, Pojman's definitions align with those of Jeppe von Platz, "The Principle of Merit and the Capital-Labour Split," *Economics and Philosophy* 38, no. 1 (March 2022): 3, https://doi.org/10.1017/S0266267120000450.

36. Pojman, "Justice as Desert," 92.

37. Pojman, "Justice as Desert," 93.

38. Pojman, "Justice as Desert," 93.

39. Pojman, 'Justice as Desert', 96.

40. Louis P. Pojman, "Introduction," in *What Do We Deserve? A Reader on Justice and Desert,* ed. Louis P. Pojman and Owen MacLeod (Oxford University Press, 1999), 6.

41. Pojman, "Introduction," 6.

42. Monbiot and Hutchison, *Invisible Doctrine,* 3.

43. Monbiot and Hutchison, *Invisible Doctrine,* 5.

44. Monbiot and Hutchison, *Invisible Doctrine,* 57.

45. John Wesley, "The Late Work of God in North America," in *The Works of John Wesley, Volume 3: Sermons, III,* 71–114, ed. Albert C. Outler, The Bicentennial Edition of the Works of John Wesley (Abingdon Press, 1986), 600.

46. Melvin J. Lerner, *The Belief in a Just World: A Fundamental Delusion, Perspectives in Social Psychology* (Plenum Press, 1980), 11.

47. Zick Rubin and Letitia Anne Peplau, "Who Believes in a Just World?", *Journal of Social Issues* 31, no. 3 (July 1975): 68, https://doi.org/10.1111/j.1540-4560.1975.tb00997.x.

48. Claudia Dalbert, "Belief in a Just World," in *Handbook of Individual Differences in Social Behavior,* ed. Mark R. Leary and Rick H. Hoyle (Guilford Press, 2009), 288.

49. See, as examples, Zick Rubin and Anne Peplau, "Belief in a Just World and Reactions to Another's Lot: A Study of Participants in the National Draft Lottery," *Journal of Social Issues* 29, no. 4 (October 1973): 89, https://doi.org/10.1111/j.1540-4560.1973.tb00104.x; Richard M. Sorrentino and Jack E. Hardy, "Religiousness and Derogation of an Innocent Victim," *Journal of Personality* 42, no. 3 (September 1974): 372–82, https://doi.org/10.1111/j.1467-6494.1974.tb00681.x.

50. Carolyn L. Hafer and Robbie Sutton, "Belief in a Just World," in *Handbook of Social Justice Theory and Research*, ed. Clara Sabbagh and Manfred Schmitt (Springer New York, 2016), 150, https://doi.org/10.1007/978-1-4939-3216-0_8.

51. Rubin and Peplau, "Who Believes in a Just World?," 73.

52. Rubin and Peplau, "Who Believes in a Just World?," 73.

53. Rubin and Peplau, "Who Believes in a Just World?," 73.

54. Rubin and Peplau, "Who Believes in a Just World?," 84.

55. Rubin and Peplau, "Who Believes in a Just World?," 68.

56. Florian Znaniecki, *The Laws of Social Psychology* (University of Chicago Press, 1925), 148, http://archive.org/details/lawsofsocialpsyc00znan.

57. The Church of England, The Common Worship Psalter, https://www.churchofengland.org/prayer-and-worship/worship-texts-and-resources/common-worship/daily-prayer/psalter/psalm-28

58. Pojman, "Introduction," 3–4.

59. Monbiot and Hutchison, *Invisible Doctrine*, 58.

60. Michael J. Sandel, *The Tyranny of Merit: What's Become of the Common Good?* (Penguin Books, 2021), 33–58.

61. Sandel, *The Tyranny of Merit*, 35–37.

62. Sandel, *The Tyranny of Merit*, 41.

63. Sandel, *The Tyranny of Merit*, 59.

64. Rubin and Peplau, "Who Believes in a Just World?," 76.

65. A. P. MacDonald Jr., "More on the Protestant Ethic," *Journal of Consulting and Clinical Psychology* 39, no. 1 (August 1972): 120, https://doi.org/10.1037/h0033156.

66. John Wesley, "The One Thing Needful," in T*he Works of John Wesley, Volume 4: Sermons, IV*, 115–151, ed. Albert C. Outler, The Bicentennial Edition of the Works of John Wesley (Abingdon Press, 1987), 356.

67. John Wesley, "The Imperfection of Human Knowledge," in *The Works of John Wesley, Volume 2: Sermons, II*, 34–70, ed. Albert C. Outler, The Bicentennial Edition of the Works of John Wesley (Abingdon Press, 1985), 582.

68. John Wesley, "The Signs of the Times," in *The Works of John Wesley, Volume 2: Sermons, II*, 34–70, ed. Albert C. Outler, The Bicentennial Edition of the Works of John Wesley (Abingdon Press, 1985), 527.

69. Theodore W. Jennings Jr., "Wesley and the Poor: An Agenda for Wesleyans," in *The Portion of the Poor: Good News to the Poor in the Wesleyan Tradition*, ed. M. Douglas Meeks (Kingswood Books, 1995), 19.

70. John Wesley, "Thoughts on the Present Scarcity of Provisions," in *The Works of the Reverend John Wesley, A. M, Volume VI* (New York: J. Emory and B. Waugh, for the Methodist Episcopal Church, 1831), 274–78, https://archive.org/details/worksofreverendj06wesl/page/278/mode/2up.

71. Donald W. Dayton, '"Good News to the Poor": The Methodist Experience After Wesley', in *The Portion of the Poor: Good News to the Poor in the Wesleyan Tradition*, ed. M. Douglas Meeks (Kingswood Books, 1995), 69.

72. John Wesley, Journal Entry for Thursday 8 February 1753, in *The Works of John Wesley, Volume 20: Journal and Diaries, III*, 1743–1754, ed. W. Reginald Ward and Richard P. Heitzenrater, The Bicentennial Edition of the Works of John Wesley (Abingdon Press, 1991), 445–445.

73. John Wesley, "On Visiting the Sick," in *The Works of John Wesley, Volume 3: Sermons, III*, 71–114, ed. Albert C. Outler, The Bicentennial Edition of the Works of John Wesley (Abingdon Press, 1986), 387.

74. Rubin and Peplau, "Who Believes in a Just World?" 76.

75. There are positive benefits to belief in a just world, see Claudia Dalbert, "Beliefs in a Just World as a Buffer Against Anger," *Social Justice Research* 15, no. 2 (1 June 2002): 123–45, https://doi.org/10.1023/A:1019919822628.

76. Rubin and Peplau, "Who Believes in a Just World?" 86.

77. Sandel, *The Tyranny of Merit*, 37.

78. John Wesley, "On Pleasing All Men," in *The Works of John Wesley, Volume 3: Sermons, III*, 71–114, ed. Albert Cook Outler, The Bicentennial Edition of the Works of John Wesley (Abingdon Press, 1986), 425.

79. Tim Macquiban, "Friends of All? The Wesleyan Response to Urban Poverty in Britain and Ireland, 1785–1840," in *The Poor and the People Called Methodists, 1729–1999*, ed. Richard P. Heitzenrater (Kingswood Books, 2002), 132.

80. G. B. Hindle, "A Venture in Charity, 1791–1803," *Proceedings of the Wesley Historical Society* 36 (June 1967): 44, https://biblicalstudies.org.uk/pdf/whs/36-2.pdf.

81. "Stranger's Friend Society Annual Accounts, 1786–91," The Museum of Methodism & John Wesley's House, accessed 14 July 2024, https://www.wesleysheritage.org.uk/object/strangers-friend-society-annual-accounts-1786–91/; John J. Vincent, "Poor, The," *A Dictionary of Methodism in Britain and Ireland*, accessed 14 July 2024, https://dmbi.online/index.php?do=app.entry&id=2202.

82. See Theodore W. Jennings Jr, "Wesley and the Poor: An Agenda for Wesleyans," in T*he Portion of the Poor: Good News to the Poor in the Wesleyan Tradition*, ed. M. Douglas Meeks (Kingswood Books, 1995), 19–37; Dayton, "'Good News to the Poor': The Methodist Experience After Wesley."

83. John Wesley, "The Danger of Riches," in *The Works of John Wesley, Volume 3: Sermons, III*, 71–114, ed. Albert Cook Outler, The Bicentennial Edition of the Works of John Wesley (Abingdon Press, 1986), 231.

84. John Wesley, "The Danger of Increasing Riches," in *The Works of John Wesley, Volume 4: Sermons, IV*, 115–151, ed. Albert C. Outler, The Bicentennial Edition of the Works of John Wesley (Abingdon Press, 1987), 181.

85. John Wesley, "Thoughts upon Methodism," in *The Works of John Wesley, Volume 9: The Methodist Societies: History, Nature, and Design*, ed. Rupert E. Davies, The Bicentennial Edition of the Works of John Wesley (Abingdon Press, 1989), 529.

86. Wesley, "Thoughts upon Methodism," 530.

87. Wesley, "The Use of Money," 269.

88. Wesley, "The Use of Money," 274.

89. Robeyns, *Limitarianism*, 97–118.

Bibliography

Boas, Taylor C., and Jordan Gans-Morse. "Neoliberalism: From New Liberal Philosophy to Anti-Liberal Slogan." *Studies in Comparative International Development* 44, no. 2 (June 2009): 137–61. https://doi.org/10.1007/s12116-009-9040-5.

Campbell, John. *Margaret Thatcher, Volume One: The Grocer's Daughter*. Pimlico 456. Pimlico, 2001.

Dalbert, Claudia. "Belief in a Just World." In *Handbook of Individual Differences in Social Behavior*, edited by Mark R. Leary and Rick H. Hoyle, 288–97. Guilford Press, 2009.

———. 'Beliefs in a Just World as a Buffer Against Anger'. *Social Justice Research* 15, no. 2 (1 June 2002): 123–45. https://doi.org/10.1023/A:1019919822628.

Dale, C. A. W. 'Letter to the Editor'. *The Times*, 11 July 1977, 13. https://archive.org/details/NewsUK1977UKEnglish/Jul%2011%201977%2C%20The%20Times%2C%20%2360052%2C%20UK%20%28en%29/page/n12/mode/1up.

Dayton, Donald W. "'Good News to the Poor': The Methodist Experience After Wesley." In *The Portion of the Poor: Good News to the Poor in the Wesleyan Tradition*, edited by M. Douglas Meeks, 65–96. Kingswood Books, 1995.

Filby, Eliza. *God & Mrs Thatcher: The Battle for Britain's Soul*. Biteback Publishing, 2015.

Hafer, Carolyn L., and Robbie Sutton. "Belief in a Just World." In *Handbook of Social Justice Theory and Research*, edited by Clara Sabbagh and Manfred Schmitt, 145–60. Springer New York, 2016. https://doi.org/10.1007/978-1-4939-3216-0_8.

Herzog, Lisa. *Inventing the Market: Smith, Hegel, and Political Theory*. Oxford University Press, 2013. https://doi.org/10.1093/acprof:oso/9780199674176.001.0001.

Hindle, G. B. "A Venture in Charity, 1791–1803." *Proceedings of the Wesley Historical Society* 36 (June 1967): 41–48. https://biblicalstudies.org.uk/pdf/whs/36-2.pdf.

Jennings, Theodore W., Jr. "Wesley and the Poor: An Agenda for Wesleyans." In *The Portion of the Poor: Good News to the Poor in the Wesleyan Tradition*, edited by M. Douglas Meeks, 19–37. Kingswood Books, 1995.

Jennings, Theodore W., Jr. "Wesley and the Poor: An Agenda for Wesleyans." In *The Portion of the Poor: Good News to the Poor in the Wesleyan Tradition*, edited by M. Douglas Meeks, 19–37. Kingswood Books, 1995.

Lerner, Melvin J. *The Belief in a Just World: A Fundamental Delusion*. Perspectives in Social Psychology. Plenum Press, 1980.

MacDonald, A. P., Jr. "More on the Protestant Ethic." *Journal of Consulting and Clinical Psychology* 39, no. 1 (August 1972): 116–22. https://doi.org/10.1037/h0033156.

Macquiban, Tim. "Friends of All? The Wesleyan Response to Urban Poverty in Britain and Ireland, 1785–1840." In *The Poor and the People Called Methodists, 1729–1999*, edited by Richard P. Heitzenrater, 131–60. Kingswood Books, 2002.

Monbiot, George, and Peter Hutchison. *The Invisible Doctrine: The Secret History of Neoliberalism (& How It Came to Control Your Life)*. Allen Lane, 2023.

Oxfam GB. "Wealth of Five Richest Men Doubles since 2020, as Wealth of Five Billion People Falls," 15 January 2024. https://www.oxfam.org.uk/mc/hffm8s/.

Platz, Jeppe von. "The Principle of Merit and the Capital-Labour Split." *Economics and Philosophy* 38, no. 1 (March 2022): 1–23. https://doi.org/10.1017/S0266267120000450.

Pojman, Louis P. "Introduction." In *What Do We Deserve? A Reader on Justice and Desert*, edited by Louis P. Pojman and Owen MacLeod, 1–9. Oxford University Press, 1999.

———. "Justice as Desert." *QUT Law Review* 1, no. 1 (1 August 2001): 88–109. https://doi.org/10.5204/qutlr.v1i1.64.

Robeyns, Ingrid. *Limitarianism: The Case Against Extreme Wealth*. Allen Lane, 2024.

Rogers-Vaughn, Bruce. *Caring for Souls in a Neoliberal Age*. Palgrave Macmillan US, 2016.

Rubin, Zick, and Anne Peplau. "Belief in a Just World and Reactions to Another's Lot: A Study of Participants in the National Draft Lottery." *Journal of Social Issues* 29, no. 4 (October 1973): 73–93. https://doi.org/10.1111/j.1540-4560.1973.tb00104.x.

———. "Who Believes in a Just World?" *Journal of Social Issues* 31, no. 3 (July 1975): 65–89. https://doi.org/10.1111/j.1540-4560.1975.tb00997.x.

Sandel, Michael J. *The Tyranny of Merit: What's Become of the Common Good?* London: Penguin Books, 2021.

Somers, Margaret R. "Dedemocratizing Citizenship: How Neoliberalism Used Market Justice to Move from Welfare Queening to Authoritarianism in 25 Short Years." *Citizenship Studies* 26, no. 4–5 (2022): 661–74. https://doi.org/10.1080/13621025.2022.2091250.

Sorrentino, Richard M., and Jack E. Hardy. "Religiousness and Derogation of an Innocent Victim." *Journal of Personality* 42, no. 3 (September 1974): 372–82. https://doi.org/10.1111/j.1467-6494.1974.tb00681.x.

Spencer, Nick. "Margaret Thatcher (1979–90)." In *The Mighty and the Almighty: How Political Leaders Do God*, edited by Nick Spencer, 1–10. London: Biteback Publishing, 2017.

Steger, Manfred B., and Ravi K. Roy. *Neoliberalism: A Very Short Introduction*. 2nd ed. Oxford: Oxford University Press, 2021. https://doi.org/10.1093/actrade/9780198849674.001.0001.

Thatcher, Margaret. "Speech at Jagiellonian University in Krakow." Margaret Thatcher Foundation, 3 October 1991. https://www.margaretthatcher.org/document/108284.

———. "Speech at St Lawrence Jewry." Margaret Thatcher Foundation, 4 March 1981. https://www.margaretthatcher.org/document/104587.

———. "Speech to Greater London Young Conservatives (Iain Macleod Memorial Lecture – 'Dimensions of Conservatism')." Margaret Thatcher Foundation, 4 July 1977. https://www.margaretthatcher.org/document/103411.

Thatcher, Margaret, and Bruce Anderson. "Interview for *Sunday Telegraph*." Margaret Thatcher Foundation, 26 June 1987. https://www.margaretthatcher.org/document/106660.

Thatcher, Margaret, and Ronald Butt. "Interview for *Sunday Times*." Margaret Thatcher Foundation, 1 May 1981. https://www.margaretthatcher.org/document/104475.

The Museum of Methodism & John Wesley's House. "Stranger's Friend Society Annual Accounts, 1786–91." Accessed 14 July 2024. https://www.wesleysheritage.org.uk/object/strangers-friend-society-annual-accounts-1786-91/.

Treanor, Paul. "Neoliberalism: Origins, Theory, Definition," 20 May 2023. https://web.archive.org/web/20230520180529/http://web.inter.nl.net/users/Paul.Treanor/neoliberalism.html.

United Methodist Church (USA). *The Book of Discipline of the United Methodist Church, 2016*. The United Methodist Publishing House, 2016. https://find.library.duke.edu/catalog/DUKE008404106.

Vickers, Mark. *God in Number 10: The Personal Faith of the Prime Ministers, from Balfour to Blair*. Society for Promoting Christian Knowledge, 2022.

Vincent, John J. 'Poor, The." A Dictionary of Methodism in Britain and Ireland. Accessed 14 July 2024. https://dmbi.online/index.php?do=app.entry&id=2202.

Weiss, Antonio E. "The Religious Mind of Mrs Thatcher." Margaret Thatcher Foundation, 14 June 2011. https://www.margaretthatcher.org/document/112748.

Wesley, John. "Circular Letter on 1770 Minutes." In *The Works of John Wesley, Volume 28: Letters IV: 1766–1773*, edited by Randy L. Maddox, 395–98. The Bicentennial Edition of the Works of John Wesley. Abingdon Press, 2023.

———. "Journal Entry for Thursday 8 February 1753." In *The Works of John Wesley, Volume 20: Journal and Diaries, III, 1743–1754*, edited by W. Reginald Ward and Richard P. Heitzenrater, 445. The Bicentennial Edition of the Works of John Wesley. Abingdon Press, 1991.

———. "Justification by Faith." In *The Works of John Wesley, Volume 1: Sermons,*

I, 1–33, edited by Albert C. Outler, 181–99. The Bicentennial Edition of the Works of John Wesley. Abingdon Press, 1984.

———. "Letter: To the Rev. Charles Wesley." In *The Works of John Wesley, Volume 28: Letters IV: 1766–1773,* edited by Randy L. Maddox, 406–7. The Bicentennial Edition of the Works of John Wesley. Nashville, TN: Abingdon Press, 2023.

———. "On Pleasing All Men." In *The Works of John Wesley, Volume 3: Sermons, III,* 71–114, edited by Albert Cook Outler, 416–26. The Bicentennial Edition of the Works of John Wesley. Abingdon Press, 1986.

———. "On Visiting the Sick." In *The Works of John Wesley, Volume 3: Sermons, III,* 71–114, edited by Albert C. Outler, 385–97. The Bicentennial Edition of the Works of John Wesley. Abingdon Press, 1986.

———. "On Working Out Our Own Salvation." In *The Works of John Wesley, Volume 3: Sermons, III,* 71–114, edited by Albert C. Outler, 199–209. The Bicentennial Edition of the Works of John Wesley. Abingdon Press, 1986.

———. "Salvation by Faith." In *The Works of John Wesley, Volume 1: Sermons, I,* 1–33, edited by Albert C. Outler, 117–30. The Bicentennial Edition of the Works of John Wesley. Abingdon Press, 1984.

———. "The Danger of Increasing Riches," in *The Works of John Wesley, Volume 4: Sermons, IV,* 115–151, edited by Albert C. Outler, 178–86. The Bicentennial Edition of the Works of John Wesley. Abingdon Press, 1987.

———. "The Danger of Riches," in *The Works of John Wesley, Volume 3: Sermons, III,* 71–114, edited by Albert Cook Outler, 228–46. The Bicentennial Edition of the Works of John Wesley. Abingdon Press, 1986.

———. "The Imperfection of Human Knowledge." In *The Works of John Wesley, Volume 2: Sermons, II,* 34–70, edited by Albert C. Outler, 568–86. The Bicentennial Edition of the Works of John Wesley. Abingdon Press, 1985.

———. "The Late Work of God in North America." In *The Works of John Wesley, Volume 3: Sermons, III,* 71–114, edited by Albert C. Outler, 595–608. The Bicentennial Edition of the Works of John Wesley. Abingdon Press, 1986.

———. "The Lord Our Righteousness." In *The Works of John Wesley, Volume 1: Sermons, I,* 1–33, edited by Albert C. Outler, 449–65. The Bicentennial Edition of the Works of John Wesley. Abingdon Press, 1984.

———. "The One Thing Needful." In *The Works of John Wesley, Volume 4: Sermons, IV,* 115–51, edited by Albert C. Outler, 352–59. The Bicentennial Edition of the Works of John Wesley. Abingdon Press, 1987.

———. 'The Repentance of Believers'. In *The Works of John Wesley, Volume 1: Sermons I,* 1–33, edited by Albert C. Outler, 335–52. The Bicentennial Edition of the Works of John Wesley. Abingdon Press, 1984.

———. "The Signs of the Times." In *The Works of John Wesley, Volume 2: Sermons, II,* 34–70, edited by Albert C. Outler, 522–33. The Bicentennial Edition of the Works of John Wesley. Abingdon Press, 1985.

———. "The Use of Money." In *The Works of John Wesley, Volume 2: Sermons, II,* 34–70, edited by Albert C. Outler, 263–80. The Bicentennial Edition of the Works of John Wesley. Nashville, TN: Abingdon Press, 1985.

———. "Thoughts on Salvation by Faith." In *The Works of John Wesley, Volume 13: Doctrinal and Controversial Treatises II,* edited by Paul Wesley Chilcote and Kenneth J. Collins, 553–56. Nashville, TN: Abingdon Press, 2013.

———. "Thoughts on the Present Scarcity of Provisions." In *The Works of the Reverend John Wesley, A. M, Volume VI,* 274–78. New York: J. Emory and B. Waugh, for the Methodist Episcopal Church, 1831. https://archive.org/details/worksofreverendj06wesl/page/278/mode/2up.

———. "Thoughts upon Methodism." In *The Works of John Wesley, Volume 9: The Methodist Societies: History, Nature, and Design,* edited by Rupert E. Davies, 527–30. The Bicentennial Edition of the Works of John Wesley. Abingdon Press, 1989.

Znaniecki, Florian. *The Laws of Social Psychology.* University of Chicago Press, 1925. http://archive.org/details/lawsofsocialpsyc00znan.

4. BEYOND THE HOLOCENE

Implications of Determining Our Geological Age for the Future of Methodism and the Planet

Joerg Rieger

Introduction

People who think in terms of geological epochs are aware that we may be finding ourselves at the end of the age of the Holocene that began with the end of the Ice Age about 11,000 years ago. What comes next is hotly debated, with some arguing that the current age is better characterized as the Anthropocene, the age when human beings determine the future of the planet.[1] Others argue that we find ourselves in the age of the so-called Capitalocene,[2] as what determines the fate of the planet is not primarily the collective presence of large numbers of human beings on the planet but extraordinary concentrations of money and power, unlike anything the world has ever seen. For theologians, this debate gains urgency if it can be argued that geological ages have implications for theology. Using the example of the Capitalocene, concentrations of money and power appear to determine not only economics and politics but also all other relationships, including culture and religion. This is the argument developed in my book *Theology in the Capitalocene*.[3]

The differences between discourses that feature the notion of the Anthropocene and discourses that argue for the notion of the Capitalocene go deep. Take the example of carbon footprint calculators. These instruments were invented by British Petroleum in the early 2000s to shift a sense of responsibility for CO2 emissions from producers to consumers. Much of the discussion of the Anthropocene takes place within this horizon: any and all human beings who burn fossil fuels supposedly are at fault for the climate crises, consumers get the blame for consumption and overconsumption, humanity as such is said to be the main problem, there are too many people living on the planet, it is claimed, and so on. Discussions of the Capitalocene, by contrast, remind us that 71 percent of CO2 emissions are produced in conjunction with the interests of only 100 corporations,[4] that large-scale consumption is driven by the interests of large producers in whose economic interest it is to produce and sell as much as possible, and that the problem is not humanity in general but a system that develops its influence by exploiting both people and the planet.

Anthropocene or Capitalocene? Theological Challenges

For theologians, where we position ourselves in these conversations makes a profound difference, and even those who do not think in these terms are often found in the dominant camp, which assumes that we find ourselves in the Anthropocene. Those who primarily think in terms of the Anthropocene tend to blame the problems of our age on human failures, such as lack of care for creation, consumerism, greed, hatred, disregard for other people, lack of care for the environment, and so on. The theological underpinnings presuppose notions of sin tied to individual and collective human failure that are sometimes considered structural but do not engage the largest systemic structures. In this paradigm, for instance, individualism and the fragmentation of relationships are lamented rather than the large-scale exploitation of people and planet that marks our age. Communitarianism is often seen as the appropriate response, assuming that the widely lamented deterioration of human community (sin) can be fixed by the formation of new communities (salvation). In ecological circles, communitarianism includes concern for the breakdown of community between human and other-than-human beings and calls for the renewal of such communities. What is missing here is a deeper understanding of the underlying problems of our age, which are not necessarily individualism and fragmentation as such, which are symptoms, but foundational relationships of exploitation of both people and the planet, which curtail human and other-than-human agency and therefore need to be addressed if the formation of community is the goal.

Those who are beginning to reflect on the theological implications of the Capitalocene can, of course, learn much from the proliferation of reflections on the Anthropocene, but they need to engage some of the questions differently. Here, the problems of our age are not primarily individual human failures and shortcomings but profound structural distortions of the world, rooted in the systemic exploitation of people and planet for the profit of the few rather than the many. This changes at its core how we think about theological categories of sin, evil, and salvation, approaching classical theological definitions of sin as total depravity, a sense of original sin, and requires a search for more robust visions of salvation. Sin, in the framework of the Capitalocene, is not merely human failure or generic shortcomings of humanity as a whole. Sin is a specific structural distortion of particular relationships between humans as well as between humans and other-than-humans, including relationships with God. Talking about the Capitalocene, therefore, reminds us of the magnitude of the reality of sin, the blame for which cannot be put on the back of individuals, lumping together eight million human beings, but needs to be investigated further in a serious search for adequate solutions, which requires more robust visions of the doctrine of salvation.

The Predicament of the Capitalocene

For theologians engaging the Wesleyan and Methodist traditions, these conversations are particularly significant. Talking about Methodism in terms of the Anthropocene is counterproductive for various reasons. Already John Wesley's eighteenth-century insights into the structural problems of his time push beyond what is now called the Anthropocene. Wesley famously understood, for instance, that what he called "provisions" were scarce not because England was overpopulated or because the land could not produce enough food. Wesley saw some of the problems that mark the early beginnings of what we are now calling the Capitalocene, including the fact that the many were pushed off their lands by the few who were creating monopolies,[5] and that natural resources such as grains were only limited because they were misappropriated for the economic gain of the few. In Wesley's analysis, this included the complex problem of alcohol distilling for hard liquors that started with the requisition of grain for the production of alcohol, which he felt could have been used for feeding people,[6] and ended in the selling of alcohol to the working majority, thereby producing dependencies that were economic, psychological, and spiritual. At the heart of the problem, Wesley argued, was the luxury of the rich, which he considered to be "the most terrible [cause] of all, and the most destructive of both personal and social happiness."[7] These problems, and Methodism's solutions to them, point us to the horizons of the Capitalocene rather than the Anthropocene.

Likewise, Wesley understood some of the harms of imperial relations of his time, as Theodore Jennings has shown. These included a wide-ranging critique, starting with the violent conquest of Latin America by the Spanish and the Portuguese, but extending also to Dutch, French, and British schemes that led to the extermination of whole nations around the globe. At the root of it in Britain was "British policy regarding the mercantile subjugation of India and the conduct of the slave trade,"[8] which are early markers of the Capitalocene. What is particularly interesting is that Wesley in various places compares these policies of Britain as a Christian nation with policies of non-Christian nations, noting that the British exploitation of India was far worse than anything.[9]

Equally devastating is Wesley's critique of the slave trade, pointing out the dynamics of early capitalism that drove it, with specific attention to the money of the merchants and the plantation owners that enabled the systemic cruelty of slavery. At the heart of it all, he addressed the British nation in theological terms, talking about the "principal sin of our nation" in terms of "the blood that we have shed in Asia, Africa, and America." In this sin, Wesley made it clear that the slave trade as well as the trading in East India "seem very nearly allied." The underlying problem, according to Wesley, was the nobility's and gentry's contempt for and neglect of "the solemn worship of Almighty God."[10] The goal of these deliberations for Wesley was not mere protest and critique but a call to repentance: "Let us follow the example of the Ninevites. Let us 'break off our sins by repentance.'"[11] Limiting our theological reflections to the Anthropocene would, therefore, miss some of the central topics that Wesley's engagement of the problems of the dawn of the Capitalocene reveals.

Before addressing some of the ecological implications, consider the implications for human relationships and for religion. Unlike the discourse of the Anthropocene, the Capitalocene draws our attention to a distortion of human relationships that is most visible in labor relations, which shape the 99 percent (who have to work for a living) deeply if only because most people are spending so many of their waking hours at work. Unfortunately, this is still rarely discussed in theological and religious circles, perhaps because it is easier to talk about sin in terms of sexuality than in terms of economic relationships. One of the foundational pillars of the Capitalocene is the exploitation of labor relations, which distorts not only human relationships but also the practice of religion. The reality of class exploitation was discovered decades before Karl Marx, who is usually seen as the first pointing out this problem at the heart of capitalism, by Wesley's contemporary Adam Smith. Smith, often called the father of capitalism, knew that this economic system was built on unequal class relationships, giving employers the advantage. In situations of disagreement, for instance, Smith notes that masters can hold out much longer than workers, due to their greater resources. Smith also notes that the masters are typically better connected and organized than the workers.[12]

For the churches, this reflection on labor relations has special significance, as those whom Smith calls the masters tend to call the shots not only in financial but also in theological matters. Most pastors know very well what they can and cannot afford (figuratively and literally) to say from the pulpits, and whole church bodies, including many bishops, follow suit.

While proponents of the Anthropocene might recognize class differentials as well, the problem does not weigh centrally on the conversation. Proponents of the Capitalocene, on the other hand, start with the insight that there are power differentials among humanity that have grave consequences not only for human relationships but also for the planet and for religion. Take the example of religious images and ideas. Throughout the Holocene, the past 11,000 years since the Ice Age during which human civilizations and religious reflection emerged, images of the divine have been shaped by images of the powerful. Images of God as king gained prominence, although they run counter to the many images of God in the Hebrew Bible as worker (as potter, gardener, tailor, shepherd, including jobs that were relegated to women in ancient society).[13] The same is true for images of Christ as emperor, which run counter to the ministry of Jesus and were not part of early Christian imagery but followed Christianity's ascent to positions of power in the Roman Empire, especially post Constantine in the fourth century, BCE. Today, images of God still line up with traditional images of power. When God's power is perceived as absolute and top down, today this resembles more closely the power of captains of industry and CEOs than anything else, in contrast even to the power of top politicians, which is typically subject to some kinds of checks and balances, and in contrast to kings and emperors, who had clear mandates to care for the community as a whole, which captains of industry and CEOs have not.[14]

Reflecting on the Capitalocene, therefore, includes accounts of the large-scale shifts that mark our age and that make it impossible for anyone, including faith communities, to pull themselves up by their own bootstraps. This is at the core of many traditional doctrines of sin that are reflected in Methodism. Such large-scale shifts affect everyone, whether people are aware of it or not. The most prominent result of these shifts today is climate change, which is the consequence of ongoing relationships of exploitation of both people and the planet, and which has the potential to end life on the planet as we know it. These large-scale shifts are linked also with dominant religious practices, whose power is grounded in various colonialisms. The rise of European Christianity, for instance, goes hand in hand with the Conquest of Latin America, and Christianity in the United States has been riding the waves of success of American-style hegemony and capitalism, whether faith communities are aware of this or not.[15]

Yet the point of investigating the predicaments of the Capitalocene is not hypercriticism and despair; just the opposite. In the Wesleyan spirit, the point of investigating sin is to investigate what alternatives might be emerging fueled by divine grace, and what God is doing in the midst of it all to make a difference. This, rather than anthropological pessimism that gets stuck with human depravity, is the point of theological investigations of sin, especially in the Methodist traditions.

Sin, Salvation, and Grace in the Capitalocene

In the Wesleyan traditions, as well as in the holiness traditions more broadly conceived, there have always been strong concerns for sin and sinfulness. John Wesley himself noted that on this topic he came as close to Calvinism as he possibly could. Accordingly, a sense of "total depravity" formed one of the pillars of his theology, together with the pillars of justification and sanctification.[16] What may come as a surprise is that this puts Wesley in the proximity of liberation theologies. While liberal theologies tend to find notions of total depravity and sin too negative and depressing, liberation theologies—by contrast—have picked up strong notions of sin and sinfulness. In contrast with many conservative theologies, the reason for engaging sin and sinfulness is to overcome them at their roots, with a view toward the sanctification of the whole world.

At the root of these conversations for both holiness and liberation theologians is not theological correctness but profoundly traumatizing experiences that things are not the way they are supposed to be.[17] Moreover, for both holiness and liberation theologians, the world, and humanity within it, are subjects of systemic distortions that transcended individual human sin and personal evil. The goal of these conversations, for the holiness movements as well as for liberation theologies, is not to put people down and make them feel bad but to deal with the structures of sin and to move toward sanctification and thus salvation. The context for all of this is broader than humanity, as all creation has been impacted by sin, and salvation therefore takes place in the broader context of the restoration of creation. For good reasons, M. Douglas Meeks finds in Wesley "a theology knit together by trust in God's promise to create all things anew and an abiding confidence in the presence of the new creation as premise and power of the Christian life."[18]

Reflections on Methodism in the Capitalocene, therefore, may have to contribute something that transcends Methodism and even Christianity and narrow definitions of religion. The core insight that goes back to Wesley and his ancestors is that sin and sinfulness can only be seen in light of what he called "prevenient grace." In other words, sin needs to be investigated not in itself but in light of an encounter with something that transcends sin. For Wesley, this was an encounter with God's grace. And since grace for Wesley was always a matter of personal relationships with God, we might extend his insight to other relationships that resist the shapes that sin has taken on in our own time. Examples include personal relations that have proven to be somewhat resilient to the capitalist spirit of exploitation, including relations of parents and children, lovers, and some relations between human and other-than-human beings. For Christians, that such relationships exist, even if they are not perfect, are signs that God is at work in the world, and they can guide us into deeper relationships with Godself, which is at the heart of it all.

Salvation, in this context, is not an escape into an ethereal heaven that leaves the world behind but a transformation of relationships in the world at all levels, here and now. John Wesley says as much in one of his most elemental sermons, "The Scripture Way of Salvation" (based on Eph 2:8: "ye have been saved" [KJV]), where he points out that salvation is most fruitfully discussed neither as the going to heaven after death nor as eternal happiness. Rather, Wesley emphasizes that salvation is what takes place here and now: "ye are saved" or "ye have been saved" is how Wesley translates the passage from Ephesians.[19] This has implications both for humans and other-than-humans, as we shall see. And once it can be shown that salvation is real before death, its reality after death might be more fruitfully discussed as well.

In the Capitalocene, this means that people of faith need to be liberated from the deep-seated and fatalistic assumption that the end of the world is more likely than the end of capitalism. What would sanctification and holiness mean in this context? While Wesleyan theology has traditionally dwelled on the implications for human relationships, in what follows we will take a closer look at ecological relationships as well.

Social Religion, Human, Other-Than-Human, and Divine

John and Charles Wesley agreed that there can be no religion but social religion, no holiness but social holiness.[20] Their point was not merely the commonplace that faith can only flourish in communities of faith; they argued that faith always needs to be connected to the world, or it vanishes. Religion, in John Wesley's words, "cannot subsist at all without society, without living and conversing" with other people.[21] These others include not only other Christians but also those who most Christians would rather avoid, like people who, according to Wesley, "do not obey, perhaps do not believe, the gospel of our Lord Jesus Christ" and others who are hungry and naked.[22]

While John Wesley's concern for salvation was for all of humanity, it was never limited to humanity. He cared for the well-being of animals and his hope for the ultimate deliverance of humans applied to the ultimate deliverance of animals as well.[23] This hope resonates with the apostle Paul's hope "that the creation itself will be set free from its enslavement to decay and will obtain the freedom of the glory of the children of God" (Rom 8:21). Wesley's theological reason for this hope is that "all things" are "full of God."[24] These concerns of Wesley have been picked up again recently by indigenous Wesleyan theologians in the Pacific and elsewhere, with an awareness that the realities in the Capitalocene prevent us from developing and deepening our theological understanding of the relation of God with everything else. According to Upolu Vaai, "The neoliberal capitalist philosophy of growth thrives with this one-dimensional narrative"[25]—that is, the discounting of the nonhuman world, according to which the earth is considered merely an afterthought or, to use the language of business, an externality that does not have to be accounted for.

The consequences of failing to address the realities of the Capitalocene can be seen in understandings of sanctification that stay on the surface and fail to go deeper. Take, for example, Methodist efforts in the United States to promote what is often called "creation care." This term is designed as a reminder that people of faith are called not only to care for human beings but also for the environment and for the planet as a whole. While well-intentioned efforts of care for the environment have made a positive difference in many ways—not caring is always worse—the theological shortcoming of projects of creation care is that notions of sin, and therefore notions of salvation, tend to be underdeveloped. Is the underlying problem of ecological devastation and climate change merely one of neglect and omission, the simple lack of care for the environment and the planet? Those who focus on the current age in terms of the Anthropocene are likely to agree, especially when they offer critiques of the anthropocentrism of modernity (not only in religion but also in science) that follow in the footsteps of Lynn White's still often-quoted critique that dates back to the 1960s.[26] From the perspective of the Capitalocene, however, a very different problem emerges that challenges theologians to deepen the notions of sin and salvation further.

Vaai's Pacific Wesleyan theology, which he calls "eco-relational theology," helps deepen theological reflections in two ways: by taking yet another look at the notion of sin and by emphasizing the "primacy of the relationality of God,"[27] which was central to Wesley's theology and what we might consider to be the ultimate goal of salvation. Regarding sin, "the greatest sin that we have to deal with," according to Vaai, is a "thirst for power where we go to great lengths to protect systems and structures that secure such power."[28] This insight can be expanded by taking a closer look at whose thirst for power matters most and is most damaging in the current situation. While thirst for power may be widespread, as Vaai insinuates, only the most privileged few occupy the seats of power that shape the fate of Capitalocene and therefore the fate of the planet. This is often overlooked due to a common confusion of privilege and power. In terms of racism, for instance, all white people have privilege but surprisingly few have power. The same is true for sexism and nationalism, where privilege is widely shared but power remains in the hands of the elite few.[29] To describe what is going on as a "human-centric economy," as Vaai does,[30] overlooks that relatively few human beings truly benefit from what is going on.

The second contribution of the Pacific experience is that, in Vaai's words, "relationality is not one-dimensional or human-centric. It is a complex, multidimensional, and cosmological whole. It sees the world as a complex cosmic community that includes God, human beings, others, and the environment that are the elusive constellations of embodied life."[31] For Pacific islanders, this means that the nonhuman environment is perceived as part of their body.[32] This implies another broadening of the notion of salvation. Emphasizing Wesley's insight that all things are full of God, Vaai puts it well when he says that "*all* is Wesley's magic word."[33] This insight needs to be developed further by Wesleyan theologians today, as Wesley was not yet able to fully embrace what this "all" could possibly mean, especially when it comes to other-than-human nature. Indigenous Pacific cultures in particular can help us explore the meaning of this "all," in conversation with eco-relational thinking in various places, including other native traditions around the globe, perhaps even certain strands of European romanticism and US naturalism, as well as new materialism and eco-socialism, as long as they bear in mind and keep investigating the wide-ranging distortions of the Capitalocene.

The emphasis on the close relationship of humanity and the environment that includes a relationship with God also has parallels in African contexts. Simagaliso Kumalo and Kisitu Gyaviira, writing from Kwazulu-Natal in South Africa, observe that "indigenous knowledge systems and African eco-friendly cultural values see the physical environment not as a slave to humanity but as sacred and as something spiritual through which the ancestors communicate to the living."[34] Moreover, they note a parallel between the wisdom of the Akans of Ghana and Christianity. Where the Akans believe that "the universe is living because the divine is actively involved in it," Christians assume that "creation has dignity because God dwells in it through His Spirit and sustains it."[35] Kumalo and Gyaviira quote John Wesley saying that "the wisdom as well as the power of God is abundantly manifest in his creation."[36] For Kumalo and Gyaviira, these theological emphases feed back into the defense and protection of the environment that resembles John Wesley's defense of the poor.[37] We might need to take this insight one step further, as this notion of defense of environment and the poor leaves open the question of agency, and investigate what contribution might the environment and the poor make to overcoming sin and working toward salvation.

Emerging Alternatives

Digging deeper into the logic of the Capitalocene, Timothy Eberhart identifies "one of the central errors of capitalist economic logic" as "the denial of the fundamental primacy of land and nature in the production and sale of commodities for financial profit."[38] Reversing this mistake, Eberhart follows Vandana Shiva's argument that "nature is the world's dominant producer."[39] Here, sin is the failure to recognize and value that which contributes to the flourishing of human and other-than-human nature. This is the question of agency that is central to Wesleyan notions of salvation and sanctification, and which for Christian theologians is always rooted in the primary agency of God, extending from there to human and other-than-human nature. From here, we can explore further the core of theological accounts of alternatives to the Capitalocene.

A revised account of Paul Tillich's concept of the "ultimate concern," which he considers to be the subject matter of theology, provides a first step. According to Tillich, this ultimate concern is a matter of being and not being, which he found in the topics of existential philosophy, including questions of meaning and meaninglessness, still at the heart of much theology and many Sunday sermons.[40] From a Wesleyan perspective, however, putting Tillich back from his head on his feet, it can be argued that the ultimate concern is more closely related to agency, something that people do—that is, living a sanctified life. This agency can be expanded beyond humanity, as other-than-human agency also affects matters of being and not being. Theologians need to remind themselves of the obvious but mostly ignored fact that no life exists without the productive and reproductive agency of people and the planet, making it the principal stuff of being and not-being, starting for humans and other mammals with the gestational labor of our mothers.

Theologically speaking, making constructive contributions to the flourishing of life is what is at the heart of holiness and sanctification. Without the synergy of divine, human, and other-than-human agency there would be no being at all, only not-being. In the Capitalocene, we also need to remind ourselves that not even productive labor would exist without reproductive labor. Reproductive labor is foundational, even though in the Capitalocene, essential reproductive labor has been relegated to minorities, women, and nonhuman beings in massive ways, exploiting even some of our most basic and intimate relationships. Moreover, there would be no biological life without the reproductive labor of many nonhuman entities, beginning with single-cell organisms and bacteria.

All this has implications for productive labor as well, which are strangely under-reflected both in theological circles and in faith communities. Productive labor is at the heart of the genesis of the Capitalocene, for without the exploitation of productive labor power broadly conceived, there would be no profit for the few on which everything else rests (including the much-decried financial capitalism), and the extreme power differentials we are seeing today would not exist. As a result, productive labor that manages to overcome its exploitation and alienation is a major factor in overcoming the basic structures of the Capitalocene. Note that this labor is always accomplished by the majority of people and the planet and therefore always diverse both in terms of identity (do not imagine it in the dominant image of white men in hard hats) and in terms of what it does (always including differently abled people and other mostly overlooked agents, contrary to entrenched ableisms). A theological revaluation of these contributions that locates the divine there and expands the conversations of salvation and sanctification, in conjunction with insights from around the world, would be a major step in the right direction.

Reclaiming agency is, therefore the first step toward identifying alternatives to the Capitalocene, where the exploitation of productive and reproductive labor of people and the planet is what accounts for the growing wealth gap and the tremendous power of the few over the many.[41] For Wesley, as Eberhart points out, in contrast to the logic of the Capitalocene, "the primary purpose of economic life . . . is not the increase of short-term, abstract financial value but rather the material sustainment and bodily health of creaturely life." As a result, "for Methodist Christians today, that must entail engaging in the production, distribution, and consumption of real goods and services that foster the flourishing of human and more-than-human others as a means of faithfully worshiping the Father/Mother in economic life."[42] Whether Eberhart intended this or not, engaging in production is indeed first, followed by matters of distribution and redistribution, a fact which is missed in widespread contemporary critiques of capitalism that focus on distribution and redistribution alone.[43]

The centrality of productive and reproductive agency becomes even clearer when thinking about sin in the Capitalocene: what fuels its power and influence is precisely the exploitation of human and other-than-human labor, which is where profit is ultimately anchored. Add to that the related mechanisms of extraction, particularly of fossil fuels, and talking about "fueling" power and influence is no longer merely a metaphor.[44] Theological notions of sin are further deepened in this context, as the structural reality of sin is now more profoundly understood in terms of the ultimate distortions of relationships between humans, other-than-humans, and God, which is at the heart of the classical definitions of sin.

Nevertheless, locating sin in the Wesleyan holiness traditions is also always the beginning of locating salvation. If the understanding of sin is deepened in light of systematically distorted relations of labor and agency, which affect our relationship to others, to the world, and to God—our understanding of salvation can be deepened here as well. First, if labor, productive and reproductive, human and other-than-human, is at the heart of the Capitalocene to such an extent that it is "essential" in the truest sense of the word, labor is a place where resistance can form. If nothing else, the Covid-19 pandemic has provided a sense of the essential nature of much of work, without which there would be only not-being rather than being. No one could ever assume that "only a dead worker is a good worker," the unfortunate statement made about many human beings in history. And to state it clearly so that this will not be missed: this labor, productive and reproductive, human and other-than-human, always includes the work of God, which is the core of the "ultimate concern."

Second, alternative forms of productive and reproductive labor are already being developed, organized, and networked, although the broader public is often not aware of it. What is most exciting for theologians is that these forms of work can feed back into new ways of living the Christian faith and being the church, if faith and labor are put in conversation with each other. Worker cooperatives, for instance, are embodying substantial ways of working together that turn the logic of the Capitalocene on its head because profit is no longer produced for the few but appropriated by the many, decisions are made by the many instead of by the few, and democratic relations are established in areas where democracy is typically absent. This cooperative logic extends to the practice of religion in the Capitalocene as well, which can now develop some resilience against the lures of big money and contribute to the flourishing of life.[45] Moreover, this cooperative logic extends not only to humanity but also to other-than-human nature and ultimately to encounters of the divine. As biologists have shown, there is a tremendous amount of cooperation going on in nonhuman nature, from rhizome systems that connect trees to collaborations among animals.[46] Salvation here, developed in terms of holiness notions of sanctification inspired by Wesleyan theology, amounts to new forms of agency and new ways of life that subvert and overcome sinful structures to such a degree that a qualitative difference is made.

These reflections on production take us back to different ways of agency that mark the Christian life, traditionally called discipleship, in sync with the agency of God in Christ through the power of the Holy

Spirit. In the Wesleyan traditions, divine agency in the world always develops in synergy with human agency, inviting people into emerging relationships that start with prevenient grace and grow toward some sort of perfection. And since not even Wesley claimed perfection for himself, the point of talking about perfection is the journey toward qualitatively different ways of life rather than perfectionist utopias or arrogance. Sanctification, which in the Wesleyan traditions is the process of moving forward in terms of somewhat imperfect perfections (Wesley excluded human limitations from his definition of perfection[47]), can therefore be understood as new ways of agency and productivity that mirror the old slogan of socialist movements "from each according to their abilities, to each according to their needs." It is unfortunate that the two parts of this statement have so often been separated from each other, as if socialism—and the ministry of Christianity—is only a matter of welfare and taking care of others, and not also a matter of agency and encouraging people to make use of their God-given abilities to make a positive difference in the world.

Conclusions

If sin is not merely a matter of personal morality and failure to care, salvation needs to be more than self-improvement and the development of virtues. Wesleyan traditions have developed broader understandings of salvation that continue to deepen today. In past decades, we have developed a much-needed sense of the political aspects of sin and salvation; today we are developing a more profound sense of the economic aspects. All this needs to go hand in hand with the emerging ecological aspects, which can no longer be ignored if humanity is to have a future on this planet.

The notion of the Capitalocene reminds us of what is ultimately at stake: blaming humanity in general, as proponents of the notion of the Anthropocene often do, is just as unhelpful as blaming sin in general for our current predicament. As we begin to understand what and who is driving our disastrous present, we can begin to develop alternatives. The structural realities of exploitation and extraction (which are the foundation of often-lamented relations of oppression and marginalization) need to be addressed head-on by transforming the exploitation of labor and agency (human and other-than-human) and the ever more violent extraction of natural resources that is detrimental to the flourishing of the planet.[48]

For the sake of the future of the planet, this means that romantic notions of ecology are not helpful, as they neglect the heart of the problem. The same is true for shallow notions of sanctification and salvation. Indigenous notions of embodiment may be better suited to address these topics, especially if they are developed in light of what we are up against. This is where Pacific Islanders' concern, expressed by Vaai, that "others are enjoying life from our death"[49] can shake us out of our slumbers, especially if it sinks in that this can illuminate the situation of the majority of humanity, the 99 percent who have to work for a living even in the countries of the North Atlantic. And if the world is indeed indwelled by God's presence, God is affected by this more than we know. Yet as we "work on your own salvation with fear and trembling" (Phil 2:12 NRSVue) in all of these relationships, we should remind ourselves of John Wesley's famous words on his deathbed that "the best of all is that God is with us."

Notes to Chapter 4

1. Even though scientists rejected the notion of the Anthropocene in 2024, the term is still in wide use. "Geologists Reject Declaration of Anthropocene Epoch," *The Guardian*, 22 March 2024, https://www.theguardian.com/science/2024/mar/22/geologists-reject-declaration-of-anthropocene-epoch.

2. Jason W. Moore coined the term Capitalocene. For its origins, see Jason W. Moore, "Anthropocene or Capitalocene? Nature, History, and the Crisis of Capitalism," in *Anthropocene or Capitalocene? Nature, History, and the Crisis of Capitalism*, ed. Jason W. Moore (PM, 2016), 1–12.

3. Joerg Rieger, *Theology in the Capitalocene: Ecology, Identity, Class, and Solidarity* (Fortress Press, 2022).

4. Rebecca Solnit, "Big Oil Coined 'Carbon Footprints' to Blame Us for Their Greed: Keep them on the Hook," *The Guardian*, 23 August 2021, https://www.theguardian.com/commentisfree/2021/aug/23/big-oil-coined-carbon-footprints-to-blame-us-for-their-greed-keep-them-on-the-hook. See also the fact check in Grace Rahman, "Are 100 Companies Causing 71% of Carbon Emissions?," *Full Fact*, 1

November 2018, https://fullfact.org/news/are-100-companies-causing-71-carbon-emissions/.

5. John Wesley, "On the Present Scarcity of Provisions," in *The Works of the Rev. John Wesley*, ed. Thomas Jackson, 3rd ed. (Wesleyan Methodist Book Room, 1872; reprinted Peabody, MA: Hendrickson, 1986), hereafter cited as Jackson, *Works*, XI, 56.

6. Wesley, "On the Present Scarcity," 54–55.

7. Wesley, "On the Present Scarcity," 56. This includes also the use of oats for increasing number of horses to pull the carriages of the wealthy and the waste that is produced in "the kitchens of the great, the nobility and gentry, almost without exception."

8. Theodore W. Jennings, "John Wesley," in *Empire and the Christian Tradition: New Readings of Classical Theologians*, ed. Kwok Pui-lan, Don Compier, and Joerg Rieger (Fortress Press, 2009), 261–62, reference to Wesley's sermon "A Caution Against Bigotry."

9. Jennings, "John Wesley," 263.

10. John Wesley, "A Seasonable Address to the More Serious Part of the Inhabitants of Great Britain," Jackson, *Works* XI, 126–27.

11. Wesley, "A Seasonable Address," 128.

12. Adam Smith, *Inquiry into the Nature and Causes of the Wealth of Nations*, edited with an introduction and notes by Andrew Skinner (Penguin, 1999), book I, chap. 8.

13. Robert Banks, *God the Worker: Journeys into the Mind, Heart, and Imagination of God* (Judson, 1994).

14. According to widely accepted conventions that have become law in some cases, business leaders are exclusively responsible to their shareholders. In more recent conversations, this is sometimes expanded to stakeholders, including consumers, but never to workers.

15. For historical accounts of how big money shapes much of Christianity see, for instance, the work of Kevin Kruse, *One Nation Under God: How Corporate America Invented Christian America* (Basic Books, 2015).

16. See John Wesley, "Minutes of Some Late Conversations Between the Rev. Mr. Wesley's [sic] and Others," in Jackson, *Works*, VIII, 285.

17. For a very helpful investigation of Wesleyan approaches tying together holiness and liberation theologies, while also pointing out some distinctions, see Donald W. Dayton, "'Good News to the Poor': The Methodist Experience after Wesley," in *The Portion of the Poor: Good News to the Poor in the Wesleyan Tradition*, ed. M. Douglas Meeks (Kingswood, 1995), 65–96.

18. M. Douglas Meeks, "Wesleyan Perspectives on the New Creation: An Introduction," in *Wesleyan Perspectives on the New Creation*, ed. M. Douglas Meeks (Kingswood Books, 2004), 13.

19. John Wesley, "The Scripture Way of Salvation," in *Works*, 2:156

20. "The gospel of Christ knows of no religion, but social; no holiness but social holiness." John and Charles Wesley, "List of Poetical Works," in Jackson, *Works*, XIV, 321.

21. John Wesley, "Upon Our Lord's Sermon on the Mount: Discourse the Fourth," in *Works*, 1:533–34.

22. Wesley, "Upon Our Lord's Sermon on the Mount," 535, 546. For a more extended engagement of these arguments, see Joerg Rieger (with contributions by Paulo Ayres Mattos, Helmut Renders, and José Carlos de Souza), *No Religion but Social Religion: Liberating Wesleyan Theology* (Wesley's Foundery Books, 2018), introduction.

23. Randy Maddox, "Nurturing the New Creation: Reflections on a Wesleyan Trajectory," in *Wesleyan Perspectives on the New Creation*, ed. M. Douglas Meeks (Kingswood Books, 2004), 21–52, emphasizes the later Wesley's increased concern not only for socioeconomic structures but also the renewal of the wider cosmos, including the deliverance of animals, ibid., 49.

24. Reference in Theodore Runyon, *The New Creation: John Wesley's Theology Today* (Abingdon Press, 1998), 206.

25. Upolu Luma Vaai, "Others Are Enjoying Life from Our Death," in *Methodist Revolutions: Evangelical Engagements of Church and World*, ed. Joerg Rieger and Upolu Luma Vaai (Wesley's Foundery Books, 2021), 179.

26. Lynn White, "The Historical Roots of Our Ecologic Crisis," *Science* 155, no. 3767 (10 March 11967).

27. Vaai, "Others Are Enjoying Life from Our Death," 194. "Although relationality was not part of Wesley's language, at the heart of his theology was his faith in the relationality of God as expressed in God's free grace for all," ibid., 182.

28. Vaai, "Others Are Enjoying Life from Our Death," 194

29. For a sustained argument on the difference and relation of privilege and power see Rieger, *Theology in the Capitalocene*, chapter 4.

30. Vaai, "Others Are Enjoying Life from Our Death,"180.

31. Vaai, "Others Are Enjoying Life from Our Death," 187

32. Vaai, "Others Are Enjoying Life from Our Death," 188.

33. Vaai, "Others Are Enjoying Life from Our Death," 185, in reference to Wesley's sermon "Free Grace," emphasis in original.

34. R. Simangaliso Kumalo and Kisitu Gyaviira, "Methodist Environmentalism in African Context: Retrieving John Wesley's Ethics of Care and Environmental Protection," in *Methodist Revolutions*, 167–68.

35. Kumalo and Gyaviira, "Methodist Environmentalism in African Context," 169, the second quotation is taken from Nico Voster, *Created in the Image of God: Understanding God's Relationship with Humanity* (Pickwick, 2011), 91.

36. Kumalo and Gyaviira, "Methodist Environmentalism in African Context," 163, quoting from John Wesley's sermon, "The Wisdom of God's Counsels."

37. Kumalo and Gyaviira, "Methodist Environmentalism in African Context," 171.

38. Timothy R. Eberhart, "Sustaining the Planetary Household: Methodist Contributions to an Ecological Economy," in *Methodist Revolutions*, 135.

39. Eberhart, "Sustaining the Planetary Household," 136, quoting Vandana Shiva, *Earth Democracy: Justice, Sustainability, and Peace* (South End, 2005), 16; Shiva continues that "human production shrinks to insignificance in comparison with nature," ibid.

40. Paul Tillich, *Systematic Theology*, vol. 1 (University of Chicago Press, 1951), 14, 49. For a more extensive engagement of Tillich on this matter see Rieger, *Theology in the Capitalocene*, 99–100.

41. This is my argument in Rieger, *Theology in the Capitalocene*, chapter 3.

42. Eberhart, "Sustaining the Planetary Household," 138.

43. This is one of the key shifts I proposed in Joerg Rieger, *No Rising Tide: Theology, Economics, and the Future* (Fortress Press, 2009).

44. It is often argued that the biggest profits are made in the realm of financial capital, but none of this could stand without anchors in exploitation and extraction, which are "essential" in the truest sense of the word. This is even more true when the bubbles of finance are periodically bursting.

45. For examples see the work of the Wendland-Cook Program in Religion and Justice at Vanderbilt University Divinity School (www.religionandjustice.org) and some of its collaborations with the Southeast Center for Cooperative Development (www.co-opsnow.org). For a deeper theological investigation of what is at stake for faith communities and theology see chapter 1 of Rieger, *Theology in the Capitalocene.*

46. For examples see Juliet B. Schor and Craig J. Thompson, "Cooperative Networks, Participatory Markets, and Rhizomatic Resistance: Situating Plenitude within Contemporary Political Economy Debates," in *Sustainable Lifestyles and the Quest for Plenitude: Case Studies of the New Economy*, ed. Juliet B. Schor and Craig J. Thompson (Yale University Press, 2014), 240–41.

47. John Wesley, "Christian Perfection," in *Works*, 2:100–104, notes that perfection does not include perfected knowledge, freedom from mistakes, including mistakes in interpreting the Bible, freedom from weaknesses, imperfections, or temptations.

48. For the connection of exploitation and extraction see Joerg Rieger, "Extraction, Exploitation, and Religious Surplus in the Capitalocene," forthcoming in *Religions*.

49. See the title of Vaai's chapter, "Others Are Enjoying Life from Our Death," 173.

Bibliography

Banks, Robert. *God the Worker: Journeys into the Mind, Heart, and Imagination of God.* Judson, 1994.

Carrington, Damian. "Geologists Reject Declaration of Anthropocene Epoch." *The Guardian.* 22 March 2024.

Dayton, Donald W. "'Good News to the Poor': The Methodist Experience after Wesley," *The Portion of the Poor: Good News to the Poor in the Wesleyan Tradition,* ed. M. Douglas Meeks. Kingswood Books, 1995.

Eberhart, Timothy R. "Sustaining the Planetary Household: Methodist Contributions to an Ecological Economy," in *Methodist Revolutions,* ed. Joerg Rieger and Upoplo Luma Vaai. Wesley's Foundery Books, 2022.

Jennings, Theodore W. "John Wesley," in *Empire and the Christian Tradition: New Readings of Classical Theologians*, ed. Kwok Pui-lan, Don Compier, and Joerg Rieger. Fortress Press, 2009

Kruse, Kevin. *One Nation Under God: How Corporate America Invented Christian America.* Basic Books, 2015

R. Simangaliso Kumalo and Kisitu Gyaviira. "Methodist Environmentalism in African Context: Retrieving John Wesley's Ethics of Care and Environmental Protection," in *Methodist Revolutions*, ed. Joerg Rieger and Upoplo Luma Vaai. Wesley's Foundery Books, 2022

Maddox, Randy. "Nurturing the New Creation: Reflections on a Wesleyan Trajectory," in *Wesleyan Perspectives on the New Creation,* ed. M. Douglas Meeks. Kingswood Books, 2004.

Meeks, M. Douglas. "Wesleyan Perspectives on the New Creation: An Introduction," *Wesleyan Perspectives on the New Creation,* ed. M. Douglas Meeks. Kingswood Books, 2004.

Moore, Jason W. "Anthropocene or Capitalocene? Nature, History, and the Crisis of Capitalism," in *Anthropocene or Capitalocene? Nature, History, and the Crisis of Capitalism*, ed. Jason W. Moore. PM, 2016.

Rahman, Grace. "Are 100 Companies Causing 71% of Carbon Emissions?," *Full Fact*, 1 November 2018, https://fullfact.org/news/are-100-companies-causing-71-carbon-emissions/.

Rieger, Joerg (with contributions by Paulo Ayres Mattos, Helmut Renders, and José Carlos de Souza). *No Religion but Social Religion: Liberating Wesleyan Theology.* Wesley's Foundery Books, 2018.

———, *Theology in the Capitalocene: Ecology, Identity, Class, and Solidarity.* Fortress Press, 2022.

Runyon, Theodore. *The New Creation: John Wesley's Theology Today*. Abingdon Press, 1998.

Schor, Juliet B. and Craig J. Thompson. "Cooperative Networks, Participatory Markets, and Rhizomatic Resistance: Situating Plenitude within Contemporary Political Economy Debates," in *Sustainable Lifestyles and the Quest for Plenitude: Case Studies of the New Economy*, ed. Juliet B. Schor and Craig J. Thompson. Yale University Press, 2014.

Smith, Adam. *Inquiry into the Nature and Causes of the Wealth of Nations*, edited with an introduction and notes by Andrew Skinner. Penguin, 1999.

Soinit, Rebecca. "Big Oil Coined 'Carbon Footprints' to Blame Us for Their Greed: Keep them on the Hook," *The Guardian*, 23 August 2021, https://www.theguardian.com/commentisfree/2021/aug/23/big-oil-coined-carbon-footprints-to-blame-us-for-their-greed-keep-them-on-the-hook.

Voster, Nico. *Created in the Image of God: Understanding God's Relationship with Humanity*. Pickwick, 2011.

Wesley, John. "Christian Perfection," ed. Albert C. Outler, The Works of John Wesley, volume 2. Abingdon Press, 1985.

———. "Minutes of Some Late Conversations Between the Rev. Mr. Wesley's [sic] and Others," ed. Thomas Jackson, Vol. 8, *The Works of the Rev. John Wesley*, 3rd ed. Wesleyan Methodist Book Room, 1872; reprinted Hendrickson, 1986.

———. "On the Present Scarcity of Provisions," ed. Thomas Jackson, Vol. 11 *The Works of the Rev. John Wesley*, 3rd ed. Wesleyan Methodist Book Room, 1872; reprinted Hendrickson, 1986.

———. "A Seasonable Address to the More Serious Part of the Inhabitants of Great Britain," ed.Thomas Jackson, Vol. 11 *The Works of the Rev. John Wesley*, 3rd ed. Wesleyan Methodist Book Room, 1872; reprinted Hendrickson, 1986.

———. "The Scripture Way of Salvation," ed. Albert C. Outler, *The Works of John Wesley*, volume 2. Abingdon Press, 1985.

———. "Upon Our Lord's Sermon on the Mount: Discourse the Fourth," edited by Albert C. Outler, *The Works of John Wesley*, volume 1. Abingdon Press, 1985.

Wesley, John and Wesley Charles. "List of Poetical Works," ed. Thomas Jackson, Vol. 14 *The Works of the Rev. John Wesley*, 3rd ed. Wesleyan Methodist Book Room, 1872; reprinted Hendrickson, 1986.

White, Lynn. "The Historical Roots of Our Ecologic Crisis," *Science* 155, no. 3767, 10 March 1967.

Vaai, Upolu Lumai. "Others Are Enjoying Life from Our Death," in *Methodist Revolutions: Evangelical Engagements of Church and World*, ed. Joerg Rieger and Upolu Luma Vaai. Wesley's Foundery Books, 2021.

5. JOHN WESLEY'S CRITIQUE OF RACE AND RACISM

Five Models

Tamara E. Lewis

On Thursday evening, March 6, 1788, a riot occurred at the New Room, Bristol, England, when John Wesley delivered an antislavery sermon. He later described the event:

> I preached on that ancient prophecy, "God shall enlarge Japhet. And he shall dwell in the tents of Shem; and Canaan shall be his servant." About the middle of the discourse, while there was on every side attention still as night, a vehement noise arose, none could tell why, and shot like lightning through the whole congregation. The terror and confusion were inexpressible. You might have imagined it was a city taken by storm. The people rushed upon each other with the utmost violence; the benches were broke in pieces; and nine-tenths of the congregation appeared to be struck with the same panic. In about six minutes, the storm ceased, almost as suddenly as it rose; and, all being calm, I went on without the least interruption. It was the strangest incident of the kind I ever remember.[1]

By preaching on Genesis 9:25-27, Wesley challenged biblical interpretation of the "Curse of Ham," used to justify the enslavement of Africans in the eighteenth century. Wesley argued that this scripture indicates the origins of institutional human slavery, a manifestation of original sin, not the perpetual subjugation of Ham's progeny, the offspring of his son Canaan.[2] Instead, as Wesley stressed in a 1791 letter to William Wilberforce, slavery was the wickedness sustained by diabolical forces no earthly effort could overcome without God's power.[3]

Although by the 1770s and the publication of *Thoughts upon Slavery* (1774), Wesley was publicly known as an abolitionist, this had not always been the case. Wesley had always been opposed to slavery but not actively engaged in movements to abolish slavery and the trade. For example, he had previously evangelized enslaved persons in America and England without protesting their condition of servitude.[4] Over time, however, Wesley's consciousness was transformed. Several high-profile legal cases in England drew his attention.[5] He was also acquainted with evangelical preachers who bought, sold, and/or owned enslaved persons, including Jonathan Edwards, the New England Congregationalist, and George Whitefield, Calvinist Methodist and former member of the Oxford Holy Club, both of whom argued passionately for the right to own slaves on biblical grounds.[6] Whitefield not only lobbied for the legalization of slavery in the colony of Georgia and promoted the Bethesda Orphanage, an institution that profited from slave labor, but also wrote treatises defending his actions.[7] In contrast, Wesley established contacts with prominent abolitionists and consumed resources that helped guide his thinking toward an uncompromising stance against all forms of slavery and the slave trade.

I argue that along with attacks on slavery, Wesley developed helpful critiques deconstructing the ideology of race upon which slavery and other racist systems are based. These critiques are found in Wesley's writings, particularly the treatise *Thoughts upon Slavery*, as well as sermons, journal entries, and publications in the *Arminian* magazine, forming five helpful models: First, by critiquing the idea of race based on Enlightenment teachings of African inferiority and European superiority, second, by refuting racist propaganda denying the history of African civilizations, third, by dispelling biblical interpretations that justify God's punishment and condemnation of certain groups of people, fourth, by fighting against racism in legal and sociopolitical structures, and fifth, by promoting racial inclusion, these five models offer instructive guidelines regarding the issues of race and racism for today's Wesleyan leaders.

Before addressing these Wesleyan models, two questions arise.

One, why should we deconstruct race?

Although the societal domination and subordination of some human beings in relation to others is as old as civilization itself, and slavery is an ancient institution that has varied historically, the transatlantic iteration of slavery was particularly heinous. The transatlantic trade not only turned human beings into physical chattel but also functioned in breaking the mind, erasing the identity, and obliterating the soul. Propagators of this version of the institution utilized a novel modern construct, novel as in new and innovative—a distinctive ideology. This distinctive ideology is the Enlightenment construct of race, which created a form of caste that was immutable and unchangeable in developing the modern world. Race marked and stereotyped groups with an indelible, essentialized imprint recognizable by physical characteristics. And it worked. Worked so well, in fact, that following the abolition of the very system, transatlantic slavery, that race was constructed to support, racism attached to systemic institutions and lived on to fight another day. Race, endemic to racism, has managed to adapt remarkably to changing times. And, if race and racism go hand in hand, deconstructing the ideological roots of the construct of race will assist in efforts to dismantle racist systems.

Two, what are the origins of the racial construct?

The modern construct of race emerged in the writings of Enlightenment philosophers, men like the German Johann Blumenbach and the Frenchman George- Louis Declerc. These and others contributed to the systematization of concepts that surprisingly had their origins in religious discourse. Early modern Protestant discourse contains ideas that foreshadow the emergence of race as a construct. These texts use dogmatic language, stressing Protestant emphases on original sin and total depravity, asserting that certain kinds of people are considered innately and irreparably sinful according to nature. These kinds of people included Africans, the Irish, Muslims, or simply pagans. Many Enlightenment philosophers sprang from devout Christian backgrounds and subtly transferred these notions of election into hypotheses supported by pseudo-scientific and pseudo-empirical methods. Swedish taxonomist Carl Linneaus, for example, called "Prince of the Botanists," was a pastor's son and created a system categorizing various species, including human races, in which Africans are lowest on the scale.[8] The Scottish historian David Hume, who had a Presbyterian background, argued that differences in phenotype, including skin color, hair texture, and facial features, denote essentialized characteristics among humans, arranged on a continuum from white, superior, to black, inferior.[9] The German philosopher Immanuel Kant, who grew up in a devout Lutheran family, concurred, postulating that all blacks are ontologically othered and innately unintelligent.[10] John Locke, who championed natural rights theory, had English Puritan parents. His appeal to natural rights holds that all human beings are endowed innately with the right to liberty and equality, ideas that were ironically adopted by abolitionists. However, Locke believed that Africans were essentially nonhuman and had no qualms about investing in the slave trade.[11]

Wesley's five models critiquing race help develop ideas about deconstructing race and thereby effectively dismantling racist systems.

First, Wesley critiqued Enlightenment assumptions of African inferiority and European superiority. Wesley recognized that, in his day, ideas about African inferiority used to justify slavery were becoming increasingly common.[12] During his stay in Georgia, Wesley read the English missionary Morgan Godwyn's 1680 treatise *The Negro and Indian's Advocate, suing for their admission into the church.* Godwyn, writing from experience as a missionary in Barbados and Virginia, complains bitterly that English planters refused to allow preachers on their plantations because enslaved Africans were "Unsoul'd."[13] In *Thoughts upon Slavery*, Wesley attacks this notion by addressing slave traders. He writes, "You have forced them into your ships like an herd of swine, them who have souls immortal as your own." Similarly, the German philosopher Immanuel Kant argued "the Black is not a human . . . the Negroes of Africa have by nature no feeling that rises above the trifling. . . ."[14] Wesley rejected this view, also writing in *Thoughts upon Slavery,* "the African is in no respect inferior to the European."[15] By stressing African equality, Wesley directly challenged the Enlightenment construct of race. His sermon "The Imperfections of Human Knowledge," based on 1 Corinthians 13:9, asks,

> And who cares for thousands, myriads, if not millions, of the wretched Africans? Are not whole droves of these poor sheep (human, if not rational beings), continually driven to market, and sold, like cattle, into the vilest bondage, without any hope of deliverance but by death?[16]

This statement stressing African rationality must be understood within its Enlightenment as well as ecclesial context. The key defining characteristic of human nature, according to eighteenth-century philosophers, was rationality, the function of the mind. This explains René Descartes's infamous quote, "I think, therefore I am." The mind, sequestered from the body, becomes the only consideration in determining the human essence. Reason, the ability to think, became the fundamental criterion for full inclusion in the human family.[17] John and Charles Wesley, men of their time and faithful clergy of the Church of England, which designates scripture, tradition, and reason as interpretative sources of authority, recognized the significance of rationality in addressing the race question.[18] The September 1790 edition of John Wesley's *The Arminian Magazine* includes a poem by William Cowper stressing African rationality despite differences in phenotype.

> Forc'd from home and all its pleasures,
>   Africa's coast I left forlorn;
> To increase a stranger's treasures,
>   O'er the raging billows borne.
> Men from England bought and sold me,
>   Paid my price in paltry gold;
> But though their's they have enroll'd me,
>   Minds are never to be sold.

(And the concluding verse reads):

Skins may differ, but affection
Dwells in white and black the same.[19]

Kant anticipated Charles Darwin's theory of natural selection by suggesting that Africans were not only inferior but developed separately as a species from the more advanced white race. Kant wrote, "The black is a black man; that is to say that as the result of a series of aberrations of affect, [the black man] is established at the core of a universe from which he must be extricated . . . because there are two camps, the white and the black . . . two metaphysics . . . fundamental is the difference between these two races of man."[20] This assertion implies that blacks and whites have distinct origins and lack a common ancestor. In response, Wesley wrote, "God is the Father of the spirits of all flesh who hast mingled of one blood all the nations upon earth."[21] Wesley described Africans as "works of God's own hands, the purchase of thy Son's blood."[22] Wesley's model of directly confronting suppositions about race and racial inferiority challenges us to examine our own internalized beliefs and assumptions about race. By bringing these ideas to the forefront, we can begin dispelling the myths, prejudices, and stereotypes disseminated by a society structured around race and racist ideas.

Second, Wesley attacked the social and cultural propaganda fostered by the Enlightenment that claimed Africa had no viable or impactful civilization or history. Although George Hegel wrote, "Africa is no historical part of the world; it has no movement or development to exhibit," during the nineteenth century, these ideas were in firm rotation during Wesley's day.[23] In *Thoughts upon Slavery,* Wesley includes material based on actual travelogues compiled by others, including the Quaker abolitionist Anthony Benezet, describing several West and Central African polities located in what is now Benin, Congo, and Angola.[24] Their general organization, especially governmental, juridical, economic, bureaucratic, and administrative structures, are outlined. Although he was not the first to disseminate this kind of information, Wesley capitalized on his prominence as a well-regarded religious leader to challenge racist myths about

Africa as uncultured, primitive, and barbarous. He concludes, "Upon the whole, therefore, the Negroes who inhabit the coast of Africa . . . are so far from being the stupid, senseless, brutish, lazy barbarians, the fierce, cruel, perfidious savages they have been described."[25] Wesley's insistence on utilizing hard evidence to refute ideas of African inferiority is noteworthy because the materials included in his work depict kingdoms and polities later destroyed through the invasion and warfare instigated by European conquest. This, I believe, demonstrates Wesley's perhaps unconscious insight that claims of African barbarity would continue to be used for centuries in the political and economic exploitation of the continent. Although Wesley wrote over a century before the 1884 Berlin Conference which divided the African continent among European powers in the systemic siphoning of natural resources that continue to this day, his writings seem to anticipate the colonialist erasure, obscuration, and misinformation regarding African history and culture. Wesley's model of acquiring and disseminating accurate sources about African societies and civilizations is a challenge for today's leaders in the church and society to work in correcting distortions and falsifications about Africa in educational curricula and other resources.

Third, Wesley's theology emphasizes the equality of humanity. In contrast with early English religious discourse that emphasizes divine election and predestination, using metaphor and metonymy to signify the reprobate as Ethiopian or Black, Wesleyan theology argues that the irresistibility of prevenient grace bestows God's covering on all humanity despite sin. Wesley believed in God's eternal love for all human creation, thus in the sermon "Free Grace," he preached, "How freely does God love the world! While we were yet sinners, Christ died for the ungodly. While we were dead in our sin, God spared not his own Son, but delivered him up for us all." Thus, Wesley rejected biblical interpretations used to justify African slavery and inferiority like the Hamitic Curse. Rather than referring to Africans as cursed, Wesley, in *Thoughts upon Slavery*, refers to them as "the noblest creatures in the visible world."[26] Wesley rejected any theological system that limits the ability of humans to move in the direction of divine power through grace. May we, as Wesleyan and Methodist ministers, scholars, and administrators, draw encouragement from Wesley's model emphasizing the equality of love, grace, and mercy toward all humans in our service to God.

Fourth, Wesley renounced political or legal systems that cripple the fundamental liberties of any group. Wesley rejected the legal deprivation of human rights by governments, rights that he argued are innately bequeathed by nature. Human beings, including Africans, as indicated in *Thoughts upon Slavery*, are born with natural rights. Laws of institutions are therefore not authorized by natural law, to, as Wesley wrote, "burst asunder all the ties of humanity."[27] Therefore, the structural imposition of inequality, whether based on the idea of race, or any reason, was outrageously unjust, unethical, and ungodly. As Wesley quipped, "Can law, human law, change the nature of things?"[28] Although Wesley remained a Tory to his dying day, a supporter of the British monarchy and Parliament, no style of governance, in his view, based on any system in any land could ever justly sanction human degradation. He stated, "An Angolan, has the same natural right as an Englishman."[29] Thus, he was indignant upon reading in *The Interesting Narrative of the Life of Olaudah Equiano, or Gustavus Vassa,* that according to American law "a man who has a black skin, being wronged or outraged by a white man, can have no redress; it being a law in all our Colonies that the oath of a black against a white goes for nothing."[30] Wesley's model resisting sociopolitical, legal, and economic inequities challenges us today as Christian leaders to be diligent in advocating for systemic justice in the contemporary world.

Fifth, Wesley promoted racial inclusion. For example, Africans were regular members of the Methodist societies in England.[31] Wesley writes of a May 7, 1780, encounter with a black woman at the Whitehaven society who "semed (sic) to be fuller of love than any of the rest . . . [with] words . . . chosen and utter with a peculiar propriety."[32] Her faith, he claimed, was stronger than any he had ever discerned in England or America. On Friday, March 10, 1786, Wesley also recorded that he baptized a "young negro" who was part of the Bristol society. Further, Wesley used print media to challenge Enlightenment ideas of African inferiority by regularly showcasing stories highlighting the gifts and talents of Africans. In 1781,

The Arminian Magazine began publishing extracts of the poetry of Phyllis Wheatley and other features on exceptional Africans, including a story of an enslaved man named Benjamin Rush, who happened to be a mathematical genius.[33] The importance of Wesley's model of racial inclusion goes without saying. Benefits of diversity include acknowledgment of the breadth and depth of God's rich human creation.

Although the average person may not think consciously about the Enlightenment on a regular basis, underlying suppositions regarding race from this period are still with us. Racial categorizations not only remain firmly embedded in our conceptualizations of human identity, but these notions have extended obliquely into mainstream perceptions of the natural world and its resources. An ever present yet invisible racial hierarchical scale, hovering in our midst like those ubiquitous screens featuring big brother in George Orwell's *1984*, is alive and well. This scale constantly assigns societal value and worth to all aspects of creation. Many people are surprised to learn that throughout history, groups, regions, and individuals operated with degrees of fluidity regarding ethnicity and identity. But in the modern world, one cannot choose or change one's race. In fact, attempting to change one's race, unlike gender, is almost universally condemned and unacceptable, as several high-profile cases have demonstrated.

Wesley's rejection of the Enlightenment construct of race challenges us to think more about our unconscious internalizations of these concepts as well as ordinary ways society fosters these notions through structural racism. Until race is effectively deconstructed ideologically, the possibility of effectively abolishing racism is futile. In other words, deconstructing race is directly related to the dismantling of sociopolitical and economic systems historically structured and perpetually maintained through racial hierarchies.

What about ways that race has been co-opted by various groups and redefined as a positive source of identity? Victor Anderson, professor of theology and ethics at Vanderbilt Divinity School, questions what he describes as "ontological Blackness," or the black metaphysical essentialism projected onto communities of African descent due to racism yet reconfigured by those same communities as new forms of identity and resistance, especially self-love, pride, and respect in an anti-black world.[34] Anderson's critique of ontological blackness, another way of describing race, reminds me of Audre Lorde's famous quote, "The master's tools will never dismantle the master's house." Race, a racist construct, cannot free us from racism. As Kwame Anthony Appiah, professor of philosophy at Princeton University, writes, "There is a danger in making racial identities too central to our conceptions of ourselves; while there is a place for racial identities in a world shaped by racism . . . we shall have, in the end, to move beyond current racial identities."[35] Are there ways that racial healing, inflicted through centuries of racist oppression, can be effectively promoted while working to dismantle our understanding of racial constructs? If so, does this entail holding on to some forms of racial essentialism, even if temporarily, in the curative process?

Finally, Wesley's model, which demonstrates the incompatibility of racial constructs with the goal of human flourishing invites questions of the ways that race, ethnicity, and nationality are enmeshed in modern perceptions. This is already happening. More and more people, no longer forced to pigeonhole themselves into one racial classification, are claiming biracial and multiracial identities. Yet, by these assertions, aren't they really affirming multiple ethnic or national identities, not racial? Clarifying definitions of race, ethnicity, and nationality will be necessary moving forward.

In closing, I am drawn to Wesley's famous last words to William Wilberforce in reflecting upon the hope that racial essentialism, structural racism, and all the isms—especially the various forms of slavery that continue to exist throughout our world—will one day be completely abolished. Wesley's model, I submit, is a mandate for us to go on in the name of God until all these forms of oppression vanish away before the sun.

Notes to Chapter 5

1. John Wesley, diary entry for Monday, March 3, 1788 7:359–60 in *The Journal of the Rev. John Wesley, A.M.* 8 vols., Nehemiah Curnock, ed. [hereafter Curnock] (Epworth Press, 1938).

2. Irv A. Brendlinger, *Social Justice Through the Eyes of Wesley: John Wesley's Theological Challenge to Slavery* (Joshua Press, 2006), 35.

3. *Evangelical Advocacy: A Response to Global Poverty*, "Last Writing of John Wesley (a letter to William Wilberforce)" (2012). Papers, PDF Files, and Presentations. Book 10. http://place.asburyseminary.edu/engaginggovernmentpapers/10.

4. Brendlinger, *Social Justice Through the Eyes of Wesley*, 35.

5.The 1772 Somerset v Stewart case was an English Court of King's Bench judgment, sensationalized throughout England, America, and the colonies, which ruled that an enslaved person brought from the British colony of Jamaica could not be forcibly deported for sale as property because domestic slavery was not English law. The ruling had no effect in the colonies but arguably strengthened the abolitionist cause. See Stephen Usherwood, "The Abolitionists' Debt to Lord Mansfield," *History Today* Vol. 31, No. 3 (1981), 40.

6. See Kenneth P. Minkema, "Jonathan Edwards on Slavery and the Slave Trade," The William and Mary Quarterly 54, no. 4 (1997): 823–34; Stephen J. Stein, "George Whitefield on Slavery: Some New Evidence," *Church History* 42 No. 2 (2009): 243–56.

7. Stephen Stein makes a convincing case that the anonymous London 1743 publication *A Letter to the Negroes Lately Converted to Christ in America*, a theological apology for slavery, was written by George Whitefield.

8. Gunnar Broberg, Carl Linnaeus (Swedish Institute, 2006), 7. See also Frank N. Egerton (2007), "A History of the Ecological Sciences, Part 23: Linnaeus and the Economy of Nature," *Bulletin of the Ecological Society of America* 88 no. 1: 72–88.

9. David Hume, quoted in Immanuel Kant, *Observations on the Feeling of the Beautiful and the Sublime*, John T. Goldthwait, trans. (University of California Press, [1764], 2004), 2:253. See David Hume, History of England, *Containing the Commonwealth, and the Reigns of Charles II and James II*, Vol. II (London: A Millar in the Strand, 1759). Andrew Sabl, *Hume's Politics: Coordination and Crisis in the History of England* (Princeton University Press, 2012).

10. Lucy Allais, "Kant's Racism," Philosophical Papers 45 no. 1 (2016): 1–36. Elvira Basevich, "Reckoning with Kant on Race," *Philosophical Forum* 51 no. 3 (2020): 221–45. Robert Bernasconi, "Kant and Blumenbach's Polyps: A Neglected Chapter in the History of the Concept of Race," in *The German Invention of Race*, ed. Sara Eigen and Mark Larrimore (SUNY Press, 2006), 73–90.

11. Locke was a major investor in the seventeenth century "Company of Royal Adventurers Trading to Africa," a business devoted to West African slave trading.

12. Brendlinger, *Social Justice Through the Eyes of Wesley*, 14–18.

13. Morgan Godwin, *The Negro and Indian's Advocate, Suing for their Admission Into the Church* (1680), 17: 24; University of Michigan Library Collections, accessed January 9, 2026, https://quod.lib.umich.edu/e/eebo2/A42949.0001.001?rgn=main ;view=fulltext.

14. Immanuel Kant, *Observations on the Feeling of the Beautiful and the Sublime*, John T. Goldthwait, trans. (University of California Press, [1764], 2004), 110–11.

15. John Wesley, *Thoughts upon Slavery* (London, 1778), 47; scanned, Academic Affairs Library, UNC-CH University of North Carolina at Chapel Hill, accessed January 9, 2026, docsouth.unc.edu, https://docsouth.unc.edu/church/wesley/wesley.html.

16. John Wesley, "Imperfection of Human Knowledge," *The Sermons of John Wesley*, ed. Thomas Jackson (London, 1872), Sermon 69; scanned Wesley Center Online, accessed December 30, 2025, Wesley.nnu.edu, https://wesley.nnu.edu/john-wesley/the-sermons-of-john-wesley-1872-edition/the-sermons-of-john-wesley-thomas-jacksons-numbering/.

17. See Catherine Molineux, *Faces of Perfect Ebony: Encountering Atlantic Slavery in Imperial Britain* (Harvard University Press, 2012), 180.

18. The year after his ordination as deacon Wesley read a play entitled Oroonoko, or the Royal Slave by Thomas Southerne (1696), based on Aphra Behn's novel, Oroonoko (1688), the story of an African prince who started a slave rebellion after being kidnapped and sold into slavery. Aphra Behn is considered to be the first English woman fiction author. See Brendlinger, *Social Justice Through the Eyes of Wesley*, 16. See also John Wesley, Journals and Diaries in *Works*, 18:410.

19. William Cowper, "On the Slave Trade," *The Arminian Magazine*, Vol. XIII, 502–03, accessed January 9, 2026, Duke Divinity School, divinity.duke.edu, https://divinity.duke.edu/sites/default/files/documents/36_Arminian_Magazine_%281785-91%29.pdf.

20. Kant, *Observations on the Feeling of the Beautiful and the Sublime*, 64. See also Edward Long, The History of Jamaica (London, 1774). Although Kant did not support polygenesis, he did stress black inferiority in relation to white.

21. Wesley, *Thoughts upon Slavery*, 56–57.

22. Wesley, *Thoughts upon Slavery*, 56–57.

23. Georg Hegel, *The Philosophy of History*, trans. J. Jibree (Dover, 1956), 99.

24. Wesley incorporates data directly from Anthony Benezet's *Historical Account of Guinea* (1771) and *A Short Account of that Part of Africa Inhabited by the Negroes* (1762). Benezet's material is a compilation of commentaries and journal notes from multiple travelers in Africa.

25. Wesley, *Thoughts upon Slavery*, 14.

26. Wesley, *Thoughts upon Slavery*, 24.

27. Wesley, *Thoughts upon Slavery*, 38.

28. Wesley, *Thoughts upon Slavery*, 33.

29. Wesley, *Thoughts upon Slavery*, 34.

30. John Wesley, "To William Wilberforce, February 24, 1791," in *The Letters of John Wesley*, VIII, accessed January 6, 2026, Wesley Center Online, https://wesley.nnu.edu/john-wesley/the-letters-of-john-wesley/wesleys-letters-1791/#Eighteen.

31. John Wesley, *The Journal of the Rev. John Wesley, A.M.* 8 vols., 8:144, in Curnock.

32. John Wesley, *The Journal of the Rev. John Wesley, A.M.* 8 vols., 6:277–78, Curnock.

33. Brendlinger, *Social Justice*, 39.

34. Victor Anderson, *Beyond Ontological Blackness: An Essay on African American Religious and Cultural Criticism* (Continuum 1999), 11.

35. K. Anthony Appiah, "Race, Culture, Identity: Misunderstood Connections," in *The Tanner Lectures on Human Values* (University of Utah, 1993–1994), 55.

Bibliography

Antsey, Roger. *The Atlantic Slave Trade and British Abolition 1760–1810*. Macmillian Press Ltd., 1975.

Ayling, Stanley. *John Wesley*. Collins, 1979.

Bready, J. Wesley. *England, Before, and After Wesley, the Evangelical Revival and Social Reform*. Harper & Brothers, Publishers, 1938.

Brendlinger, Irv A. *Social Justice Through the Eyes of Wesley: John Wesley's Theological Challenge to Slavery*. Joshua Press, Inc., 2006.

Clarkson, Thomas. *History of the Rise, Progress and Accomplishment of the Abolition of the African Slave-Trade by the British Parliament*. Longman, Hurst, Reese, and Orme, 1808.

Curnock, Nehemiah, ed., *The Journal of the Rev. John Wesley, A.M.* VII. Epworth Press, 1938.

Curtin, Philip D. *The Image of Africa, British Ideas and Action, 1780–1850*. The University of Wisconsin Press, 1964.

Davis, David Brion. *The Problem of Slavery in Western Culture. Ithaca*. Cornell University Press, 1966.

Drescher, Seymour. *From Slavery to Freedom: Comparative Studies in the Rise and Fall of Atlantic Slavery*. New York University Press, 1999.

Fogel, Robert William. *Without Consent or Contract: The Rise and Fall of American Slavery*. Norton, 1989.

Furneaux, Robin. *William Wilberforce.* Hamish Hamilton Ltd., 1974.

Fryer, Peter. *Staying Power: Black People in Britain since 1504.* Humanities Press, 1984.

Gossett, Thomas F. Race: *The History of an Idea in America.* Schocken, 1965.

Hall, Kim F. *Things of Darkness: Economies of Race and Gender in Early Modern England.* Cornell University Press, 1995.

Hendricks, Margo and Patricia Parker, eds. *Women, "Race," and Writing in the Early Modern Period.* Routledge, 1994.

Molineux, Catherine. *Faces of Perfect Ebony: Encountering Atlantic Slavery in Imperial Britain.* Harvard University Press, 2012.

Pritchard, Elizabeth. *Religion in Public: Locke's Political Theology: Cultural Memory in the Present.* Stanford University Press, 2013.

Rice, C. Duncan. *The Rise and Fall of Black Slavery.* Macmillan, 1975.

Smith, Warren Thomas. *John Wesley & Slavery.* Abingdon Press, 1986.

Thompson, Edgar. *Nathaniel Gilbert, Lawyer and Evangelist.* Epworth Press, 1960.

Wesley, Charles. *The Journal of the Rev. Charles Wesley, M.A.* 2 vols., ed. Thomas Jackson. Wesleyan Methodist Book Room, 1849.

Wesley, John. *Explanatory Notes Upon the New Testament.* William Bowyer, 1765.

———. *The Letters of the Rev. John Wesley, A. M.* 8 vols., ed. John Telford. The Epworth Press, 1931.

———. *The Works of John Wesley,* 3rd ed., 14 vols., ed. Thomas Jackson. Wesleyan Conference Office, 1872.

Williams, Eric. *Capitalism and Slavery.* Epworth Press, 1960.

6. JOHN WESLEY'S *THOUGHTS UPON SLAVERY*

An Argumentative Fabric, with a Finely Interwoven Biblical Reference, and a Loose Thread End

Helmut Renders

When I was invited to this panel, I immediately asked back whether I was a good choice, especially concerning the question of representation. As it was guaranteed that this key question had been considered, I accepted, mainly, because racism is still an essential attitude toward ethnic otherness widely seen "among the fair faced natives of Europe" (a phrase used by Welsey in *Thoughts upon Slavery*) and their descendants living today in other continents.

Racism poisons relations, hinders development, and causes tremendous unacceptable suffering. To fight racism, I published over the years several texts. Among them, a bilingual edition of *Wesley's Thoughts upon Slavery* and six of his letters to abolitionists, with two long introductions by myself and a translation by Prof. Dr. Filipe Maia.[1] Another one was an article, "Structural racism and social or structural sin: conceptional approximations,"[2] sparked by the murder of Alberto Silveira Freita on

November 20, 2020, in a Brazilian supermarket by the local guards, and the outraging reaction of representatives of the Brazilian government. The main objective was to remember the concept of social or structural sin, used by such theologians as those of the social gospel, integral mission, and liberation theology, even with variations between them, as an important tool for both analysis of racism and the struggle to overcome it. Another text was a book chapter investigating the "ethical" justification of the letter of resignation of the Minister of Education, Milton Ribeiro,[3] under the presidency of Bolsonaro, and, finally, a longer article in the actually last publication of the Theological Seminary of the Methodist Church in Brazil, before the dismissal of its faculty and its technical administrative staff (in December 2023), titled "Wesleyan Theology and the Challenge of Overcoming Racism and Prejudice."[4] Here, in this panel, I shall focus on John Wesley's *Thoughts upon Slavery*.

The Ethical Argumentation in John Wesley's *Thoughts upon Slavery*

One of the commonplace ideas concerning John Wesley's *Thoughts upon Slavery*[5] is that he mainly compiled texts of others, and that it lacks specific biblical or theological argumentation. This idea is incorrect. The composition of the texts in five chapters counts with three original contributions from John Wesley: the first and the fifth or last chapter, and the continuous use of the biblical ethical double term "justice and mercy" with which Wesley knitted all five parts of his *Thoughts* together.

In the other three parts, II to IV, it is true that Wesley widely quotes several texts from Antoine Bénezét[6] (1713–1785), Granville Sharp[7] (1738–1813), starting with a definition by Francis Hargrave[8] (1741–1821). Bénezét, Sharp, Hargrave, and Wesley contributed different aspects to build up the argument of the *Thoughts*. Actually, the text is the product of an ongoing direct exchange between Bénezét, Sharp, and Wesley, which involved the exchange of letters and books. The cooperation and interchange of ideas linked two continents—America and Europe—two generations—Sharp and Hargrave were between 25 to 28 years younger than Wesley—

and different religious backgrounds—Bénezét was a Quaker, Sharp an Anglican, and Wesley Anglican and head of the Methodist Movement. What brings Mr. Wesley's *Thoughts upon Slavery* to our table today?

- An exercise of respecting different cultures, their otherness or alterity, as a first and fundamental antidote against racism;
- a self-critical comprehension of one's own culture and its racist structures protected by unjust national laws and religious and cultural narratives to justify atrocities;
- the exercise of establishing a biblical argument, in spite of biblical argumentations defending slavery (and the necessity to be very careful in the use of biblical narratives and their *Wirkungsgeschichte* or reception history);
- the openness to work together with different fields of knowledge, and people from different religious backgrounds, to describe and comprehend racism—before the term was even coined[9]—and to look for ways to end it;
- the challenge to be aware that even in case of good efforts, we are not there yet and often still reproduce racist attitudes and prejudices; and
- the fundamental necessity of learning to see the presence of racism with the eyes of those who have been and still are discriminated by it.

Respect for Different Cultures, Their Otherness or Alterity as an Antidote against Racism

The great contribution of Antoine Bénezét to the *Thoughts* was to share a positive narrative about the people of West Africa, from the North to the South of its Atlantic coast. He did this in several books, from which Wesley quotes at least two, maybe three. The people of Africa are described as living in organized societies, hardworking or industrious people, knowing what is right and what is wrong, and paying attention to the elderly in need. They are described as people of religion, defending a moral code, concerning marriage, for example. As Maurice Jackson says:

> Using the travelers' narratives was a brilliant rhetorical strategy [. . .] He told his reader in the first pages of *Some Historical Account of Guinea* that he had "extracted from authors of credit; mostly such as have been principal officers in the English, French and Dutch factories, and who resided for many years in those countries." Benezet combined this knowledge of Africa with both religious and philosophical attacks on slavery, thus creating a new framework for the debate on slavery.[10]

Wesley follows Bénezét in quoting European travelers, who were probably more interested in this narrative of "stability" because it was good for business. But Bénezét and Wesley hitchhiked these reports, and transformed them into something new, an argument against the central element of the economic model of what we today call in the Atlantic world: enslavement. Bénezét understood that racism is always about supposed and imposed cultural, religious, ethnical, technical, linguistic, logical, ethical, and sexual superiority and inferiority, and that to overcome it, we need a new narrative about otherness to turn the tide.

A Self-Critical Comprehension of One's Own Culture and Its Racist Structures

For me, one of the most impressive moments of Wesley's *Thoughts* is what seems to me a kind of adaptation of the biblical motive of the peregrination of the nations (to Zion). We know its Jewish origin, its adaptation by Christianity, and its application in the Americas. My point here is that the peregrination of the nations in passages like Isaiah 2:3 always had to do with ethics, justice, knowing and recognizing what is right and what is wrong, or genuine honesty:

> *Our forefathers!* Where shall we find at this day, among the fair faced natives of Europe, a nation generally practicing the justice, mercy, and truth, which are found among these poor Africans? Suppose the preceding accounts are

> true, (which I see no reason or pretense to doubt of) and we may leave England and France, to seek genuine honesty in Benin, Congo, or Angola.[11]

The European nations have to relearn what is right and what is wrong, visiting Africa. Europe can only find itself again with the help of Africa. So it is not sufficient to read good narratives, we have to experience them by living together. And by living together, what in good case scenarios involves open hearts, open minds, and open arms, we have the chance to see ourselves in a new way.[12] Wesley seemed to me to be convinced that European culture, by opting for slavery as an essential part of its economic system, revealed that it had come to a critical point, a dead end, a tipping point. The way to relearn what justice and mercy are about is an encounter with Africa in Africa, a place of otherhood itself to understand what brotherhood and sisterhood are about.

The Exercise to Establish a Biblical Argument, in Spite of Biblical Argumentations Defending Slavery

Few people have paid attention to the use of the double term "justice and mercy" in Wesley's *Thoughts*. We find it ten times,[13] three times as "justice, mercy, and truth."[14] [15] One who did pay attention was Manfred Marquardt in his *Ethics of John Wesley*[16]; another, more recently, was David Nugent Field.[17] Although Marquardt mentions the use, nonetheless, he does not explore it; and Field left out its biblical dimension.[18] Probably a reason why this exploration was laid aside is that Wesley himself says in his *Thoughts* that he will not enter into a biblical discussion: "I would now inquire, whether these things can be defended, on the principles of even heathen honesty; whether they can be reconciled (setting the Bible out of the question) with any degree of either justice or mercy."[19]

But, in this case, we suggest, we should not take Wesley literally at his word for several reasons. First: we already mentioned the application and inversion of the motive of the peregrination of the nations. Second: the double term "justice and mercy" is a transversal and central moral concept and ethical theme in the Old and the New Testaments, which appears in key biblical passages such as Micah 6:8 and the Sermon of the Mount.[20] Combining the words is an original contribution of John Wesley to the *Thoughts*, as Bénezét refers in his texts a lot to mercy[21] and divine mercy,[22] but never to justice; and Sharp, in general, to law or natural law,[23] but not to justice or to mercy, not even when he discussed questions of the biblical interpretation.[24] A clearly theological use of the double term by Wesley has been already shown by Randy Maddox, as it played a fundamental role in Wesley's narrative against the doctrine of double predestination.[25] And this, again, is at least indirectly connected with our text, as the respective biblical key reference against this doctrine, Psalm 145:9, appears at the end of Wesley's *Thoughts.*[26] [27] Fourth, Wesley refers three times to "justice, mercy and truth,"[28] which is for sure biblical language,[29] as it already appeared here and then in his sermons.[30] Fifth, in four of the seven paragraphs of the fifth chapter,[31] we find this typical biblical "quilting" we know from his sermons: parts of biblical verses, rearranged in new combinations.[32] As a reminder, the organization into five chapters is John Wesley's creation. That means that his biblical documentation is applied within the *Thoughts* only to fight slavery, by denouncing it as not Christian and appealing for a world without slavery. Sixth, and this is for sure one of the very problematic, not sensible, and contradictive parts of the *Thoughts*, the stanza which ends the whole text refers to Genesis 9:25 and echoes, at least partially, its racist reception history. We return to this question in our last section.

On the whole, and in dialogue with the contribution of David Fields, we like to push our argument a little bit further and beyond a mere observation that John Wesley introduced a biblical foundation to the overall argument of the *Thoughts*. We wonder whether one should not go even so far as to say that the discussion about enslavement leads Wesley to a special biblical hermeneutics, characterized by two elements. First, very similar to Martin Luther's biblical hermeneutic, namely the use of an underlying principle to consider biblical texts as more essential or peripheral (*Was Christum treibet* or "what promotes Christ"), Wesley understands that those biblical passages which refer to or promote justice and mercy are more central than others to discuss different cultures and the institution of slavery. By this hermeneutic, these passages have preference over other texts which refer to the institution of slavery, even in a more explicit and direct and defensive or tolerating way. This is at least the implicit impression which the biblical argumentative fabric of the *Thoughts* gives us. Different than Luther, Wesley's hermeneutics then emphasizes in the particular question of slavery those texts which promote the love of one's neighbor instead of those texts which describe slavery or servantry eventually as common practice among the people of God. Second, Wesley comes to this decision by studying the real life of slavery, racism, and European supremacy. So it seems to us that Wesley's choice to move from real life to the biblical texts, not only from the biblical texts to real life, gives him a certain liberty. In the end, his hermeneutics relates life and Bible in a circular movement: from life to text and from text to life. In that particular case, real life experience is the criterion to illuminate the textual choices. Consequently, human experience is not only the field for an existential proof of the biblical truth—a classical interpretation within Wesleyan studies. But this hermeneutic also has the power to change real life for the better, to challenge enslaving political, economic, and social systems. It is deeply rooted in the gospel message of the Bible, which is assumed as in its essence about justice and mercy.

The Openness to Work Together with Different Fields of Knowledge, People from Different Religious Background, to Comprehend Racism and Establish Ways to Overcome It

Wesley made himself useful in a movement that was beyond him or the Methodist movement. He teamed up, learned with others, promoted others, and contributed to others. He looked for and connected new narratives with older ones. He related discussions about civil law and religious law, so called economic rules and necessities and what we may call a biblical argument concerning their apparently endless extension or application.

Wesley seems very aware of the established proximity between the missionary impulse and call of the Christian churches to work overseas and the enslaving exploitation established by the European nations in exactly the same territories. His understanding of this proximity is astonishingly "modern," considering his proposal that a *moratorium* of mission activity might be the only acceptable attitude until slavery is banned. Mission, we may say, is not seen as humanizing the living conditions of enslaved people—one of the arguments used in the defense of slavery—but the institution of slavery is always brutalizing the practitioners of the Christian religion and permanently contradicting the basic elements of the gospel. Wesley seems already to predict that slavery is a long-term vaccine against the Christian religion. They cannot coexist, and where they do so Christianity loses and the devilish slavery wins. This may be one of his most astonishing conclusions, which questions in the end his own involvement in oversea mission activities and his not only ambiguous but, in the end, very negative and not at all affectionate descriptions of native people, first nations, or indigenous communities around Georgia in his diaries.

He teamed up with a Quaker, not his most favored religious people, and a young advocate, whom he believed to be not very religious. We know that when it became available, he read the *vox africanum*, too, as expressed in the autobiography of Olaudah Equiano.[33] Unfortunately, Wesley did not submit his *Thoughts* to an African. So we may say that the *Thoughts upon Slavery* reveals Wesley as an abolitionist networker. This abolitionist networking attitude would be confirmed and even amplified by his efforts to keep the public informed and guided toward abolitionist attitudes and support by the *Arminian Magazine,* which started in 1789. On the one hand, in the magazine we find additional examples of travel reports but, beside these, also first original African voices. Here we may mention five poems from Phillis Wheatley (1753–1784), an enslaved woman[34] who today is considered one of the first African-American poets.[35] The first four poems can be found in a book published in 1773 of her authorship.[36] Wesley published them in two books in 1781 and 1784 following the sequence found in her book and added a fifth poem from an unknown source:

- *On the Death of a young Lady of Five Years of Age*[37] (published under the title On the Death of a Child, five Years of Age in the *Arminian Magazine* 1781, v. 4, p. 676;

- *On the DEATH of a young GENTLEMAN,*[38] published in the *Arminian Magazine* 1781, v. 4, pp. 676–77;

- *THOUGHTS on the Works of PROVIDENCE,*[39] published in the *Arminian Magazine* 1781, v. 4, pp. 677–80;

- *To the Right Honourable WILLIAM, Earl of Dartmouth, His Majesty's Principal Secretary of State for North-America,*[40] published under the title *To the right honourable William, Earl of D-t-th, when Secretary of State for North America,* in the *Arminian Magazine* 1784, v. 7, pp. 394–95;

- *An elegy on leaving,* published in the *Arminian Magazine* 1784, v. 7, pp. 395–96.

The second example is a report of two Africans together with a sailor about their experience of enslavement as part of a trial in England:

- *An Extract from the Depositions of William Floyd, of the City of Bristol, Mariner, and Little Ephraim Robin-John, and Ancona Robin Robin-John, of Old Town, Old Calabar, on the Coast of Africa. In the Court of King's-Bench,* published in the *Arminian Magazine,* 1783, v. 5, pp. 98-99 and pp. 211-212.

In conclusion, we find after 1774 some signs of progress considering the networking, including now Afro-American and African voices.

The challenge is to be aware that even in case of good efforts, we are not yet there and often are still reproducing racist attitudes and prejudices.

At least in two instances, Wesley's *Thoughts* stay behind its own proposal: within chapter three there is an expression which signaled pity and not respect: "These poor Africans."[41] And a poem at its end reproduces the narrative of the curse of Ham (!) and literally relates African traditional religion to idolatry:

The servile progeny of Ham
Seize as the purchase of thy blood!
    Let all the Heathens know thy name:
    From idols to the living God
The dark Americans convert,
And shine in every pagan heart![42]

The poetry is from 1758, probably written by Charles Wesley.[43] It is part of a collection of hymns that focuses on the universal character of God's grace, including indiscriminately all humankind, as in the third stanza of a hymn called "For the heathens."

The hymnbook treats, in general, different groups of Great Britain's society. The above stanza belongs to a small group of four songs:

Hymn 32: For the Jews

Hymn 33: For the Turks

Hymn 34: For the Heathen

Hymn 35: For the Arians, Socinians, Deists, Pelagians, etc.

The way that Wesley refers, in general, to African practitioners of religion may lead us to recognize diverse reasoning involved in the logic of including this stanza. As the only direct references to religion practiced in Africa in the *Thoughts* is to Islam ("Mahometan[s] Negroes," chapter II, §5.7). "Mahometan and pagans" (and not "heathens") appears once in chapter V, §5. In all cases, Wesley stresses the moral integrity of these religious adaptations. On the other hand, African traditional religions are not only not specifically positively mentioned, they are only mentioned once: in this stanza. So, it seems to us that Wesley distinguishes between Jewish or Islamic religions practiced among Africans as real religions and African traditional religions as non-religions or idolatry. Charles Wesley's hymn titles (Jews, Turks, Heathens) seem to be underlined by a similar understanding.

Beside this, there is a second problem, and this refers to the reception history of Genesis 9:25ff. The "Hamitic Curse" had for a long time been abused by all three major Mediterranean scripture-based religions—Judaism, Christianity, and Islam—as a racist narrative based on a monogenetic theory of the creation of mankind combined with a theory of degeneration of specific populations.[44] Mentioning this narrative, relating "Ham and servitude!" to "Dark Americans." looks like an uncritical reception or even acceptance of this narrative. Maybe not in 1758, but at least in 1774, this was not any more a publicly undiscussed or unquestioned position and so, maybe, a kind of understandable or even acceptable position. The pattern "from idol to the living good" represents an inversion of the underlying religious degeneration theory but still relates to it. Interesting is here a comparison with a text from Granville Sharp challenging a biblical defense of slavery, published two years earlier. It also ends with a poem: "An Elegy On the miserable STATE of an African SLAVE, by the celebrated and ingenious William Shenstone."[45] The text focuses on suffering, Christian cruelty, and divine justice. And concerning the Ham narrative, Sharp simply states in the same book (on p. xi): "[. . .] nor can the sons of Ethiopia, with any degree of clearness, be proved to have descended from any of those nations who so came under the Divine displeasure as to be brought into servitude." Actually, this understanding was not unfamiliar to John Wesley at all. He himself, in 1765, in his *Explanatory Notes on the Old Testament*, had already dismissed this reception history and had related Genesis 9:25 only to future conquests of Israel:

> A servant of servants—That is, the meanest and most despicable servant shall he be, even to his brethren. Those who by birth were his equals, should by conquest be his lords. This certainly points at the victories obtained by Israel over the Canaanites, by which they were all either put to the sword, or put under tribute. Jos 9:23 Jud 1:28,30,33,35, which happened not "till about eight hundred years after this."[46]

Actually, Wesley cites here nearly verbatim a commentary by Matthew Henry, who already in 1702 did not relate the text to the enslavement of Africans at all.[47] On the other hand, the following quotation from John Wesley's tractate *The doctrine of original sin, according to scripture, reason, and experience*[48] published one year before the stanza appears again in the *Thoughts*, reveals an understanding not so far developed:

> And yet most certain is, that God has in other cases actually punished men's sins on their posterity. Thus, the posterity of Canaan, the sons of Ham, is punished with slavery for his sin (Gen. 9:25, 27). Noah pronounced the curse under divine afflatus, and God confirmed it by his providence. So we do in fact suffer Adam's sin, and that too by the sentence inflicted on our first parents.

It is correct that Wesley even here does not relate nor restrict this biblical passage to the enslavement of Africans, native people, first nations, or indigenous communities. But the passage still does affirm the institution of slavery as biblical and justified as godly punishment. So we may conclude that Charles Wesley's stanza from 1758 and the quotation from John Wesley's *The doctrine of original sin* from 1757 represent a similar mindset.

On the other hand, John Wesley already made the first clear public stand against enslavement in 1756 in *Explanatory Notes Upon the New Testament,* 1 Timothy 1:10: "*Manstealers*—The worst of all thieves, in comparison of whom, highwaymen and housebreakers are innocent. What then are most traders in negroes, procurers of servants for America, and all who list soldiers by lies, tricks, or enticements?" The description of enslavers as "the worst of all thieves" follows Richard Baxter (1673) who refers to them as "one of the worst sort of thieves in the world." The reference to 1 Timothy 1:10, accompanied by a comparison with other contemporary types of criminals, is found in a publication of his father, Samuel Wesley, who compares them to "murderers of fathers and mothers."[49] John Wesley takes up the idea again, but, following the model, uses other examples. Considering that the poor have neither carriages nor houses, we find here a good dose of social criticism, because we can imagine how the same people who probably complained about these types of crimes were eventually enjoying the profits from businesses related to slavery. The note then does not represent a brand-new idea or positioning but more a kind of reminder of a position already made and probably known at least among Puritans.

In the end, the stanza at the end of the *Thoughts* is a strange corpus within the presented line of argumentation, still reproducing racist prejudices or seemingly ignoring this possible interpretation.[50] If it is not understood as an accident or textual carelessness which happen then to re-affirm what Wesley already rejected in 1774, it still may be understood as an indication of a kind of total misunderstanding or [dis]qualification of African Traditional Religions as non-religions, religions of inferior quality, or religions practicing idolatry. Actually, looking again a little further and searching how Wesley handled this question in the *Arminian Magazine*, the understanding of African Traditional Religions as non-religions appears in an uncommented letter from Francis Gilbert in which he upholds that "the Negroes have no religion, except these two which were in England with my brother, who have not only retained their faith, but have received an abundant increase of it."[51] And there is another quote, from a travel report, *An Account of Mr. SILAS TOLD [written by himself]*, where the understanding of African Traditional Religion as diabolic is also reproduced:

> ONE day I accompanied King Arigo on shore for the benefit of my health (as the Captain had almost put an end to my life) and continued there for the space of six weeks, and slept with the King's son, Prince Arigo, during the same. One morning I was suddenly seized with a racking pain in my head. I acquainted the Queen, in Moorish, with the cause of my indisposition; she informed his black Majesty therewith, who ordered me some "doctor," as they term it. On this about half a dozen of his ladies took me into a back yard, and stripping me quite naked, even to my skin, sat me on a joint-stool, and gave me some yabba (or water) with a cloth to dry myself. I could not conceive what they purposed to do with me, as the elder lady invented divers stratagems to get me into a studious frame of mind. [. . .] When I entered the house, I was struck with uncommon amazement at the sight of forty or fifty men's heads hanged round this palaver house. Here I was inexpressibly terrified, as I had received a very pious and Christian education; so that their diabolical and gross proceedings created great horror upon my soul. At length they commenced the usual sacrifice to their gods [. . .][52]

So, it seems to us that Wesley, whereas he defended that enslavement of others can never be justified, even if that meant not evangelizing, and learned to appreciate African government and moral system, traditional religion is still not given positive appraisal. For sure, this did not hinder him from rejecting slavery nor from thinking about the necessity of a missionary moratorium. But it also does not yet indicate a way toward a dialogue between Christianity and African Traditional Religion as it has been established in Africa in the twentieth century, with important Methodist participation.[53] Although the question can be asked whether the poem gives the overall tone for all the text or not, its strategic position as a final word represents a dangerously loose end of an argumentative fabric with the potential to nullify at least partially the general narrative of the *Thoughts*. It is also true that in his days Wesley was not alone with the ambiguous position within the abolition movement. We can see the same ambiguity in the symbol of the abolition movement, showing a kneeling African in chains saying: "Am I not your brother?" Why does he kneel? Why did Wesley put this poem at the end of his thoughts? Why did he maintain similar comments, at least two times, in the *Arminian Magazine*? We cannot find an acceptable answer, except that it serves as a reminder how all our attempts to overcome racism are embedded in a racist culture and we have to read with the eyes of the victims of racism what we are writing. Wesley's *Thoughts* are still a result of fair-faced male natives of Europe talking about enslaved people, quoting fair-faced male natives of Europe. It cannot be claimed these voices stand on direct talks with the enslaved.

But, let us take a last look into the *Arminian Magazine*. In the end of 1790, near to his death, we find as so often a poem finishing the monthly edition. This specific one was written by William Cowper (1731–1800). Unlike other antislavery poems published by Wesley, and more like those from Hannah More,[54] who actually was a friend to Cowper and who shared his attitude that she should use her gift to support the abolitionist cause, this poem is all about African agency and not European paternalism:

The Morning Dream

'Twas in the glad season of spring,
Asleep at the dawn of the day,
I dream'd what I cannot but sing,
So pleasant it seem'd as I lay.
I dream'd that on ocean afloat,

Far hence to the westward I sail'd,
While the billows high lifted the boat,
And the fresh blowing breeze never fail'd.

In the steerage a woman I saw,
Such at least was the form that she wore,
Whose beauty impressed me with awe,
Ne'er taught me by woman before:
She sat, and a shield at her side
Shed light like a sun on the waves,
And, smiling divinely, she cried—
"I go to make freemen of slaves."

Then, raising her voice to a strain,
The sweetest that ear ever heard,
She sung of the slave's broken chain
Wherever her glory appear'd.
Some clouds which had over us hung
Fled, chas'd by her melody clear,
And me thought, while she liberty sung,
'Twas liberty only to hear.

Thus swiftly dividing the flood,
To a slave-cultured island we came,
Where a demon, her enemy, stood,
Oppression his terrible name:
In his hand, as a sign of his sway,
A scourge hung with lashes he bore,
And stood looking out for his prey,
From Africa's sorrowful shore.

But soon as, approaching the land,
That goddess-like woman he view'd,
The scourge he let fall from his hand,
With blood of his subjects imbrued.
I saw him both sicken and die,
And, the moment the monster expir'd,
Heard shouts that ascended the sky,
From thousands with rapture inspir'd.

Awaking, how could I but muse
At what such a dream should betide,
But soon my ear caught the glad news,
Which serv'd my weak thought for a guide—
That Britannia, renown'd o'er the waves,
For the hatred she ever has shown
To the black-sceptred rulers of slaves,
Resolves to have none of her own.[55]

If my PhD student Domingos Gaspar from Angola is right, and I believe he has good reasons to believe so, we may have here an early written echo of the memory of the Angolan warrior queen Mwene Njinga Mbandi (1582–1663) who fought the Portuguese for thirty years. She became a legendary figure of resistance and was later rediscovered for the fight of the independence of Angola. If he is right, Cowper created his version of this myth, which may have come to his attention through John Newton, with whom he worked and who proposed a more radical abolitionist approach. [56]

Some Intermediate Considerations

We believe that, seeing all these parts together, we should consider one important contribution of Wesley's *Thoughts*—namely, it presents an argumentative fabric, with finely interwoven biblical references, knitted together with a discussion about natural law, English law, foreign and home cultures, economic argumentation and biblical values. Why is this important to us? First, we point out the matter of biblical argumentation because we believe that we have a forever established task to fight racism among our people in the church biblically. Second, this means that we must offer to every new generation a hermeneutics, a state-of-the-art interpretation of the Bible text to assist our reading of our culture, socioeconomic and political realities, and an analysis of the principal assumptions underlying current science, so that we are able to connect the loose ends which still promote racism. We have to be aware how the Bible, science, economics, and politics were used and still are used as bulwarks to excuse or even defend racism. To do so, we have to talk with interlocutors from different departments of theology and beyond theology, especially learning to understand from those who suffer(ed) racism.

And we will do a little bit better when our voice, even if it is the voice of a still predominately white church, speaks in resonance with the voices of the enslaved, old and new, hearing their stories, welcoming their experiences, willing to be confronted by a considerable number of surly and always "unpleasant" and "uncomfortable" reminders. Memories of enslavement cannot necessarily serve harmony. Stating injustice and fighting for justice, respect, and recognition probably always destroy our longing for harmony but may offer instead an experience of peace. Maybe then we choose to speak about the horrific reasons why today so many Africans still have to fear Europeans, although we live in a time and world where we are surrounded by so many narratives which want to make us believe that it is the other way round and that Europeans and North Americans should be afraid of Africans. This cannot go on. In the end, Wesley shares with us his hope that even nations and ethnicities can repent, even more, that they can be transformed, when they become aware of the beauty of the other and one's own sin, when they are humble to recognize their ongoing shortcomings and blind spots, their deep involvement, including the academic world, when they embrace their mutual importance and interdependence as members of one humankind, brother- and sisterhood.

Notes to Chapter 6

1. Helmut Renders, *John Wesley e a luta abolicionista: com edição bilíngue dos seus Pensamentos sobre a escravidão* (Editora da HASTE, 2019).

2. Helmut Renders, "Racismo estrutural como pecado social ou estrutural: aproximações conceituais e implicações pastorais". Caminhando 25. 3 (2020): 115–39 DOI: 10.15603/2176-3828/caminhando. v25n3p115-139.

3. Helmut Renders. "Minha honra, minha família e meu país": pilares éticos apresentados por um ministro evangélico do governo Bolsonaro. Eduardo Meinberg de Albuquerque Maranhão (orgs.). *Deus de Bolsonaro acima de tudo: Poder e religião no governo Bolsonaro* (Florianópolis. AMAR / Fogo, 2023). (Coleção Poder, Educação, Gênero e Religião; v. 8).

4. Helmut Renders, "Teologia Wesleyana e o desafio da superação do racismo e preconceito." Jonadab Domingues (ed.). *Anuário Litúrgico da Igreja Metodista 2024* (São Bernardo do Campo, SP: Editeo, 2023), 44–46.

5. John Wesley, *Thoughts upon Slavery* (Printed by R. Hawes, 1774 [1ª ed.]).

6. Before 1774: Anthony Bénezét, *Short account of that part of Africa, inhabited by the Negroes; with respect to the fertility of the country; the good disposition of many of the natives, and the manner by which the slave trade is carried on* (Philadelphia: [s.n.], [1762]); Anthony Bénezét, A Caution and Warning to Great Britain and her Colonies (Philadelphia: 1766); Anthony Bénezét, *Some historical account of Guinea, its situation, produce, and the general disposition of its inhabitants: with an inquiry into the rise and progress of the slave trade, its nature, and lamentable effects* (W. Owen, 1772). After 1774, one finds two letters published in the Arminian Magazine, one after Wesley's death: Anthony Bénezét, "A letter to John Wesley," *The Arminian Magazine* 10.1 (1787): 44–51; Anthony Bénezét, "A Letter on the Slave-Trade," *The Arminian Magazine* 16.10 (1793): 532–33.

7. Before 1774: Granville Sharp, *A representation of the injustice and dangerous tendency of tolerating slavery* (Benjamin White; Robert Horsfield, 1769); Granville Sharp, *An appendix to the representation (printed in 1769) of the injustice and dangerous tendency of tolerating slavery* (Benjamin White, 1772); Granville Sharp, *An essay on slavery, proving from Scripture its inconsistency* (Isaac Collins, 1773); after 1774: Granville Sharp, *The just limitation of slavery in the laws of God: compared with the unbounded claims of the African traders and British American slaveholders* (B. White; E. and C. Dilly, 1776); Granville Sharp, *The law of liberty recommended to slaveholders*, 1776; Granville Sharp, *The law of passive obedience, or Christian submission to personal injuries*, 1776; Granville Sharp, *The law of retribution . . . against tyrants, slave-holders, and oppressors*, 1776; Granville Sharp, *The just limitation of slavery in the laws of God: compared with the unbounded claims of the African traders and British American slaveholders* (Printed for Benjamin White; E. and C. Dilly, 1776); Granville Sharp, *A tract on the law of nature: and principles of action in man* (B. White; E. and C. Dilly, 1777).

8. Francis Hargrave, *An argument in the case of James Sommersett a negro, lately determined by the court of King's bench: wherein it is attempted to demonstrate the present unlawfulness of domestic slavery in England. to which is prefixed a state of the case by Mr. Hargrave, one of the counsel for the negro* (Hargrave & Otridge, 1772).

9. Following Gene Demby, "The ugly, fascinating history of the word 'racism.'" NPR.org (12-06-2014). Accessed November 11, 2016, the first use was in 1902 and related to indigenous populations in the US.

10. Maurice Jackson, *Let This Voice Be Heard: Anthony Benezet, Father of Atlantic Abolitionism* (University of Pennsylvania Press, 2009), 73.

11. Wesley, *Thoughts*, chapter II, §11.

12. I personally rely heavily on the thoughts of Miroslav Volf in *Exclusion and Embrace, Revised and Updated: A Theological Exploration of Identity, Otherness, and Reconciliation* (Abingdon Press, 2010) and its very precise and helpful Christological foundation, in the tradition of Dietrich Bonhoeffer, and the contribution of Walter Wink and his "Powers trilogy"—*Naming the Powers: The Language of Power in the New Testament* (Fortress, 1984); *Unmasking the Powers: The Invisible Forces That Determine Human Existence* (Fortress, 1986); *Engaging the Powers: Discernment and Resistance in a World of Domination* (Fortress Press, 1992)—as its follow-ups—*When the Powers Fall: Reconciliation in the Healing of Nations* (Fortress Press, 1998); *The Powers That Be: Theology for a New Millennium* (Doubleday, 1999).

13. Wesley, *Thoughts*, chapter 2, § 11; chapter 4, §§ 1, 2 [2x], 3, 5 [2x], 6, 7; chapter 5, §7

14. Wesley, *Thoughts*, chapter 2, § 11; chapter 4, §§ 4, 6.

15. See appendix I.

16. Manfred Marquardt, *Praxis und Prinzipien der Sozialethik John Wesleys* (Vandenhoeck & Ruprecht, 1977), p. 87.

17. David Nugent Field. "Imaging the God of justice and mercy: theological allusions in John Wesley's *Thoughts upon Slavery*," *Studia Historiae Ecclesiasticae*, 47.1 (2021): 1–20.

18. Although, only by reading his article I was able to understand how the double term has actually a bridging function between religious and humanist thinking.

19. Wesley, *Thoughts*, chapter 4, §1.

20. These biblical double terms can be found in prophetic (Hosea 10:12 and 12:6; Zechariah 7:9; Micah 6:8; Daniel 4:27; Isaiah 16:5) and sapiential literature (Psalm 45:4, 85:10 [including "truth"], 89:14, 101:1, 103:17, 119:149, 145:7) as in the Letters (Ephesian 5:9 [including "truth"]; Titus 3:5) and the Gospel (Matthew 5:6-7, considering that the beatitudes follow a chiastic structure, and Matthew 23:23). Matthews 5:6 Wesley reads "righteousness," but relates it with truth and justice (§II.13).

21. Bénézet, *Short account*, pp. 49, 53; Bénezét, Some historical, p. 51, 73, 79, 88, 92, 94.

22. Bénezét, *Short account*, pp. 39, 40, 42, 53, 62, 63, 64; Bénezét, Some historical, p. 123.

23. Sharp, *A representation*.

24. Sharp, *An essay*.

25. Randy Maddox. "The Rule of Christian Faith, Practice and Hope: John Wesley and the Bible," *Epworth Review*, p. 29, April 2011.

26. Wesley, *Thoughts*, chapter V, §7,

27. People normally do not relate the doctrine of double predestination to the promotion of slavery. In the person of Whitefield, they are related.

28. Wesley, *Thoughts*, chapter II, §11; chapter IV, §§4 and 6.

29. Psalm 85:10; Ephesian 5:9.

30. The three terms appear also together in the sermons Salvation by faith (§I.1) and Catholic spirit (§I.12)

31. Wesley, *Thoughts*, chapter V, §§3, 5, 6, 7.

32. Following its appearance: Wesley, *Thoughts*, §V.3: James 2:13; Genesis 15:16 or Matthew 23:32; Hebrews 12:7; Ezekiel 3:18 or Acts 18:6; Mark 6:11a; Psalm 95:7-8; Hebrews 3:15; Psalm 23:1; Hebrews 13:6; Job 2:4; Matthew 10:39 and 16:25; §V.5: 1 Timothy 1:10; Genesis 4:10; Amos 5:19. §V.6: 2 Timothy 2:24. §V.7: Psalm 145:9; Hebrews 12:9; Psalm 86:5b; Acts 17:26; Ezekiel 16:5; Psalm 35: 2b or 44:26a; 2 Samuel 14:14 or Psalm 22:14; Psalm 138:8.2; 2 Chronicles 6:37; Psalm 119:169a; 2 Samuel 22:2c; 2 Chronicles 30:9; Psalm 126:4; Nahum 1:13; and John 8:36. See Appendix II with the example of Chapter five, paragraph seven.

33. Olaudah Equiano, *The Interesting Narrative of the Life of Olaudah Equiano* (London: 1789).

34. Vincent Carretta, *Phillis Wheatley: Biography of a Genius in Bondage* (The University of Georgia Press, 2014).

35. Debora Deborah, *Phillis Wheatley: First Published African-American Poet* (The Child's World, 2004).

36. Phillis Wheatley, *Poems on various subjects, religious and moral. Negro Servant to Mr. John Wheatlev; of Boston, in New England* (A Bell, 1773).

37. Wheatley, *Poems on various subjects, religious and moral*, 25–26.

38. Wheatley, *Poems on various subjects, religious and moral*, 27–28.

39. Wheatley, *Poems on various subjects, religious and moral*, 43–50.

40. Wheatley, *Poems on various subjects, religious and moral*, 73–75.

41. Wesley, *Thoughts*, chapter II, §11.

42. Wesley, *Thoughts*, chapter V, §7.

43. [Charles Wesley,] *Hymns of intercession for all mankind* (Farley, 1758), 28.

44. See, for example, David M. Goldenberg, *The Curse of Ham: Race and Slavery in Early Judaism, Christianity, and Islam* (Princeton University Press, 2003) and David M. Goldenberg, *Black and Slave: the Origins and History of the Curse of Ham* (De Gruyter, 2017.

45. Sharp, *An essay on slavery*, 1772, 26–28.

46. John Wesley, *Explanatory Notes Upon the Old Testament*, Genesis 9:25.

47. See the first volume of Matthew Henry, *Matthew Henry's Commentary on the Whole Bible* (Marshall, 1706–[172?])

48. E. Farley, 1757, part II, chapter I, §5.

49. Arthur Alan Torpy, "Samuel Wesley, senior: A Late Seventeenth-century English Abolitionist," *Methodist History* 47.1 (2008): 5–15. http://hdl.handle.net/10516/234.

50. There is an interesting comment by Thomas Coke about the reception of the Thoughts among Methodists which may be explained by this. Mentioning a visit to a slave holder he said: "Friday 13: I preached at Bent-chapel, belonging also to the Church of England, to an attentive people. At night I lodged at the house of Mr. Dillard, a most hospitable man, and as kind to his negroes as if they were white servants. It was quite pleasing to see them so decently and comfortably clothed. And yet I could not beat into the head of that dear man, the evil of keeping them in slavery, although he has read Mr. Wesley's *Thoughts on Slavery*; (I think he said) three -times over: but his good wife is strongly on our side." Thomas Coke. Journal of Bishop Coke [Friday 13 May 1785]. *Arminian Magazine* 1:8 (1789): 393. In this case it is the American version of the *Arminian Magazine*, edited by Francis Asbury and Thomas Coke.

51. Francis Gilbert Letter 246 to Rev. Mr. Wesley; Antígua.18/06/1763. *Arminian Magazine* 5. (1782): 384.

52. Silas Told, *An Account of Mr. SILAS TOLD* [written by himself]. *Arminian Magazine* 10.4 (1787): 183–84.

53. See, for example: Bolaji Idowu, *African Traditional Religion: a Definition* (Orbis Books, 1973); R. W. Omotoye, "African Traditional Religion Scholarship: E. Bolaji Idowu and John S. Mbiti," in *The Palgrave Handbook of African Traditional Religion, Aderibigbe*, ed. I. S., Falola, T. (Palgrave Macmillan, 2022): 589–97. https://doi.org/10.1007/978-3-030-89500-6_44; M. Gabriel Setiloane, *African theology: an introduction* (Skotaville Publishers, 1986); Gabriel M. Setiloane (1978), "How the traditional worldview persists in the Christianity of the Sotho-Tswana," in *Christianity in Independent Africa*, ed. Edwards Fasholé-Luke, et al. (Rex Collings, 1978): 402–12; Gabriel M. Setiloane, *The Image of God among the Sotho-Tswana* (Rotterdam: 1976); Fulgence Nyengele, "African spirituality and the Wesleyan spirit: implications for spiritual formation in a multicultural church and culturally pluralistic world," 13º *Oxford Institute of Theological Studies*. https://oxford-institute.org/wp-content/uploads/2013/10/2013-4-nyengele.pdf.

54. Hannah More, "An Extract from a Poem on Slavery," *Arminian Magazine* 11.10 (1788): 5558–560. This only the first part of Hannah More's famous poem. Unfortunately, I had no access to the 12th volume from the year 1789.

55. Thomas Cowper, "A morning dream," *Arminian Magazine* 13.10 (1790): 558–60.

56. The motive of a warrior queen is not new to Cowper. See his poem "Boadicea. An Ode." William Cowper, 1731–1800, *Poems: by William Cowper, of the Inner Temple, Esq.* (T. Bensley 1782): 354–57. In this poem a British warrior queen, tortured by Romans, hears the prophecy of her religious leader, a Druid. He foresees the end of the Roman Empire—4th stanza: "Rome shall perish—write that word / In the blood that she has spilt; / Perish hopeless and abhorr'd / Deep in ruin as in guilt"—and proclaims the rise of the British Empire—7th and 8th stanza: "Then the progeny that springs / From the forests of our land,/ Arm'd with thunder, clad with wings, / Shall a wider world command. // Regions Caesar never knew, Thy posterity shall sway, / Where his eagles never flew, / None invincible as they." Seeing both poems together, one wonders whether six years later, Cowper widened his horizon to the point to dreams about an African warrior queen, putting an end to British caused enslavement.

Bibliography

Aderibigbe, I. S., Falola, T., eds. *The Palgrave Handbook of African Traditional Religion*, Palgrave Macmillan, 2022

Bénezét, Anthony. *A Caution and Warning to Great Britain and her Colonies* (Philadelphia: 1766)

———. "A letter to John Wesley." The *Arminian Magazine* 10.1 (1787)

———. "A Letter on the Slave-Trade." *The Arminian Magazine* 16.10 (1793)

———. *Short account of that part of Africa, inhabited by the Negroes*; with respect to the fertility of the country; the good disposition of many of the natives, and the manner by which the slave trade is carried on (Philadelphia: [s.n.], [1762])

———. *Some historical account of Guinea, its situation, produce, and the general disposition of its inhabitants*: with an inquiry into the rise and progress of the slave trade, its nature, and lamentable effects (London / Philadelphia: W. Owen, 1772)

Carretta, Vincent. *Phillis Wheatley Biography of a Genius in Bondage*, Athens & London: The University of Georgia Press, 2014

Coke, Thomas. "Journal of Bishop Coke [Friday 13 may 1785]." *Arminian Magazine. 1*:8, 1789

Cowper, Thomas. "A morning dream." *Arminian Magazine* 13.10 (1790)

Cowper, William. "Boadicea. An Ode". *Poems: by William Cowper, of the Inner Temple, Esq.*, T. Bensley, 1782

Deborah, Debora. *Phillis Wheatley. First Published African-American Poet.* The Child's World, 2004

Demby, Gene. "The ugly, fascinating history of the word 'racism.'" NPR.org. (12-06-2014)

Equiano, Olaudah. *The Interesting Narrative of the Life of Olaudah Equiano,* London: 1789

Field, David Nugent, "Imaging the God of justice and mercy: theological allusions in John Wesley's *Thoughts upon Slavery*". Studia Historiae Ecclesiasticae, 47.1 (2021): 1-20.

Gilbert, Francis. "Letter 246 to Rev. Mr. Wesley; Antígua.18/06/1763." *Arminian Magazine* 5.

Goldenberg, David M. *The Curse of Ham: Race and Slavery in Early Judaism, Christianity, and Islam.* Princeton University Press, 2003

———. *Black and Slave: The Origins and History of the Curse of Ham.* De Gruyter, 2017

Hargrave, Francis. *An argument in the case of James Sommersett a negro, lately determined by the court of King's bench: wherein it is attempted to demonstrate the present unlawfulness of domestic slavery in England. to which is prefixed a state of the case. by Mr. Hargrave, one of the counsel for the negro.* Hargrave & Otridge, 1772.

Henry, Matthew. *Matthew Henry's Commentary on the Whole Bible,* London: Marshall, 1706– [172?].

Idowu, Bolaji. *African Traditional Religion: A Definition.* Orbis Books, 1973.

Jackson, Maurice. *Let This Voice Be Heard: Anthony Benezet, father of Atlantic abolitionism.* University of Pennsylvania Press, 2009

Marquardt, Manfred. *Praxis und Prinzipien der Sozialethik John Wesleys.* Vandenhoeck & Ruprecht, 1977.

More, Hannah. "An Extract from a Poem on Slavery," *Arminian Magazine* 11.10 (1788).

Nyengele, Fulgence. "African spirituality and the Wesleyan spirit: implications for spiritual formation in a multicultural church and culturally pluralistic world," *13º Oxford Institute of Theological Studies*. https://oxford-institute.org/wp-content/uploads/2013/10/2013-4-nyengele.pdf.

Renders, Helmut. *John Wesley e a luta abolicionista: com edição bilíngue dos seus Pensamentos sobre a escravidão.* São Paulo: Editora da HASTE, 2019.

———. "Minha honra, minha família e meu país": pilares éticos apresentados por um ministro evangélico do governo Bolsonaro. Eduardo Meinberg de Albuquerque Maranhão (orgs.). *Deus de Bolsonaro acima de tudo: Poder e religião no governo Bolsonaro* (Florianópolis. AMAR / Fogo, 2023). (Coleção Poder, Educação, Gênero e Religião; v. 8).

———. “Racismo estrutural como pecado social ou estrutural: aproximações conceituais e implicações pastorais”. *Caminhando* 25. 3 (2020)

———. “Teologia Wesleyana e o desafio da superação do racismo e preconceito”. Jonadab Domingues (ed.). *Anuário Litúrgico da Igreja Metodista 2024* (São Bernardo do Campo, SP: Editeo, 2023).

Setiloane, Gabriel M. *African theology: an introduction.* Skotaville Publishers, 1986.

Setiloane, Gabriel M. “How the traditional worldview persists in the Christianity of the Sotho-Tswana,” in *Christianity in Independent Africa,* ed. Edward Fasholé-Luke, Richard Gray, Adrian Hastings, and Godwin Tasie (Rex Collings, 1978).

———. *The Image of God among the Sotho-Tswana.* A. A. Balkema, 1976.

Sharp, Granville. *An appendix to the representation (printed in 1769) of the injustice and dangerous tendency of tolerating slavery.* (Benjamin White, 1772)

———. *An essay on slavery, proving from Scripture its inconsistency* (Isaac Collins, 1773).

———. *The just limitation of slavery in the laws of God: compared with the unbounded claims of the African traders and British American slaveholders* (B. White; E. and C. Dilly, 1776).

———. *The law of liberty recommended to slaveholders,* 1776 (B. White; E. and C. Dilly, 1777).

———. *The law of passive obedience, or Christian submission to personal injuries,* London 1776;

———. *The law of retribution . . . against tyrants, slave-holders, and oppressors,* 1776, printed by W. Richardson, for B. White; and E. and C. Dilly.

———. *A tract on the law of nature: and principles of action in man* (B. White; E. and C. Dilly, 1777).

———. *A representation of the injustice and dangerous tendency of tolerating slavery* (Benjamin White; Robert Horsfield, 1769).

Told, Silas. *An Account of Mr. SILAS TOLD* [written by himself]. *Arminian Magazine* 10.4 (1787).

Torpy, Arthur Alan. “Samuel Wesley, senior: A Late Seventeenth-century English Abolitionist,” *Methodist History* 47.1.

Wesley, Charles. *Hymns of intercession for all mankind.* Farley, 1758.

Wesley, John. *Thoughts upon Slavery.* (Printed by R. Hawes, 1774 [1ª ed.]).

———, *Explanatory Notes Upon the Old Testament.*

Wheatley, Phillis. *Poems on various subjects, religious and moral.* Negro Servant to Mr. John Wheatlev; of Boston. A Bell. 1773.

Wink, Walter. *Naming the Powers: The Language of Power in the New Testament.* Fortress Press, 1984.

———. *Unmasking the Powers: The Invisible Forces That Determine Human Existence.* Fortress Press, 1986.

———. *Engaging the Powers: Discernment and Resistance in a World of Domination.* Fortress Press, 1992.

———. *When the Powers Fall: Reconciliation in the Healing of Nations.* Fortress Press, 1998

———. *The Powers That Be: Theology for a New Millennium.* Doubleday, 1999.

Volf, Miroslav. *Exclusion and Embrace, Revised and Updated: A Theological Exploration of Identity, Otherness, and Reconciliation.* Abingdon Press, 2010.

Appendix I

CHAPTER I (Wesley)
I.1 Slavery – Hargave´s definition
I.2. Slavery – Wesley´s definition
I.3 Slavery – in antiquity
I.4 Slavery – its return with the Portuguese and the Spanish

Chapter II (Wesley: II.1-2; partially II.11; Bénezét (II.3 -II.10; partially II.11)
II.1-2 Introduction
II.3-5 African countries: politic, economy, and religion
II.6-11 African countries: high ethical standards II.11 ***"Justice, mercy, and truth"***

Chapter III (Bénezét III.1-III.4, 6-7; Sharp III.8-11)
III.1-4 Slaves, their capture an injustice
III.5-6 Slaves, their transport an injustice
III.7 Slaves, their selling an injustice
III.8 Slaves, their plantation life an injustice
III.9-11 The Colonies, their laws an injustice

Chapter IV (Wesley: IV.1; 5-6; Sharp: IV.2-4)

IV.1 Introduction	***"Justice or mercy"***
IV.2 Injustice authorized by the law	***"Justice and mercy"***
	"Mercy or justice"
IV.3-4 The Corpus Civilis and its justification of slavery	***"Justice as to mercy"***

IV.5 Slavery – an economic necessity?	***"Mercy or justice"***
	"Justice and Equity"
	"Equity or justice"
	"Justice, mercy, and truth"
IV.6 Slavery, not necessary to the glory of a nation	***"Justice, mercy, and truth"***
IV.7 Slavery, necessary for economy	***"Justice and mercy"***
Chapter V (Wesley)	
V.1 Whom shall be addressed?	
V2-3 To the captains	
V.4 To the merchants and salesmen	
V.5 To the slaveholders	
V6. To those who inherited slaves	***"Justice . . . mercy"***
V7: To those who finance slavery	
Final Poetry	

Appendix II

7. O thou God of love, "thou who art loving to every man, and whose mercy is over all thy works" (Ps. 145:9); thou who art "the Father of the spirits of all flesh" (Heb. 12:9), and who "art rich in mercy unto all" (Ps. 86.5b); "thou who hast mingled of one blood all the nations upon earth" (Acts 17.26); "have compassion upon these outcasts of men, who are trodden down as dung upon the earth!" (Ezek. 16.5) "Arise, and help these" (Ps.35.2b) that have no helper, "whose blood is spilt upon the ground like water!" (Ps. 22.14) Are not these "also the work of thine own hands" (Ps. 138.8), the purchase of thy Son's blood?" Stir them up "to cry unto thee in the land of their captivity" (2 Chron. 6.37); "and let their complaint come up before thee; let it enter into thy ears!" (2 Sam. 22.2c). "Make even those that lead them away captive to pity them" (2 Chron. 30.9)), and "turn their captivity as the rivers in the south" (Ps. 126.4). "O burst thou all their chains in sunder" (Nah. 1.13); more especially the chains of their sins! Thou Saviour of all, make them "free, that they may be free indeed!" (John 8.36)

Appendix III

The slide presentation accompanying this chapter featured a fabric print reproducing a quilt pattern of interlocking overlapping circles, rendered in multicolored patchwork. The pattern is consistent with designs known variously as the Double Wedding Ring or Cathedral Windows. Some historians and quilt scholars have proposed that certain geometric quilt patterns like this one were used in 19th-century America as signals to freedom seekers fleeing enslavement toward the Northern states, indicating that a particular farm offered food, shelter, or safe passage. This claim remains contested in the historiographical literature, and direct documentary evidence for a systematic quilt code is limited. The fabric print was chosen to visually introduce the chapter's engagement with the layered, interwoven, and sometimes ambiguous character of John Wesley's arguments in "Thoughts Upon Slavery," and to gesture toward the real human lives at stake in that text's reception history.

Appendix IV

7. CRITICAL REFLECTIONS FOR US-BOUND INTERNATIONAL STUDENTS AMIDST AMBIVALENCE

Lessons Learned from Various US Methodist Institutions

Jeong, Dong Hyeon

Reparative Justice for the International Students

I was an international student for thirteen years in two Methodist institutions and one Methodist-approved institution. I was also the president of the international student association in one of the Methodist institutions. In my current and fourth Methodist institution, aside from teaching biblical studies, I serve as the director of the Asian center. Reflecting upon those years and experiences, I have noticed that our presence as international students is both hyper-visible and oppressively invisible. On the one hand, we are constantly featured in the institution's brochure, website, Instagram, and other diversity-performing channels. On the other, the lived experiences of international students, particularly their partners and children, remain oppressively invisible. The smiling faces of the international students on the websites do not show how much they are struggling to make ends meet. Our stories are hard to quantify because they are anecdotal for the Association of Theological Schools, let alone if anyone wants to report it. And yet, I decided to write about the international students in this Methodist theological studies conference because presenting/writing about the international students somehow academically legitimizes our experiences. Our anecdotal becomes footnote-worthy. Becoming a quotable resource participates in unmasking the reality and confronting the dilemma the international students go through. Writing our stories as international students is like, to use Keri L. Day's expression, testifying against "the racist character of the theological enterprise even in the midst of its growing racially diverse landscape."[1] Also, I recognize that writing about our experience might be perceived as my procrustean solution to this dilemma. I do not seek to commodify our complex experience with academic bromide; rather, writing about international students is reparative. I invoke the reparative here because international students are barely mentioned in discussions on racism. And yet, we know that the transient are constant and vulnerable victims of racism.

Our precarious situation is historically and politically situated since the US–Russia Cold War. The US government fueled the growth of US-bound international student recruitment because, according to Sevan G. Terzian and Leigh Ann Osborne, "American political and educational leaders hoped that on returning home, the graduates of these academic programs would act as ambassadors and spread American political and cultural mores in their respective nations—to cultivate sympathy and understanding for American values worldwide."[2] This highly politicized legacy is deeply rooted and entangled not just in the colonized grounds of various academic campuses but also in the colonized minds of the former, current, and prospective international students. I admit that I myself have utilized my privilege in order to receive some crumbs from the master's table or this colonial machination.

This colonized mind is a result of global whiteness that endured throughout the centuries via oppressive missionary strategies and the normalization of whiteness in various parts of the world. According to Cara Cancelmo and Jennifer C. Mueller, whiteness "embodies both a material reality—connected to the disproportionate economic and political power wielded by those racialized as white, as well as a symbolic reality—shaped by the cultural meanings attached to whiteness as a form of inflated value, morality, aesthetics, and civilization."[3] Whiteness is hegemonic imposition, forced construct of white normality. Even if the futurity of whiteness is contested albeit postcolonially lingering, certain academic institutions sustain, knowingly or otherwise, their predilection for whiteness by the lack/absence of hospitality, colonially dictated rigor, and western hegemonic legacy.[4] Such projections of white normality "become the standard against which all other cultures, groups, and individuals are measured and usually found to be inferior."[5] The imposition of inferiority rings true even today and especially for the international students. Their transient circumstances become an excuse not to care for them: they will leave soon anyway, as murmured every now and then.

Such whiteness is also raised by Cristine Carnate-Atrero and Izzy Alvaran[6] in their work, "The Christmas Covenant: Toward Decolonizing UMC Polity," published in the editorial volume, *Methodism and American Empire: Reflections on Decolonizing the Church*. They argue that it is time for regionalization to emerge and become a law of The United Methodist Church. The Central Conferences, including the Philippines, have been heavily swayed and influenced by the US-based UMC churches and politics. Carnate-Atrero and Alvaran declare that the Central Conferences must "reject US-centrism and US normativity as well as colonialist/neocolonialist power dynamics, and fully commit to an identity as a global church expressing ministry regionally."[7]

If the UMC is finally trying to decenter US normativity within its denomination, then such efforts should also be expressed with reparations for their international students in their various institutions. We see this in Javier Viera's leadership at Garrett-Evangelical Theological Seminary. Viera echoes Carnate-Atrero and Alvaran's sentiments in regard to regionalism. Coming from his role as president of a US Methodist institution, Viera connects his thoughts on regionalism with caring for (international) students. That is, since regionalism "empower[s] local conferences, trusting them to know what their people need most and resourcing them to provide it . . . , [Garrett has been able] to learn how we can partner with local churches and co-create a new model of global theological education."[8] Viera connects regionalism with this renewed sense of commitment to decolonial theological education by asking: "How can we together breathe life and energy into the ministries you're already doing? How do we best discern God's Spirit and our calling in what we co-create?"[9] Viera's leadership demonstrates an expression of reparative care and justice for international students whereby the international students are invited to co-create, breathe together, and partner with the institution in addressing their educational needs and vocational discernments.

Reparative justice is an expression of anti-racist work. I follow how Jennifer Harvey finds the reparative paradigm a suitable response against whiteness. This reparative paradigm "insists that we look carefully at where we are now, in this historical moment, and at the ways the legacies we inherit continue to shape and inform our relationships. . . ."[10] Channeling Harvey's work, one can see that the reparative happens when we look carefully at where our students are now, particularly the international students. Carefully looking at their present circumstances helps us see whether or not our inherited legacies complicitly sustain oppressive structures that subjugate international students. Echoing the call for the reparative with the indigenous and racially/ethnically minoritized communities in the US, caring for international students should be part of the reparative responsibility of many academic institutions. That is, I argue that the reparative must be both indigenous and international.

In this reparative work, neoliberalism is a significant stumbling block. That is, academic institutions in the US have participated in dispossessing the indigenous people's lands, thereby replicating the regimes of dispossession and commodification of the other happening in the US and around the world.[11] Moreover, many of these academic institutions participated in dispossessing the minds and commodifying the bodies of their (international) students. In the present, neoliberalism continues this legacy of dispossession and commodification by wiping out the flourishing mind and spirit of many international students. As Wendy Brown defines it, neoliberalism is "a peculiar form of reason that configures all aspects of existence in economic terms."[12] In other words, neoliberalism commodifies the identity of international students as things to collect from. Neoliberalism creates spreadsheets that levy our names for dollar figures. Listing our bodies, minds, and spirits as mere economic numbers is an expression of neoliberal racism. That is why countering this neoliberal racism is reparative justice.

Teresa Brawner Bevis and Christopher J. Lucas remind us that international students are "individual human beings, with unique backgrounds, experiences, and aspirations . . . [and for institutions to be responsible in maximizing their] prospects for their success during their sojourn in America."[13] Inasmuch as this statement could be perceived as mundane, fulfilling this invitation and/or challenge by Bevis and Lucas is a difficult and yet radically effective process of countering racism/whiteness in many US (theological/academic) institutions. In particular, adapting Tatiana Suspitsyna's thoughts on whiteness and higher education, perhaps this reparative justice manifests when we, the Methodists, participate in the "repoliticization of internationalization."[14] That is, Methodist institutions must "acknowledge the ideological differences and inequalities between international partners, question the hegemony, ethnocentricity, and paternalism in the Global North-South encounters, examine the colonial legacy of partnering institutions and systems, and safeguard collaborations against self-serving agendas and easy solutions."[15] Furthermore, I follow Hendrik R. Pieterse's challenge, whereby he asks: "How do US theological institutions 'locate' themselves responsibly and with integrity in a global church that continues to bear the marks of our past mistakes, missteps, and shortsightedness"?[16]

Methodist institutions must continuously hope to change the world for the better while, as Christine Hong cautions, "holding a mirror up to its white supremacist, settler-colonial, and Christian hegemonic histories and practices."[17] Decolonizing efforts should not be metaphorical or turned into empty signifiers. Decolonizing Methodist institutions is chaotic because it rattles white fragility and passive aggressive niceties. As Tuck and Yang assert, decolonization should even follow an ethic of incommensurability or the moves "that unsettle innocence, stands in contrast to aims of reconciliation, which motivate settler moves to innocence."[18] To hope for a better world is not a return to innocence or providing a "hall pass" to those who do not desire to engage their messiness. Methodist institutions must be engaged with the difficult circumstances of the international students. This unsettling engagement is our Methodist duty to participate in the reparative. The technologies that produce international students in our institutions must consider ways to maximize their prospects of success with decolonial intentions. As Namsoon Kang suggests, theological educators must participate in transforming not just theological discourses but also the "concrete implementation of the discourse in the praxis of an individual theological school."[19] Kang expresses this invitation for constructive transformation with the concept of *planetarization*:

> *Planetarization* of theological education grounds itself in the geopolitical sensitivity to the power differentials between different regions of the world and seeks radical hospitality, responsibility, and cosmopolitan justice for every singular person in the world regardless of one's gender, class, race and ethnicity, ability, sexuality, or religion in its pedagogical philosophy and practices.[20]

This grounding embodies the educational. This sensitivity speaks the names of their geopolity. Kang does so in three iterations: radical hospitality, responsibility, and cosmopolitan justice. I echo Kang's planetarization by reiterating their sensitivities particularly to the reparative work for the international students. I mimic Kang by naming my three expressions as (radical) hospitality, rigor (or responsibility), and communal legacies (or cosmopolitan justice). I will also expound upon their ambivalent realities since each international student encounters them differently. Nevertheless, such critical take hopefully will provide a more realistic and holistic view in narrating the ambivalent lives of international students in US Methodist institutions.

A pause here because I have to address the elephant in the room. That is, who are the international students in relation to Wesleyan/Methodist studies? In her book *Strange Encounters*, Sara Ahmed expounds upon the relational dynamics between the recognized versus the foreign/strange. In particular, Ahmed exposes how "there are techniques that allow us to differentiate between those who are strangers and those who belong in a given space."[21] What is recognized in Wesleyan/Methodist studies is the explicit connection made with Wesleyan texts and other historical texts. What is strange is to bring up present (Methodist) concerns even if the topic (of a particular conference, explicitly formed and asked) is on racism and the concerns of international students. Moreover, the technique of differentiation or making something "strange" is when a Wesleyan/Methodist discourse is not peppered with Wesleyan quotes and historical passages. And yet, why is the discourse on the international students, a present condition in Methodism, a figure of strangeness? What is/are the very process(es) that keep such discourse recognized or strange? If these "encounters are meetings . . . which are not simply in the present: each encounter reopens the past encounters," then perhaps the strangeness of highlighting international students in a Methodist conference is a manifestation of a history of uneasiness, even of antagonism.[22] Perhaps such reluctance to this strange encounter is due to the enmeshment of the established ways of being Wesleyan and/or Methodist with these new embodiments and sensitivities that disrupt the status quo. Perhaps the sacrality of the recognized, unbothered and unfazed, is now being bothered by the strange, even labeled by some as an unholy encounter.

And yet, I write about this encounter/meeting because to not write or forget about the past further justifies the stranger-recognized dichotomy. Such dichotomy comes out of whiteness that keeps the stranger as stranger, international students as foreign/strange/unwelcome. Even if the international students are Methodists, they are strange Methodists. Since they are strange, their strangeness is perceived to be inferior and unworthy to be written down. To stop this forgetting that leads to oppression,

I argue that the process of identifying, naming, and associating a paper, event, or an encounter/meeting as Wesleyan/Methodist should be beyond the four corners of the recognized. So, how about the affective?

I became a Methodist before I knew I was a Methodist. When I introduced myself in my first US Methodist institution, I told them that I am a Methodist even though I barely knew what that particular identity meant. I felt being a Methodist because I was in a space that declares itself to be. The flames and the crosses were everywhere. The Wesleys were seen and sung. I was told that I was invited to this meeting and that event because I am a Methodist. I received this and I was asked to share that because, apparently, I am a Methodist. If I had to summarize these experiences, I would say that my first Methodist identity was affective; they were expressed and received affectively in particular through the hospitality that the institutions have provided, the academic rigor that was expected, and the communal legacies that I am asked to build and sustain. Could we explore what it means to become a Methodist in ways that are not just historical, theological, institutional, ecclesial, and academic? Can someone be a Methodist because they are affectively entangled with the community and participate in their reparative justice? Now, some of these entanglements were joyous; some of them were traumatic. I feel ambivalent about my experiences and entanglements; nevertheless, I feel like I need to share the lessons so that future international students and institutions (Methodist or otherwise) will be assisted in ways that are life-giving and holistic.

Lesson #1: Hospitality

Let's begin again with an anecdote. One of my institutions was so proud that they had given at least 50 percent scholarship to 95 percent of their students for that particular academic year. It was plastered all over the seminary's announcement billboards, community newsletters, and other communication and marketing outlets. I was miffed because I only got a 10 percent scholarship. I tried to let it go because I should be grateful that I have received even 10 percent financial aid as a foreigner. One day, one of the leaders of the international student association approached me and asked how much scholarship I had received from the institution. He told me that most of the international students didn't get good scholarship packages that particular academic year; in other words, we were the majority of the 5 percent who did not get good financial aid. I get it: international students are moneybags. This is nothing new; international students who are undergraduates pay ridiculous amounts of tuition and boarding fees every year. Nobody told or forced us to come to the US in the first place, at least that is what I have been told. What is hospitality when right from the beginning the welcome is costly, selective, and environmentally microaggressive?

According to NAFSA: Association of International Educators, there were more than one million international students in the US for the year 2022–2023. This is across the board: undergraduate to various professional degrees. On their website, they have declared that international students have brought in the total amount of $40.1 billion USD and have created directly or otherwise 368,333 jobs.[23] The numbers are based on state by state and congressional district analysis of revenue generated directly or indirectly by the international students. Their host institutions have sent the data to the US government, and NAFSA accounted for the numbers. Here, one can see how the data magnifies the financial contribution the international students offer for the US as a whole. However, as Carol W. N. Fadda and Dana W. Olwan assert, the focus is limited to the quantifiable, and their "physical presence on campus that indexes diversity."[24] I agree that there should always be room for quantifiable data because they are also helpful in determining the conditions of the community and the needs of various entities. And so, recognizing the value of such data gathering, I also asked for data from the thirteen Methodist academic institutions in the US. Interestingly, not all agreed to share their data with me. As a person who works in an institution myself, I understand the need for privacy and proprietary concerns. Those who shared were eager to do so. A few directed me to the Association of Theological School's database, which is somewhat helpful because their scope is beyond the thirteen Methodist institutions. I thought of pursuing the next steps to gather the exact numbers of international students and their financial contributions to their institutions. Then, I caught myself doing something that is colonial, voyeuristic, and even panopticon-like surveillance. Maybe I am a bit paranoid here. Inasmuch as the data are important, the reparative work should not be beholden to the numbers of enrollment and their financial contributions. So, I dropped the inquisition because I realized that I am measuring the thirteen Methodist institutions with colonial and neoliberal lenses. I am not claiming that the thirteen institutions are completely different from the undergraduate learning institutions or immune to neoliberalism; nevertheless, I do acknowledge that the thirteen Methodist institutions are relatively smaller, some are embedded in their universities, and have legacies that are complex to quantify and capture. That is why I turned my gaze to the anecdotal and yet systemic environmental microaggressions many international students are (still) facing.

There are four expressions of microaggressions: micro-assaults, micro-insults, micro-invalidation, and environmental microaggression. I argue that environmental microaggression is one of the most significant hindrances for institutions in becoming hospitable. According to Hye Jin Tina Yeo, et al.,

> Environmental microaggressions occur on an institutional level (e.g., policies and recruitment and admission practices) and are evident in the built environment (e.g., images of honor that are predominantly White, classes with one or very few students of color). In other words, these "numerous demeaning and threatening social, educational, political, or economic cues" (Sue 2010, 25) involve individual, institutional, or societal communication toward marginalized groups. Environmental microaggressions are generally unnoticeable by majority and privileged groups. However, they are often quite visible to minority and underrepresented groups such as domestic students of color and international students. Specific examples of environmental microaggressions for international students include policies and practices related to obtaining student visa and work permits; lack of legal, financial, social, and culturally relevant resources and supports; and being viewed as economic commodities during recruitment-related activities. Examining racialized campus climates facilitates understanding and theorizing international students' racial experience and racial identity development in U.S. institutions of higher education.[25]

To propose the primacy of environmental microaggression does not negate the lingering presence of other microaggressions; they still happen and have evolved in ways that are less conspicuous. I highlight environmental microaggression because its evolution has tapped into the chicanery of neoliberal machination of hyper-capitalistic efficiency. The usual rhetoric is as such: we cannot do this, we cannot do that because we do not have the budget for it; by the way, we just hired another sinecure position. That is why Yeo et al. narrate how "responsibilities for adjustment are often treated as an individual-level problem to be addressed by international students and with their own resources. . . . Asian international students often mistakenly explain discrimination as though they are implicitly responsible."[26] Some institutions have policies and offices that assist international students; and yet, their techniques of hospitality are usually curtailed in the name of budgetary restrictions and so-called strategic relevancy. Others might invoke individualism's mantra of "I don't want to be disturbed or told what to do" in order to cover their indifference and transfer blame to the individual. The irony is that hospitality has become a ground zero for hostility. Hospitality, which is supposed to be acts of joy and welcome, has turned into sources of anxiety, resentment, and even xenophobia.

Jacques Derrida has touched a nerve on this very issue of hospitality, a sensitive matter particularly for those who consider themselves as the host. Derrida's fluid wordplay interrogates how hospitality is enmeshed with hostility (*hostis*), turning into a portmanteau, "*hostpitality.*" That is, the foreigner (*hostis*) slips in its connotation both as a guest and an enemy.[27] *Hostpitality* evokes the need for the host to maintain sovereignty over their home (or institution) in order to sustain the provision of hospitality to the other. And yet, the transgressions of providing to the foreign/international student "risk of becoming their hostage" because hospitality without finitude has the possibility of dismantling the capacities of the home/institution.[28] To put it in different terms, "absolute hospitality" (or radical hospitality) requires that I "*give place*" to the foreign absolutely even if such giving has the capacity to permeate and obliterate what is home/institution for the host, thereby losing one's home.[29] The contention is antinomy. If hospitality has to be radical, unlimited, or absolute, then hospitality is tyrannical, beyond the law. Derrida argues that "the *unconditional* law of hospitality needs the laws, it *requires* [sic] them. . . . It wouldn't be effectively unconditional, the law, if it didn't have to become effective, concrete, determined. . . . It would risk being abstract, utopian, illusory. . . ."[30] *Hostpitality* then turns guests into enemies or even parasites when there are no laws to protect their selves, from each other and from the host. Such lack of the conditional is paradoxically inhospitable. Derrida leaves the issue of *hostpitality* in its deconstructed state, of its antinomous construct, and concludes the discussion with the invitation for hospitality-to-come, "a hospitality invented for the singularity of the new arrival, of the unexpected visitor."[31]

I cannot leave the issue in its deconstructed state because there is an urgent need to care for a group of new arrivals who have been visibly neglected even more than the international students themselves: their partners and their children. They have experienced not only environmental microaggression but also micro-invalidation or denial/belittling of their experiential realities.[32] Ana X. de la Serna asserts that the partners and children of international students experience not only neglect but the almost complete absence of prospect for success. Their incapacity as F2 visa holders is exacerbated with their legally imposed identity as supporters for their studying partners.[33] The so-called neoliberal efficiency demands the utmost protection of the host's sovereignty by declaring that partners and their children are unfortunately "not part of the budget" or they are financially parasitic. Caring for them will overextend the meager capacities of the institution. Again, I get it. And yet, it does not sit well with me. One of the buzzwords these days is holistic. Institutions seek to care for their students holistically; however, the reach of this holistic care apparently is limited to one paying customer. How is the well-being of a student holistically cared for when their family members are struggling? For those who need data and scientific analysis to justify the importance of the communal, particularly in supporting the families and partners of international students, Dae Seok Chai, et al., invited thousands of international students to participate in their research on the influence of family and community support in their studies. They have received and analyzed 1,436 cases. With these cases, they have concluded that there is "a reciprocal influence between personal and work domains, which supported the spillover theory (work and personal domains affect each other; [Caligiuri et al 1998]). . . . Since work and personal domains are blurred for international students, support from family members and communities is crucial to international students' outcomes."[34]

What is hospitality when hostility draws the line? What if the singularity of the new arrival (partners and children) is not the problem in terms of hospitality? What if the problem is the removal of the unexpected by codifying hospitality? What if this codification is a mask of the colonial enterprise? That is, this codifying colonial enterprise forces us to see that the conflict is just between the host and the guest. This limiting purview is codified into the law of hospitality, creating an unnecessary hostility between entities. Hospitality-to-come, as Derrida suggests, unravels this mask with reparative justice. *Hostpitality* cannot be the end or the state of affairs. Hospitality that is accompanied by reparative justice interrogates the assumed, codified inability and unwillingness, in order to welcome the other.

Taking a step back, *hostpitality* reminds me and my fellow international students that I cannot be on the moral high horse of this binarization between international students and their host institutions. As Derrida would say, I am both a host and a guest. I also embody *hostpitality* toward the other. The confluence of being home/host and hospitable/hostile resides both with the international students and with their institutions. Hostility is also found when one considers oneself a pure specimen of victimhood who denies or even condones one's own moments of oppressive behaviors and actions. In particular, I admit that my thesis and arguments are Christian-centric: hospitality for Christian international students in Methodist institutions. As Nuray Karaman would say, the homogeneity and dominance of Christianity in this chapter needs to be interrogated in its whiteness.[35] If non-Christian international students become students in my institution, will I/we be ready to radically welcome them? E. Byron Anderson brings this important inquiry as he analyzes how the higher education's negotiations with church affiliation correlate with recent discussions on globalization in various theological institutions.[36] As he lays out the different models on how institutions/universities have responded to this inquiry, Anderson highlights Elizabeth Newman's challenge to provide homes, not hotel rooms, for the other if one truly seeks to provide hospitality. Newman argues that "hospitality can only be fully practiced when a concrete sense of place sustains the life of an institution."[37] Anderson expands my horizon on hospitality because he has shown me that my hospitality toward non-Christians is wanting, at least for now. Anderson[38] even quotes Michael G. Cartwright who evinces my current "room for growth" in terms of the lack when it comes to caring for non-Christian international students: "The agency of hospitality appears to be governed more by administrative tolerance than by the kind of enriched hospitality."[39] Of course, there will always be room for growth especially when it comes to enriched/radical hospitality. Nevertheless, Anderson's invitation to reframe globalization as an opportunity to be in solidarity with the oppressed echoes and shapes the critical humility that is required in dealing with *hostpitality* in oneself and in one's institution.[40]

Lesson #2: Rigor

Here is an anecdote I can never forget. I had a conversation with a professor about applying for PhD programs in the US. I had asked him about the requirements and the expectations. He preached on the importance of intellectual rigor and that I had to be on par or better than most of the elite students. Then, he said something that took me by surprise: "You have to improve your English because listening to you sounds like biting on a small stone while eating rice." Then and there, I bit my tongue and took a bite into his cruel optimism. Lauren Berlant would ask someone like me: "Why do people stay attached to good-life fantasies—say of enduring reciprocity in couples, families, political systems, institutions, fragility, markets and at work—when the evidence of their instability, fragility, and dear cost, abounds?"[41] I hoped for this cruel optimism; I was willing to do anything to achieve this fantasy even if I knew that the odds were stacked against me. I just had to have rigor—intellectual rigor, apparently.

Because there could be only one, I had to be better than my colleagues. I had to be more efficient, productive, and resilient if I wanted to survive the unstable, fragile, and taxing world of academia. I performed and internalized model minority in the name of honoring my community that sent me. I get it. We cannot bring shame. And yet, we also know that institutions are not responsible for our honor. As a matter of fact, they do not need to operate with such cultural understanding. In a certain sense, the very idea that we are contesting the spaces of honor-shame in a foreign space is baffling. We do not have to resort to the toxic strategies of "fight, flight, or playing white" in order to be rigorous.[42] In other words, rigor does not have to be colonial and oppressive. We do not have to sacrifice each other and become stumbling blocks to the next generation of international students.

What if we could have rigor that reduces trauma of shame by creating a flourishing environment? What if we could study and work in ways that do not serve the master narrative and the neoliberal colonial enterprise? Here, I hope to respond to my own inquiries with four expressions of rigor for students, instructors, and institutions. These four inquiries are heuristic and based upon my own experience. There may be more or less; some might not apply to your context. In any case, the consistent thread is the hope for creative flourishing that leads to holistic success not just for the international students but also for the instructors and the institutions.

First, institutions must create welcoming spaces for international students before and after their arrival to the host institution's space/country/region. Institutions spend a significant amount of money when it comes to recruiting students, enticing them to join our illustrious company for the opportunity to learn from us and pay their way to honorable recognition. Could institutions also spend comparable time, energy, and finance in caring for the international students as soon as they land in the US? Institutions could pick them up from the airport, prepare welcome packages with food, water, blankets, and other forms of assistance. Moreover, this welcoming space must assist international students in settling their bank accounts, children's school registration (if needed), and even employment. Inasmuch as this welcome seems logical and obvious, others might find these expectations hostile; here, I invoke Derrida's ***hostpitality***: hostility emerges if international students are perceived simply as cash cows. Hospitality-to-come with a dose of reparative justice does otherwise because supporting the international students is an expression of undoing the trauma of colonial education. This hospitality requires the full acknowledgment and participation of the institution; in other words, this is not a job delegated to a few—a classic sign of colonial response to problems. By doing so, this hospitality becomes a meaningful gesture toward (continuously) decolonizing spaces of learning. Such a gesture hopefully will speak louder to institutions who value co-curricular pedagogies.

Second, instructors must be empowered to create generous and courageous spaces within their classrooms. I chose not to use the expression "safe space" because I follow Christine J. Hong's admonition: "To call a space 'safe' in North American society privileges heteronormativity, men, nondisabled bodies, Christianity, and whiteness. Individual and communal identities, religious, and otherwise, can hold power in one space, but remain liminal in others."[43] Courageous and generous spaces hold all entities accountable in their liminal and vulnerable selves. These spaces provide not just mutual understanding but also room for repentance and forgiveness. Many students, including international students, seek spaces in which they could express their ideologies and theologies without being cancelled immediately. Of course, hateful and harmful rhetoric are not tolerated; nevertheless, these courageous and generous spaces allow for students to actually learn from each other, receive constructive feedback, and critically reflect upon their own words and the words of others. This is crucial for international students because they have to traverse multiple and convoluted linguistic, cultural, geopolitical, and other sensitivities/barriers within and without the classroom. Moreover, our global classrooms, heightened by the shift toward online teaching modalities, have exacerbated the importance of learning each other's cultural cues, rhetorical sensitivities, and idiomatic expressions. That is why classrooms, digitized or otherwise, must hold the confluence of the critical and inviting, of the courage to learn from one another while fully expressing one's thoughts.

Third, Tat-siong Benny Liew admonishes instructors to have these courageous and generous spaces that consider "how our evaluation or assessment of students can become antiracist project."[44] Liew quotes Roderick Ferguson who also cautions against the notion of excellence and/or rigor that endorses zero sum game individualism and competitiveness under the banner of surveillance, exclusion, and measurement.[45] Liew pushes the bounds by inviting instructors to explore "something more transformative that changes the underlying cultural ethos of assessment—even or especially when traditional evaluation practices feel rational, natural, or normal."[46] Of course, I understand that this will require significant unlearning and relearning for instructors. Nevertheless, as a faculty member myself, such invitation is much needed because it keeps us grounded, open to new learning, and attuned to the needs of the present generation. In a certain sense, the accrediting (Association of Theological Schools) and ordaining (denominations and religious orders) entities should also be part of this conversation in decolonizing assessments. As a professor in a Christian seminary, these two entities are constantly in my mind as I create assessments for my courses. Perhaps this reshaping of rigor based on decolonial assessments has deeper underlying concerns that need to be unearthed/addressed. It is one thing for me to change my assessments; will these entities accept/endorse such transformative change that shifts the underlying ethos of theological education?

Fourth, institutions can create theological education that is based on *renren* or co-humanity, as K. K. Yeo asserts. According to Yeo, *renren* invites a nonbinary model of theological education in which there is room for "*communal living and reading of theology.*" This communal and co-human rigor reminds us that most of our seminary students' post-graduation work (unless they choose work that requires research writing) is not defined by individualized academic paper writing. Rather, they are thrust into the interpersonal and "cross-cultural."[47] Doing so reduces the possibility for shame because it lessens individual competitiveness where my success is not dependent upon myself alone and even the other's lacking. Moreover, *renren* reminds me of the Korean expression *woori*, which mean we/us/our. *Woori* is used to express communal identity formation and belonging. Koreans prefer to say "*woori oma,*" or our mother, even if I am only talking about my mother. Such emphasis on the communal recognizes that my mother is also a mother figure of the community. Here, I invoke Christine J. Hong's take on this expression: "*Woori* encompasses what it means to cultivate a communal theology that gives birth to a theology of selfhood, not the other way around."[48] Of course, reiterating Hong's concerns, I recognize the negative effects of this communalism where too much emphasis on it leads to the negative sacrifice of the self, "To romanticize *woori* is a colonial move that reproduces the erasure of those who have experienced the concept and embodiments of *woori* as painful and traumatizing."[49] And yet, when it is implemented with liberating and sustainable intentions, *woori* could heal wounds, protect the most vulnerable, sustain joyous environment, lessen (or if possible, eliminate) the traumatic, and recognize that international students are not just studying for themselves. We are "actually witnessing ancestors, families, cities, villages, temples, mosques, and/or churches coexisting in one body."[50]

Living out the spirit of *renren* in theological institutions also implies that international students are participating in the "technology of governance," as Ahmed asserts.[51] That is, international students should also have a voice in determining, navigating, and contributing to the flourishing of themselves and their institutions. The spirit of *renren* is not limited to the classrooms; *renren* should also manifest in the very systems that recruit, teach, and even organize the international students. In that way, theological institutions could become communities of genuine care, *renren*-filled homes that counter the poison-induced machinations of neoliberal tendencies.

Lesson #3: Communal Legacies

To my fellow international students: let's be honest. One of the reasons we seek western institutions is that we know the implications of graduating from one of these places: honor and authority. In some ways, we seek the prestigious legacy these western institutions will provide us and our communities. I get it; and yet, I am also cautious about this search for prestigious legacy because such a search for honor and authority turns into the search (knowingly or otherwise) for becoming neo-colonizers. I have seen this saddening neo-colonization manifesting with various close friends and acquaintances. They were sent to become liberators of the oppressed; unfortunately, many have returned to become neo-oppressors of their own people. They have mimicked the colonial method of going to another land, conquering it/them, and returning (or not) home with the spoils of their conquest. That is why I ask my fellow international students: what kind of communal legacies do we seek?

I do not look at western institutions with binary perspective or with complete disdain. In fact, I see that these institutions could become safe havens for those who are persecuted back in their home communities. International students who are queer, politically persecuted (particularly in Myanmar), and abused in various ways back home find healing spaces in these institutions. Albeit many of these institutions are not fully welcoming and some are actually more oppressive than their home communities, the institutions who are welcoming of the other create opportunities for the minoritized and oppressed to live and thrive.

How then can Methodist theological institutions participate in sustaining liberating communal legacies? My response to this inquiry is this Filipinx expression: *kumain ka na ba*? This expression means "have you eaten already?" Inasmuch as this expression sounds quotidian, it actually implies layers of meaning, connections, and decolonial intentions. First, the expression invites to see each other as humans, fragile and weak, in need of each other's support. We all need food no matter who we are and where we come from. This embodied provisioning addresses not just individual needs but also the need for systemic initiative that addresses the holistic needs of the individual and the community. Moreover, the ones who are invited to eat or to receive the invitation of *kumain ka na ba?* should include the international students' significant others. Their well-being is our well-being, and vice versa. The international students' well-being is the institution's well-being. Second, *kumain ka na ba?* helps institutions look at students not as numbers and revenue data. Rather, they are persons with vocational ministry, families to feed, and personal health matters to deal with. To invite someone to one's house is to make sure that they are at least fed with nourishing food. The nourishing food does not have to be extravagant; the food just needs to meet dietary requirements and cultural expectations. Third, this expression is a pushback against oppression and colonization. To care for one another with *kumain ka na ba*? means we are going to fight oppression together, one meal at a time. Communal eating is solidarity with the well-being of everyone involved. This is the kind of legacy I hope our Methodist institutions will sustain: a communal legacy in which everyone who comes will be fed with liberation and decolonization.

Conclusion

I wrote/spoke about the international students for a panel on racism at a Methodist conference because Methodism is not a relic of the past but a living entity entangled in the present church, academia, and the wider world. We are Methodist history in the making. So, when some ask, what do Wesleyans/Methodists have to say about racism, we cannot just point to the past and call it a day. We, as living Methodists, are also accountable in undoing present racism and whiteness. Methodism does not only unearth historical information; it is a living entity that, as Fadda and Olwan argue, engages in "anti-racist, anti-imperial, and anti-Orientalist frameworks, as well as to the critique of hegemonic knowledge productions that serve the university's diversity goals and imperatives."[52] Also, as Sara Ahmed in *On Being Included* reminds us, we are invited "to co-create and co-flourish in sustainable futures. To co-learn from each other; to help us see the shifting contours of oppressive behaviors and institutionalizations we cannot see for ourselves. For not to be absorbed into silence and complacency."[53] "Comfortable isolationism," as Bevis and Lucas state, "is no longer a viable option."[54] Comfortably isolating Methodist/Wesleyan studies to the historical is no longer a viable option because we are also part of and responsible for what happens in Methodism today.

Expanding the conversation further, caring for international students should also involve the divine and the nonhumans. As I said above, I became a Methodist affectively. Moreover, I am grateful for the joys brought about by the spirit of *renren/woori*. I believe that caring for the other cannot simply be an anthropocentric endeavor. It has to involve the guidance and the lessons provided by the divine and the nonhumans because of humanity's insufficiency when it comes to caring for the other. Here, the divine is not limited to the Christian deity; the nonhumans are not anthropomorphized for human consumption. Rather, the divine is a reflection of the mystical/spirit; the nonhumans are actants/agents of their own presence in this world. With these in mind, Letty M. Russell's take on hospitality as "God's *unfolding promise*" contradicts singular understanding of hospitality.[55] If the divine's revelation is constantly unfolding and revealing to all (humans and nonhumans), then such generous divine promise should empower us to courageously welcome the other. Joshua W. Jipp continues in this theological reflection by intersecting hospitality with his take on the divine mandate to care for the other: "Because God is the one who welcomes humans, that is 'the other,' into relationship with him [sic], humans are called to enact hospitality in their relations with each other. The structure of the divine-human relationship in terms of divine host and human guest is the foundation for hospitable intra-human relationships."[56] Luke Bretherton provides another theological reflection on hospitality by arguing that "Christians are not only commanded to welcome the vulnerable stranger, but to see the vulnerable stranger as representing Christ."[57] If for Jipp the divine is the host who welcomes radically, Bretherton signifies the divine as the guest/stranger. Juxtaposing Jipp and Bretherton's theological takes on hospitality echoes Derrida's take on *hostpitality*. That is, even within theological discourse, the entanglements and ontological fluidity between the host(s) and the guest(s) lingers. We unravel them with reparative justice here and now.

Again, a pause . . . .

After all of these, we need to breathe.

I accept Stephen Lewis, Matthew Wesley Williams, and Dori Grinenko Baker's invitation to CARE acronym for four adaptive moves

(Create hospitable space, Ask self-awakening questions, Reflect theologically together, Enact the next most faithful step) that "invites people to engage wholeheartedly in ways of leading profound change, ways that are deeply connected to people's inner well-being and to their communities of accountability."[58] They invite us to CARE in ways that are contrary to neoliberal expectations. We are invited to breathe because we do not need to pretend that we have figured everything out.[59] Here and elsewhere, I hope that this chapter has testified, manifested, and critically engaged our concerns enough. No pretentions, just enough for us to breathe and fight another day. So, to my fellow international students, I look forward to engaging your CARE and your invitations for hospitality, rigor, and sustaining communal legacies.

Notes to Chapter 7

1. Keri L. Day, *Notes of a Native Daughter: Testifying in Theological Education* (Eerdmans, 2021), 3.

2. Sevan G. Terzian and Leigh Ann Osborne, "Postwar Era Precedent and the Ambivalent Quest for International Students at the University of Florida," *Journal of Studies in International Education*, 10.3 (2006), 300–301.

3. Cara Cancelmo and Jennifer Mueller. "Whiteness: Introduction." www.oxfordbibliographies.com. *Oxford Bibliographies: Sociology*. Accessed 16 May 2024.

4. See Linda MartinAlcoff, *The Future of Whiteness* (John Wiley & Sons, 2015) and Alfred J. Lopez, ed, *Postcolonial Whiteness: A Critical Reader on Race and Empire* (SUNY Press, 2012).

5. Cicely Belle Blain, "How Canadian Universities Fail Black Non-Binary Students," in *Coloniality and Racial (In)Justice in the University: Counting for Nothing?* ed. Sunera Thorani (University of Toronto Press, 2022), 330–58. See also Frances Henry, Tim Rees, and Carol Tator, *The Color of Democracy: Racism in Canadian Society* (Nelson Education, 2010).

6. Cristine Carnate-Atrero and Izzy Alvara, "The Christmas Covenant: Toward Decolonizing UMC Polity," in *Methodism and American Empire: Reflections on Decolonizing the Church*, ed. David W. Scott and Filipe Maia, 173–90 (Abingdon Press, 2023).

7. Carnate-Atrero and Alvara, "The Christmas Covenant," 186.

8. Javier A. Viera "Making Room in the UMC for the Spirit's Work," *The Christian Century,* https://www.christiancentury.org/features/making-room-umc-spirit-s-work (July 2024). Accessed September 20, 2024.

9. Viera, "Making Room in the UMC for the Spirit's Work."

10. Jennifer Harvey, *Dear White Christians: For Those Still Longing for Racial Reconciliation* (Eerdmans, 2014), 251.

11. SuneraThorani, "Introduction - Present Pasts: The Anxieties of Power.]," *in* Coloniality and Racial (In)Justice in the University: Counting for Nothing? ed. Sunera Thorani (University of Toronto Press, 2022) 3–46.

12. Wendy Brown, *Undoing the Demos: Neoliberalism's Stealth Revolution* (MIT Press, 2015), 17.

13. Teresa Brawner Bevis and Christopher J. Lucas, *International Students in American Colleges and University: A History* (Palgrave Macmillan, 2007), 242.

14. Tatiana Suspitsyna, "Internationalization, Whiteness, and Biopolitics of Higher Education," *Journal of International Studies* 11.1 (2021): 59.

15.Suspitsyna, "Internationalization, Whiteness, and Biopolitics of Higher Education," 59.

16. Pieterse, Hendrik R. "Internationalizing Theological Education? Musings on a Neglected Concept," in *Locating US Theological Education in a Global Context: Conversations with American Higher Education*, ed. Hendrik R. Pieterse, 1–22 (Pickwick Publications, 2019), 18.

17. Christine J. Hong, *Decolonial Futures: Intercultural and Interreligious Intelligence for Theological Education* (Lexington Books, 2021), 1.

18. Eve Tuck and K. Wayne Yang. "Decolonization is Not a Metaphor," *Decolonization: Indigeneity, Education, & Society* 1.1 (2012): 35.

19. Namsoon Kang, "Global Politics of Knowledge and US Theological Education: From Globalization to Planetarization," in *Locating US Theological Education in a Global Context: Conversations with American Higher Education*, ed. Hendrik R. Pieterse (Pickwick Publications, 2019), 36–37.

20. Kang, "Global Politics of Knowledge and US Theological Education," 38–39.

21. Sara Ahmed, *Strange Encounters: Embodied Others in Post-Coloniality* (Routledge, 2000), 22.

22. Ahmed, *Strange Encounters,* 8.

23. Rachel Banks, "The United States of America Benefits from International Students," www.nafsa.org/economicvalue. NAFSA: Association of International Educators. Accessed December 15, 2023.

24. Carol W. N. Fadda and Dana W. Olwan. "Refusing Diversity in the Militarized Settler Academy," in *Coloniality and Racial (In)Justice in the University: Counting for Nothing?* ed. Sunera Thobani (University of Toronto Press, 2022), 318.

25. Hye Jin Tina Yeo, Ruby Mendenhall, Stacy Anne Harwood, and Margaret Browne Huntt, "Asian International Student and Asian American Student: Mistaken Identity and Racial Microaggressionsm," *Journal of International Students* 9.1 (2019): 45–46.

26. Yeo, et al., "Asian International Student and Asian American Student," 58.

27. Jaques Derrida, *Of Hospitality: Anne Dufourmantelle Invites Jacques Derrida to Respond*, trans. Rachel Bowlby (Stanford University Press, 2000), 45.

28. Derrida, *Of Hospitality*, 55.

29. Derrida, *Of Hospitality*, 25.

30. Derrida, *Of Hospitality*, 79.

31. Derrida, *Of Hospitality*, 83.

32. Yeo, et al., "Asian International Student and Asian American Student," 45.

33. Ana X. de la Serna, "One Family, Different Experiences of Identity Formation: International Graduate Students and Their Spouses," *Journal of International Students* 12:2 (2022): 376–78.

34. Dae Seok Chai, Huyen Thi Minh Van, Chih-Wei Wang, Jin Lee, and Jia Wang. "What Do International Students Need? The Role of Family and Community Supports for Adjustment, Engagement, and Organizational Citizenship Behavior," *Journal of International Students* 10.3 (2020): 583. See also Paula. M.Caligiuri, Mary Anne M. Hyland, Aparna Joshi, and Allon S. Bross, "Testing a Theoretical Model for Examining the Relationship between Family Adjustment and Expatriates' Work Adjustment," *Journal of Applied Psychology* 83 (1998).

35. Nuray Karaman, "Coding Whiteness and Racialization: Living in the Space as an Insider-Outsider," *Journal of International Students* 12.2 (2022): 135.

36. E. Byron Anderson, "Church Affiliation and Educational Mission in a Secularizing World," in *Locating US Theological Education in a Global Context: Conversations with American Higher Education*, ed. Hendrik R. Pieterse (Pickwick Publications, 2019), 82.

37. Newman, Elizabeth, "Hotel or Home? Hospitality and Higher Education," in *Conflicting Allegiances: The Church-Based University in a Liberal Democratic Society*, ed. Michael L. Budde and John Wright (Brazos, 2004), 91.

38. Anderson, "Church Affiliation and Educational Mission," 90.

39. Cartwright, Michael G. "The Mission of the University, Reincorporated?: Membership Matters at the Intentionally Pluralist Church-Related University." Paper presented at Exiles from Eden Conference, Valparaiso University. June 7, 2014.

40. Anderson, "Church Affiliation and Educational Mission," 98.

41. Lauren Berlant, *Cruel Optimism* (Duke University Press, 2011), 2.

42. Chris Derrington, "Fight, Flight, and Playing White: An Examination of Coping Strategies Adopted by Gypsy Traveller Adolescents in English Secondary Schools," *International Journal of Educational Research* 46.6 (2007): 357–67.

43. Hong, *Decolonial Futures*, 142.

44. Liew, Tat-siong Benny and Shelly Matthews, "Introduction: Racism, Classroom Teaching, and Beyond," in *Race and Biblical Studies: Antiracism Pedagogy for the Classroom*, eds. Tat-siong Benny Liew and Shelly Matthews. Resources for Biblical Study 101 (SBL Press, 2022), 7.

45. Roderick A. Ferguson, *The Reorder of Things: The University and Its Pedagogies of Minority Difference* (University of Minnesota Press, 2012), 76–102.

46. Liew and Matthews, "Introduction: Racism, Classroom Teaching, and Beyond," 7.

47. K. K. Yeo, "'Made in the USA': A Chinese Perspective on US Theological Education in Light of the Chinese Context," in *Locating US Theological Education in a Global Context: Conversations with American Higher Education*, ed. Hendrik R. Pieterse (Pickwick Publications, 2019), 150–51.

48. Hong, *Decolonial Futures*, 110.

49. Hong, *Decolonial Futures*, 108, 110.

50. Hong, *Decolonial Futures*, 102.

51. (2012), 163.

52. Fadda and Olwan, "Refusing Diversity in the Militarized Settler Academy," 322.

53. Sara Ahmed, *On Being Included: Racism and Diversity in Institutional Life* (Duke University Press, 2012), 153.

54. Bevis and Lucas, 246.

55. Letty M. Russell, *Just Hospitality: God's Welcome in a World of Difference*, ed. J. Shannon Clarkson and Kate M. Ott (Westminster John Knox, 2009), 43.

56. Joshua W. Jipp, *Saved by Faith and Hospitality*. Foreword by Christine D. Poh (Eerdmans, 201), 127.

57. Luke Bretherton, *Hospitality as Holiness: Christian Witness Amid Moral Diversity* (Ashgate, 2006), 149.

58. Stephen Lewis, Matthew Wesley Williams, and Dori Grinenko Baker, *Another Way: Living and Leading Change on Purpose,* foreword by Parker J. Palmer (Chalice Press, 2020), 1.

59. Lewis, et al., *Another Way*, 13.

Bibliography

Ahmed, Sara. *On Being Included: Racism and Diversity in Institutional Life*. Duke University Press, 2012.

_____. *Strange Encounters: Embodied Others in Post-Coloniality*. Routledge, 2000.

Alcoff, Linda Martin. *The Future of Whiteness*. John Wiley & Sons, 2015.

Anderson, E. Byron, "Church Affiliation and Educational Mission in a Secularizing World." In *Locating US Theological Education In a Global Context: Conversations with American Higher Education*, ed. Hendrik R. Pieterse, 81–106. Eugene, OR: Pickwick Publications, 2019.

Banks, Rachel. "The United States of America Benefits from International Students," www.nafsa.org/economicvalue. NAFSA: Association of International Educators, accessed December 15, 2023.

Bevis, Teresa Brawner and Christopher J. Lucas. *International Students in American Colleges and University: A History*. Palgrave Macmillan, 2007.

Berlant, Lauren. Cruel *Optimism*. Duke University Press, 2011.

Blain, Cicely Belle. "How Canadian Universities Fail Black Non-Binary Students." In *Coloniality and Racial (In)Justice in the University: Counting for Nothing?* ed. Sunera Thorani, 330–58. University of Toronto Press, 2022.

Bretherton, Luke. *Hospitality as Holiness: Christian Witness Amid Moral Diversity*. England: Ashgate, 2006.

Brown, Wendy. *Undoing the Demos: Neoliberalism's Stealth Revolution*. MIT Press, 2015.

Caligiuri, Paula. M., Mary Anne M. Hyland, Aparna Joshi, and Allon S. Bross. "Testing a Theoretical Model for Examining the Relationship between Family Adjustment and Expatriates' Work Adjustment." *Journal of Applied Psychology* 83 (1998): 598–614.

Cancelmo, Cara and Jennifer Mueller. "Whiteness: Introduction." www.oxfordbibliographies.com. Oxford Bibliographies: Sociology. Accessed 16 May 2024.

Carnate-Atrero, Cristine and Izzy Alvaran. "The Christmas Covenant: Toward Decolonizing UMC Polity." In *Methodism and American Empire: Reflections on Decolonizing the Church*, ed. David W. Scott and Filipe Maia, 173–90. Abingdon Press, 2023.

Cartwright, Michael G. "The Mission of the University, Reincorporated?: Membership Matters at the Intentionally Pluralist Church-Related University." Paper presented at Exiles from Eden Conference, Valparaiso University. June 7, 2014.

Chai, Dae Seok, Huyen Thi Minh Van, Chih-Wei Wang, Jin Lee, and Jia Wang. "What Do International Students Need? The Role of Family and Community Supports for Adjustment, Engagement, and Organizational Citizenship Behavior." *Journal of International Students* 10.3 (2020): 571–89.

Day, Keri L. *Notes of a Native Daughter: Testifying in Theological Education*. Eerdmans, 2021.

Derrida, Jacques. *Of Hospitality: Anne Dufourmantelle Invites Jacques Derrida to Respond.* Translated by Rachel Bowlby. Stanford University Press, 2000.

Derrington, Chris. "Fight, Flight, and Playing White: An Examination of Coping Strategies Adopted by Gypsy Traveller Adolescents in English Secondary Schools." *International Journal of Educational Research* 46.6 (2007): 357–67.

Fadda, Carol W. N. and Dana W. Olwan. "Refusing Diversity in the Militarized Settler Academy." In *Coloniality and Racial (In)Justice in the University: Counting for Nothing?* Edited by Sunera Thobani, 305–29. University of Toronto Press, 2022.

Ferguson, Roderick A. *The Reorder of Things: The University and Its Pedagogies of Minority Difference*. University of Minnesota Press, 2012.

Harvey, Jennifer. *Dear White Christians: For Those Still Longing for Racial Reconciliation*. Eerdmans, 2014.

Henry, Frances, Tim Rees, and Carol Tator. *The Colour of Democracy: Racism in Canadian Society*. Nelson Education, 2010.

Hong, Christine J. *Decolonial Futures: Intercultural and Interreligious Intelligence for Theological Education*. Lexington Books, 2021.

Jipp, Joshua W. *Saved by Faith and Hospitality*. Foreword by Christine D. Pohl. Eerdmans, 2017.

Kang, Namsoon. "Global Politics of Knowledge and US Theological Education: From Globalization to Planetarization." In *Locating US Theological Education in a Global Context: Conversations with American Higher Education,* edited by Hendrik R. Pieterse, 23–43. Pickwick Publications, 2019.

Karaman, Nuray. "Coding Whiteness and Racialization: Living in the Space as an Insider-Outsider." *Journal of International Students* 12.2 (2022): 124–40.

Lewis, Stephen, Matthew Wesley Williams, and Dori Grinenko Baker. *Another Way: Living and Leading Change on Purpose.* Foreword by Parker J. Palmer. Chalice Press, 2020.

Liew, Tat-siong Benny and Shelly Matthews. "Introduction: Racism, Classroom Teaching, and Beyond." In *Race and Biblical Studies: Antiracism Pedagogy for the Classroom*, edited by Tat-siong Benny Liew and Shelly Matthews. Resources for Biblical Study 101. SBL Press, 2022.

Lopez, Alfred J., ed. *Postcolonial Whiteness: A Critical Reader on Race and Empire*. SUNY Press, 2012.

Pieterse, Hendrik R. "Internationalizing Theological Education? Musings on a Neglected Concept." In *Locating US Theological Education in a Global Context: Conversations with American Higher Education*, edited by Hendrik R. Pieterse, 1–22. Pickwick Publications, 2019.

Newman, Elizabeth. "Hotel or Home? Hospitality and Higher Education." In *Conflicting Allegiances: The Church-Based University in a Liberal Democratic Society*. Edited by Michael L. Budde and John Wright, 91–105. Brazos, 2004.

Russell, Letty M. *Just Hospitality: God's Welcome in a World of Difference*, ed. J. Shannon Clarkson and Kate M. Ott. Westminster John Knox, 2009.

de la Serna, Ana X. "One Family, Different Experiences of Identity Formation: International Graduate Students and Their Spouses." *Journal of International Students* 12:2 (2022): 366–83.

Sue, Derald Wing. *Microaggressions in Everyday Life: Race, Gender, And Sexual Orientation.* Wiley, 2010.

Suspitsyna, Tatiana. "Internationalization, Whiteness, and Biopolitics of Higher Education." *Journal of International Studies* 11.1 (2021): 50–67.

Terzian, Sevan G. and Leigh Ann Osborne. "Postwar Era Precedent and the Ambivalent Quest for International Students at the University of Florida." *Journal of Studies in International Education* 10.3 (2006): 286–306.

Thorani, Sunera. "Introduction—Present Pasts: The Anxieties of Power." In *Coloniality and Racial (In)Justice in the University: Counting for Nothing?* ed. Sunera Thorani, 3–46. University of Toronto Press, 2022.

Tuck, Eve and K. Wayne Yang. "Decolonization is Not a Metaphor," *Decolonization: Indigeneity, Education, & Society* 1.1 (2012): 1–40.

Viera, Javier A. "Making Room in the UMC for the Spirit's Work." *The Christian Century*. https://www.christiancentury.org/features/making-room-umc-spirit-s-work (July 2024). Accessed September 20, 2024.

Yeo, K.K. "'Made in the USA': A Chinese Perspective on US Theological Education in Light of the Chinese Context." In *Locating US Theological Education in a Global Context: Conversations with American Higher Education*, edited by Hendrik R. Pieterse, 134-57. Pickwick Publications, 2019.

Yeo, Hye Jin Tina, Ruby Mendenhall, Stacy Anne Harwood, and Margaret Browne Huntt. "Asian International Student and Asian American Student: Mistaken Identity and Racial Microaggressions." *Journal of International Students* 9.1 (2019): 39–65.

8. ECOLOGY AND SALVATION

A Wesleyan Methodist Meditation on Stewardship

Catherine Keller

You may feel a certain redundancy in my title: why Wesleyan and Methodist? I did not mean to mark off my Methodism as truly Wesleyan versus some other versions. (I wasn't thinking of the current separation; nor was I thinking of the US Wesleyan Methodist church in their separation from the Methodist Episcopal Church in 1841—though I admire their resistance to war and to slavery.)[1]

But my redundancy did give me an excuse to engage—at last—a bit of John Wesley himself. I have been gratefully a United Methodist for three decades, when I joined a (very hip) congregation; I was already teaching in an ecumenically United Methodist seminary. And it happens that well before that I had sought out John Cobb, himself a son of Methodist missionaries to Japan, as my doctoral advisor. He was the profoundly ecumenical sort of Christian who spoke of Christ calling us to learn from other religions, which in his case had meant especially Buddhism.[2]

What I cherish most from my work with that Methodist (who passed at 99 last year) is the theology of a lively creation, of a universe made not of separate mostly dead bits but of animate interconnection between all of its parts: a cosmos in a living process of unfolding and evolving by way of these events of relationship. That process worldview was adopted from Alfred North Whitehead's profoundly ecological cosmology of the 1920s. It, of course, preceded earth's ecological crisis but not its causes. It lays out a (still) profoundly alternative worldview, in which no individual creature, the simplest or the most complex, exists in independence from its world, a vision in which the universe is a dense web of social relations and God is the most social of all beings. There in the 1970s, I couldn't miss the reverb with my feminist critique of the separative male ego.[3] Not accidentally, John Cobb was the first Christian theologian to pen a book about the ecological crisis. It was called *Is It Too Late: A Theology of Ecology*, first published in 1972.[4] That titular question echoes eerily unto this day. As I delivered this talk we found ourselves in the hottest year on record; with droughts, fires, ice melts, and the CO2 level higher than it has ever been. And as I revised it, the subsequent hottest, and . . . You know the drill. Cobb has done incalculably much over half a century to expose the economics of planetary degradation. As the degradation continues.

And key for the present conversation, his *Grace and Responsibility: A Wesleyan Theology for Today* (1995) makes clear that John Wesley's distinctive synergy of human and divine agency underlies John Cobb's eco-social theology. We are created responsible, able-to-respond. "John Wesley," according to the later John, "considered the failure to practice Christian stewardship a major threat to the spiritual health and effectiveness of the Wesleyan revival." Stewardship—I will return shortly to that troubled notion. Cobb cites Wesley writing the following in 1786: "I fear, wherever riches have increased, (exceeding few are the exceptions,) the essence of religion, the mind that was in Christ, has decreased in the same proportion. Therefore, do I not see how it is possible, in the nature of things, for any revival of true religion to continue long. For religion must necessarily produce both industry and frugality; and these cannot but produce riches. But as riches increase, so will pride, and anger, and love of the world in all its branches. . . ."[5]

What a superb exemplification of the vicious circle we often call original sin. Wesley, as Cobb then notes, "had a mounting suspicion of the acquisitiveness and consumerist dimensions of capitalism . . . [his] stewardship practice or his economic ethics is summarized in the familiar formula: earn all you can, save all you can, and give all you can. That formula was laid out clearly in his sermon entitled 'The Use of Money.'" There, Wesley asks: "How many have you found that observe the third rule, 'Give all you can?' Have you reason to believe that five hundred of these are to be found among fifty thousand Methodists?" (This bit of discouragement comes two years before his death.) So, Cobb does not draw optimism from Wesley but a prophetic call. He considered Wesley's greatest theological contribution to be "his way of affirming human responsibility for our ultimate destiny and daily life while strongly maintaining the primacy of faith."[6]

It was in this way that John Cobb prepared me to embrace, years later, Methodism. But worry not, I am not about to preach process theology to you or to argue it is the true Wesleyanism. The diversity of theologies in conversation, even at this conference, is a testimony to an ongoing strength of the Methodist tradition—a strength more like that of ecological interdependence than of unifying authority. It is a not invulnerable strength (as we know all too well). I am also not here to make anachronistic claims about the eighteenth-century theologian as prophetic environmentalist. But I might let a hint of his homiletical prophecy, a hint with a green tint, slip through. Such hints and tints have long helped motivate the meaningful work that the denomination already attempts on behalf of this little bit of the creation we call Earth. This is less a matter of an anachronistic reading than of a synchronistic one: of working our past into the present synergy of a shared future.

Crucially, the Social Principles of the *2016 Book of Discipline* include ecological responsibility. Its substantive section on "The Natural World" reads: "All creation is the Lord's, and we are responsible for the ways in which we use and abuse it. Water, air, soil, minerals, energy resources, plants, animal life, and space are to be valued and conserved because they are God's creation and not solely because they are useful to human beings. God has granted us stewardship of creation."[7]

Such "stewardship" is quite a grant! And inasmuch as we have taken that grant for granted, we now use and abuse it in ways Wesley could not have imagined. Sadly, even some of the most socially principled Methodists also take the grant for granted. They have more humanly vivid and pressing priorities. This is the case with my congregation. The pastors are gifted, visionary preachers and courageous activists on behalf of social justice: especially of race and LGBTQI urgencies, so existential for so many in our denomination, in our congregation. But the issue of ecological justice hardly arises (though they welcome my contributions). Stewardship of the creation is never denied. But the materiality of the nonhuman remains in the background of what more immediately matters. The fact that each degree of global warming will raise the degree of suffering, especially of the poor and people of color in my city and around the planet; or that the reductive understanding of "nature" that serves the US and global economy also categorizes many as sexually unnatural: such connections remain mostly abstract, distant.

In the meantime, the increasing strength of AI does deliver the facts, continually updated, of the degrees of warming and the condition of the resources, the health, the creatures, of our corner of creation. And at the same time, I just happened to learn the following about AI:

> As the tech giants compete in a global AI *arms race*, a *frenzy of data center construction* is sweeping the [US] country. Some computing campuses require as much energy as a modest-sized city, turning tech firms that promised to *lead the way* into a *clean energy future* into some of the world's *most insatiable guzzlers of power*. Their projected energy needs are so huge, some worry whether there will be enough electricity to meet them from any source.[8]

So, the indispensable tool for fighting the problem ironically increases the problem—which suggests a vicious circle of sin and stewardship. But I want here to back off from the frenzy of data and reflect with you on the symbol of stewardship in its relationship to two other theological symbols important to John Wesley: salvation and soul. These connections can help intensify a Wes-Meth environmentalism (presuming—as I still must and as you read—it is not "too late"). Each of these three symbols will be offered in the context of a particular homily of John Wesley. I am hoping that these three sermonic *s*'s—stewardship, salvation, and soul—will reverberate together in a past and future synchronism, helping us to become better stewards in and of the present. Even now.[9]

If you are involved in a wider movement of ecological theology, you know what criticism the term "stewardship" has endured. I am not referring to standard right-wing and denialist, anti-environmentalist discourse. No, I am thinking of my own language and that of most ecologically oriented theologians in mainline Christianity. Among us the critique, and even dismissal, of the trope of stewardship is almost presumed. How did that happen?

United Methodist pastor and activist Sharon Delgado captures the issue in her recent book, *The Cross in the Midst of Creation*. She writes that "as followers of the crucified and risen Jesus, we are called to live by the Spirit and do our part to bring about creation's healing and transformation."[10] In this work "the biblical term stewardship is often used to express human responsibility to care for the natural world, based on the idea that all things belong to God and that we do not own land or any other part of creation. . . . " Rather, we exhibit "stewardship over it on behalf of God. 'The earth is the Lord's and all that is in it . . .' (Ps 24)." However, she continues, "in this time of extreme ecological devastation, the concept of environmental stewardship has limited value. Although this well-meaning concept calls for responsibility and care for the earth, it reinforces the anthropocentric concept of human dominion over the natural world (Gen 1:26) and leaves intact the view that humans are somehow above and separate from the natural world." It portrays "a universe created for and centered on human beings, which devalues the rest of creation and sanctifies hierarchical ideas that have led to widespread ecocide."[11] We may derive from this superb summary of the problem that the symbol of stewardship is achieving the opposite of both its scriptural original and of its recent environmental intentions.

I could share other eco-theological repudiations of the term, such as that of Jürgen Moltmann and Michael Northcott. In a joint evaluation of the 2009 'Evangelical Declaration on Global Warming,' [Cornwall Alliance] they criticize stewardship theologies for disconnecting environmental practices from Christian spirituality by failing to show nature's own significance for God. Others point out the management ethos of stewardship which may dull the gracious awe, by which nature humbles us before God.[12]

I have for all these reasons long avoided the term. But I realize that I need a different strategy now. I will continue.to take seriously the eco-critique of stewardship. But I want to do so in order not to erase but to improve the concept of stewardship; I want the term to bolster rather than undermine the rigorous eco-theology we need. Human language is never sufficient, always part of our fallen condition. So, I want to recycle "stewardship" for the following reason: it has at once an ancient scriptural root and an immediate resonance with biblically minded folk—including, crucially in case we actually want change, more conservative and evangelical publics.

Of course, the symbol has a significant root in John Wesley, and this root brings with it a key economic meaning. In "The Good Steward" Wesley was preaching a responsibility tuned primarily to our personal bodies, properties, and money. So, it would be a mistake to think that because he was focused on economic rather than ecological stewardship, his usage is irrelevant to current environmental urgencies. After all, what is driving climate change, what is overheating the planet, what is discreating manifold species of the creation—but the neoliberal economy materializing as the organizing principle of our planetary *oikos*? Far from ecologically irrelevant, what he was thinking allows us to hook our current sense of stewardship as *oikologia* into his critical *oikonomia*. At any rate, *oikonomia* translates as stewardship. And what emerges from his sermon is a remarkable rejection of private property itself, on principle, indeed on the basis of the biblical parable of the steward.

The point reveals itself in Wesley's distinction of the debtor from the steward. Permit me to indulge here in the flow of his own words in this homily:

> We are now indebted to [God] for all we have; but although a debtor is obliged to return what he has received, yet until the time of payment comes,

> he is at liberty to use it as he pleases. It is not so with a steward; he is not at liberty to use what is lodged in his hands as he pleases, but [only] as his master pleases. He has no right to dispose of anything which is in his hands. . . . For he is not the proprietor of any of these things, but barely entrusted with them by another; and entrusted on this express condition,—that he shall dispose of all as his master orders . . . they are all, as our Lord speaks, *allotria*, belonging to another.[13]

The point comes through loud and clear—we are indebted to God for everything, but we are not normal debtors, who can do what they want with their property when they get it. Stewardship, unlike debt, is no kind of deferred or indirect ownership—of one's own resources, talents, body, or goods. The steward is one who has been conditionally "entrusted" with another's goods.

> Nor [Wesley continues] is anything properly our own, in the land of our pilgrimage. We shall not receive *ta idia*, our own things, till we come to our own country. Eternal things only are our own: . . . With all these temporal things we are barely entrusted by the Disposer and Lord of all. . . . Above all, he has committed to our charge that precious talent which contains all the rest,—money: Indeed it is unspeakably precious, if we are wise and faithful stewards of it; if we employ every part of it for such purposes as our blessed Lord has commanded us to do.[14]

Stewardship, in other words, is not only not ownership. "Steward" is an antonym of "proprietor." Even our money—precisely in its noted preciousness—is not actually our own. The economic implications are not low-key! Joerg Rieger in *No Rising Tide* emphasizes Wesley's account of God's entrustment to us of private property. He argues that according to the model of stewardship, the "only basis for having anything, is an ongoing relationship with God, which constantly provides the focus for the use of what Christians have."[15] So while we are told to earn, save, and give all we can, those who in his context have things (one even hesitates to use the term "own") enjoy nothing like the version of freedom promoted by contemporary free market economics.

Wesley's interpretations set strong limits on the prerogative of ownership. Perhaps that was easier to do in a time when private property did not yet resemble the extensive monopolies now represented by transnational corporations. But precisely because private property has taken such absolute forms and is held in such large pools, Rieger argues convincingly that Wesley's reflections are now more relevant than ever. And we might add: because of the religious right's sanctification of capitalism's rising tide, a theological response takes on intensified importance.

The politically potent religious conservatism of the United States remains of course key to liberating capitalism from all ethical, and certainly environmental, regulation. Therefore, I am better recognizing the importance of the work of seriously ecological evangelicals (not just Wesleyan ones) and distinguishing them from those evangelical organizations designed to oppose them by claiming a conservative stewardship model. The evangelical spectrum is ecologically complicated.

Crucial for the eco-evangelical potential is the 1999 Cornwall Declaration on Environmental Stewardship. It recognized "the moral necessity of ecological stewardship."[16] It asserted that the strengthening of market freedom and property rights—instead of government regulations—would be the solution to environmental problems. But in 2006, the Evangelical Environmental Network launched the Evangelical Climate Initiative (ECI), which produced the statement "Climate Change: An Evangelical Call to Action."[17] Led by Jim Ball, that Call was signed by over three hundred evangelical leaders favorable to regulation for the sake of ecological and economic justice. Soon the Cornwall Alliance reacted with "A Call to Truth, Prudence, and Protection of the Poor: An Evangelical Response to Global Warming." It began to refer to pro-regulation Christians as the "Cult of the Green Dragon." And it published a "Brief History of Environmental Exaggerations, Myths and Downright Lies."

Methodists can be found in both of these eco-evangelical publics. Which is to say: Wesley's definition of stewardship in terms resistant to private property should not be downplayed! Indeed, the sense of the steward's responsibility before God could hardly be more relevant. Is there, however, a way to make Wesley's economic stewardship more explicitly ecological—from within his own theology? To recycle the very notion of stewardship, freeing it from its capitalist misuses?

You know there is: Sermon 60, "The General Deliverance," in which Wesley can be read as an ecological prophet.[18] In its vision of salvation, the logic of stewardship reveals that so-called "brute creatures" (the term then referring to nonhuman animals, not to brutality) will also be delivered. They, too, have souls. The eco-theological importance of Wesley's attention to the souls of nonhuman animals is lucidly demonstrated by United Methodist theologian Greg Van Buskirk, who sets him in contrast with Aquinas. The latter denies "Plato's theory that the souls even of brute animals are immortal."[19] Wesley's position on the "souls of brutes" spans his entire theological career, beginning with his 1726/1727 Master's degree lectures and stretching well into his most mature sermons in the 1780s. Permit me to replay here his captivating homiletics.

"During this season of vanity"—the epoch of human domination—"not only the feebler creatures are continually destroyed by the stronger; . . . but both the one and the other are exposed to the violence and cruelty of him that is now their common enemy—man." (I let that exclusive language stand.) "And if his swiftness or strength is not equal to theirs, yet his art more than supplies that defect . . . He pursues them over the widest plains, and through the thickest forests. He overtakes them in the fields of air, he finds them out in the depths of the sea. Nor are the mild and friendly creatures"—those "duteous to his commands"—"secured thereby from more than brutal violence; from outrage and abuse of various kinds." Do take in the powerful effect of Wesley's concern! "Is the generous horse, that serves his master's necessity or pleasure with unwearied diligence, is the faithful dog, that waits the motion of his hand, or his eye, exempt from this? What returns for their long and faithful service do many of these poor creatures find? . . . The lion, the tiger, or the shark, gives them [other animals] pain from mere necessity, in order to prolong their own life; and puts them out of their pain at once: But the human shark, without any such necessity, torments them of his free choice; and perhaps continues their lingering pain till, after months or years, death signs their release" (Sermon 60).

In this extraordinary homily, the "human shark" comes off worse than any of our fellow creatures! And in the sermon's climax, Wesley's attention to animal suffering waxes eschatological:

> But will "the creature," will even the brute creation, always remain in this deplorable condition? God forbid that we should affirm this; yea, or even entertain such a thought! While "the whole creation groaneth together," (whether men attend or not,) their groans are not dispersed in idle air, but enter into the ears of Him that made them. While his creatures "travail together in pain," he knoweth all their pain, and is bringing them nearer and nearer to the birth, which shall be accomplished in its season. He seeth "the earnest expectation" wherewith the whole animated creation "waiteth for" that final "manifestation of the sons of God;" in which "they themselves also shall be delivered" (not by annihilation; annihilation is not deliverance) from the "present bondage" of corruption.

In this season of "groaning together" Wesley was of course not specifying the effects of later white capitalist exploitations and extinctions. But we can hardly avoid hearing the prophetically synchronistic ecology. [20] Randy Maddox also emphasized the ecological implications of this preaching in an essay called "Anticipating the New Creation: Wesleyan Foundations for Holistic Mission."[21] Such missionary holism today takes on increasingly eschatological intensity.

Back to Sermon 60: "Away with vulgar prejudices—" Wesley is pointing at uses of the Genesis dominion "and let the plain word of God take place. They [all creatures] 'shall be delivered from the bondage of corruption, into glorious liberty;' even a measure, according as they are capable, of 'the liberty of the children of God.'" The sermon thus includes nonhuman animals in the liberating glory—of salvation. That marks a soteriology with few precedents. It shows a glimpse of such a vision already given us "in the twenty-first chapter of the Revelation. When He that 'sitteth on the great white throne' hath pronounced, 'Behold, I make all things new.'"

So, the stewardship that characterizes the creation spirals all the way to the salvation signified by the new creation. In this the effects of the abusive misuse of dominion are not ended at the level of the redemption of human souls. Rather, the soulful life of every creature will find then its ultimate renewal. Here we witness how a universal soulfulness comes into play. Since animals have souls, it is no coincidence that Wesley became a vegetarian and strongly promoted such a diet. (Wesley's holism has bite!) Based on his doctor's recommendation he gave up meat and soon found himself, as he wrote in a letter, "free, blessed be God, from all bodily disorders."[22] He did not make this a mandate. To do so would hardly have helped the spread of Methodism! But in our time—given the economic role of cattle production in releasing methane into the atmosphere—this holism supports not just ethical treatment of animals but of all of us creatures. And given the ecological and food justice concerns of upcoming generations, this aspect of Wesley could contribute to some effectual outreach.

To help this underpublicized side of Wesleyanism sink in—the theological depth which supports it must not be ignored. It is a depth of soul—that opens into what he called "the soul of the universe." No creature at all is simply soulless. And this cosmic soulfulness then defines our relationship, all critters' relationships, to the Creator. It cannot be brushed away as some pagan animism. Neither is its key citation unfamiliar.

The passage I will read from Sermon 23, on the Sermon on the Mount, is one of the most beautiful theological statements of the Creator-creature relation on record. Wesley captures the soulful intimacy that pervades and holds every single creature of the creation. In his words:

> But the great lesson which our blessed Lord inculcates here . . . is, that God is in all things, and that we are to see the Creator in the glass of every creature; that we should use and look upon nothing as separate from God, which indeed is a kind of practical atheism; but, with a true magnificence of thought, survey heaven and earth, and all that is therein, as contained by God in the hollow of his hand, who by his intimate presence holds them all in being, who pervades and actuates the whole created frame, and is, in a true sense, the soul of the universe.[23]

This thought emerges from an odd context: the lesson Wesley is referencing pertains to Jesus's warning in Matthew 5:33 against swearing. Not just against false swearing, with its betrayal of promises made to God, but swearing in general. No, not in the recent sense of swear words, as cusses and curses! But of making vows in the name of heaven or earth or Jerusalem—the Nazarene's point being that God is in all these places, and so one risks breaking promises to God. [24]

Somehow Wesley leaps from there to make his key contribution to future creation theology: we are invited to see the Creator mirrored in every creature. In the ensouled universe he reveals, transcendence is intimately immanent (what I've sometimes dubbed transcendimmanence . . .). This is a radical expansion of the doctrine of the *imago Dei*, a universalization in the true sense: it implicates the whole universe. Even in the most creation-friendly theologies before or in his time, I do not find such explicit imagery of every creature, not just good old us, created in the image of God. So, each one, in its own way, mirrors the Creator. And Wesley adds here no distracting or diluting qualifiers about false deifications or idolizations of creatures.

Indeed, he conveys that I might as well be an atheist if I do not see God in the fly that was bugging me as I wrote this. Does that pretty much render the vast majority of so-called believers atheists? This God is no mere exterior transcendence, creating from on high—but is the very life, animacy, and soul of the universe. And because Wesley says we should not just "see" but also "use nothing as separate from God," neither should we repress the relation of this inseparability to his own later notion of stewardship. Or its pertinence to our own age's use and abuse of the earth. This "true magnificence of thought"—magnificent in the original sense, of magna, immense—suggests a cosmically embracing thinking that he wants us all to actualize. Its magnitude implicates our theology and its practice in intimate proximity to every fellow creature of our cosmos, each one becoming a mirror of the divine transcendimmanence.

Such divinity visible in the mirror of every creature, let me suggest, might offer a Wesleyan portal to all manner of fresh publics: to the young, with their strong environmental concerns; to all Christians who want to build broad eco-social alliances; but also to those more mystically than dogmatically inclined, with meditative proclivities, as in Quaker or Asian interreligious moods; and in intriguing ways to the spiritual not religious public who want solidarity and meaning.

Nonetheless, some of Wesley's language, even in this sermon, does also pose problems for an eco-social perspective: "The spirit which is in the world is directly opposite to the Spirit which is of God. It must therefore needs be, that those who are of the world will be opposite to those who are of God. There is the utmost contrariety between them."[25] The familiar theological dualism of that passage seems to weaken the chances for an ecologically viable Wesleyanism: suddenly we are hearing the old, old opposition of spirit and world—with no distinction of "world" from "creation." Taken out of context, it can cancel the sermon's own vision of God as the soul of the universe.

Perhaps then there is nothing to do but acknowledge that "world" in this usage leans directly on John 18:36, and the kingdom "not of this world" with *kosmos* naming that which directly opposes the will, the way, and the word of God. One can then insist that in that sense "the world" signifies the dominant civilization, the civilization now operating in globalized white economic and cultural opposition to the Earth itself. And we can underscore that such passages need contextualization, that in our context it is no longer responsible to use the word *world* as a pejorative. We must help *world* now to signify the universe in which the Spirit lives, the world to which God gave and gives life—world as the all of creation, *ta pan*.

For some it may be meaningful to acknowledge that Sermon 23's world-soul affords a vivid expression of what would later be called panentheism. When I pronounce that word in nonWhiteheadian publics I immediately add: do not mishear it as pantheism! For panentheism—all in God—signifies an alternative both to the transcendent God-above, which performs the separation Wesley denounces; and to its opposite, the God merely within, which flattens readily into a pantheism long dismissed (and not without reason) as heresy. But Whiteheadians didn't invent the term panentheism; actually, a theologian named Krause in the early nineteenth century did. My *Cloud of the Impossible* tracks its content as already fully anticipated in De Docta Ignorantia of Nicholas of Cusa, 1440.[26] This sense of all creatures existing within the God who is at the same time within all creatures, pervading them, does welcome the clarity of the all in God vs either all is God or God is outside of it all. Such mutual immanence always also involves mutual difference. Thus, the interrelatedness of all creatures—connected but different—reflects the God/world relation. And the metaphor of the world-soul deepens, broadens, and enlivens the language.

The anti-dualistic metaphor of the world-soul comes quite paradoxically right out of Mr. Dualism himself, Plato. A passage of Timaeus that got to me in antiquity (well, half a century ago) proposes "that this *Cosmos* has verily come into existence as a Living Creature endowed with soul and reason . . . a Living Creature, one and visible, containing within itself all the living creatures, which are by nature akin to itself."[27] That world-soul then occurred commonly in Eastern Christendom, but Augustine found it a "magna atque abdita quaestio" (a great and hidden question)[28] and never identifies the anima mundi with God. Indeed, he remains uncertain as to whether one can properly speak of a world soul and an animated universe. So then most Latin and Medieval theologians rejected the world-soul. It did, however, revive in the Renaissance. And it found distinctive support in seventeenth-century England, particularly with Henry More, and would likely have been known to the erudite Wesley.

It is not that Wesley was preoccupied with the philosophy of the world-psyche. However, his embrace of the soul of the universe can lend theological depth and breadth—and for many also an attractive metaphor—to his pleas for economically responsible stewardship. And so, importantly, to its extension into a responsible, which now means ecological theology. For if God is the very soul of the universe, then it becomes inescapable that the Earth is of inherent value. The creation, world, pan—all of it—has not merely extrinsic but intrinsic value to its creator: in Wesley's words "nature's own significance for God."

It may be that Christians need to sense the interiority to God of that value in order to fight our own most civilized habit: of rendering nonhuman nature external to our humanness. Of treating Earth and its materiality as background to what really matters—rather than as the ground not just of civilization, but of the incarnation, indeed of every enfleshment, every materialization, every creation. Bruno Latour, the leading Continental ecological theorist, may have nailed it with the title of his recent book: *If we lose the Earth, we lose our souls.* That cuts against the soul/body, spirit/earth dualism still assumed by most Christians. Interestingly, this secular thinker ends the book on a biblical note: "'Renew the face of the earth': is this not a revolutionary program?" Latour asks. With Psalm 104 he also embraces the Apocalypse, but not as the sudden End of time: he emphasizes that ecological revolution is radical but works "in detail, slowly, in a multiplicity of fields, through the reformation of a multitude of actions among billions of people."[29] Thus, the apocalypse comes through ecologically as the new creation. And we can add: as Wesley's "glorious liberty" of all the creatures of God.

In this essay, and in the spirit of John Cobb's reading of John Wesley, I hope I have brought forth the importance of our multitude of human decisions and actions. Key is that these decisions are never made independently of grace. Grace will not do our eco-social justice labor for us. It will not silence the groaning of creation. It will not fix the crisis of our age. But neither does it cease to invite us to hear and to respond: indeed, to decide ("decision" being by the way the root of the term "crisis," *krinein*). It still calls us to become critical and graced stewards of a vulnerable planet. And that spirited stewardship lets us participate more vibrantly, more hopefully, in the work of eco-social salvation—as a collective, systemic work. We can together earn, save, give.

That is one kind of saving. Yet it is not irrelevant to the work of salvation. The saving grace will keep our work cosmically soulful. That means none of our burning issues, not even the most urgently encompassing, can block the salutary flow of energy, life, and even joy. That grace brings "glad tidings of salvation in an age of crisis." The grace tunes us to the soul of the universe. Magnified in our own souls by that glimpse of magnificence, it charges us with an energy that burns no fossil fuels. In its animation, we share—in that liberty of the children of God—along with countless other nonextinct animals. All in connection with each other, and only so: "very good." All of us creatures bound—no matter what, consciously or not—by that intimate presence. All of us together in this world that is our parish.

Notes to Chapter 8

1. The name "Wesleyan" came into play around 1740 to distinguish the followers of John Wesley from other Methodists (such as "Whitefieldites" and the Countess of Huntingdon's "Connexion"). Not in formal use until the early nineteenth century, "Wesleyan" then differentiated the "Original Connexion" from its offshoots and, in Wales, from Calvinistic Methodism. Now the term Wesleyan is usually used in the broad sense of "deriving from the Wesleys" and is applied to theology held by almost all Methodist groups.

2. John B. Cobb, Jr., *Christ in a Pluralistic Age*. 1st ed. (Westminster Press, 1975).

3. Catherine Keller, *From a Broken Web: Self, Separation and Sexism.* Boston 1986. German edition: Der Ich-Wahn: Abkehr von einem lebensfeindlichen Ideal, trans. Erika Wisselinck Zürich (1989). Reissued as *Penelope verläßt Odysseus: Auf dem Weg zu neuen Selbsterfahrungen,* 2nd ed., with a preface by Jürgen Moltmann and Elisabeth Moltmann Wendel (1993).

4. John B. Cobb, Jr., *Is It Too Late: A Theology of Ecology* (Bruce, 1972). That was the first book-length Christian ecology. Notably, the first overall ecotheological book was written by a Muslim scholar, Seyyed Hossein Nasr, *Man and Nature: The Spiritual Crisis of Modern Man* (George Allen & Unwin, 1966; 2nd ed., 1997).

5. John Wesley, "Cause of the Inefficacy of Christianity" (Sermon 116, 1789), in *The Works of John Wesley*, 3rd ed., edited by Thomas Jackson, 14 vols. (Wesleyan Methodist Book Room, 1872). https://www.resourceumc.org/en/content/sermon-116-causes-of-the-inefficacy-of-christianity. Cited in John B. Cobb, Jr., *Grace & Responsibility: A Wesleyan Theology for Today* (Abingdon Press, 1995). See also Kenneth L. Carder, "John Wesley on Giving," *Interpreter*, July/August 2016. Adapted from the addresses delivered to the Giving and the Gospel Symposium (1997). https://www.umc.org/en/content/john-wesley-on-giving-pog.

6. Cobb, *Grace & Responsibility*, ibid.

7. The United Methodist Church, "Social Principles: Community of All Creation," in *The Book of Discipline of the United Methodist Church 2020/2024*. (The United Methodist Publishing House, 2024). https://www.umc.org/en/content/social-principles-the-natural-world (accessed November 2025).

8. Evan Halper and Caroline O'Donovan, "AI Is Exhausting the Power Grid. Tech Firms Are Seeking a Miracle Solution," *Washington Post*, June 21, 2024, https://www.washingtonpost.com/business/2024/06/21/artificialintelligence-nuclear-fusion-climate/.

9. Given the deadly progress of climate change over even the period of this paper's delivery and its publication, I am aware of the apocalyptic overtones of that "even now." But apocalypse, as argued elsewhere, does not mean "the end of the

world." See Catherine Keller, *Facing Apocalypse: Climate, Democracy, and Other Last Chances* (Orbis Books, 2021).

10. Sharon Delgado, *The Cross in the Midst of Creation: Following Jesus, Engaging the Powers, Transforming the World* (Fortress Press, 2022), 100, emphasis mine.

11. Delgado, *The Cross in the Midst of Creation*, 101, emphasis mine.

12. The United Methodist Church, "Social Principles: Community of All Creation," in the *Book of Discipline of the United Methodist Church 2020/2024* (The United Methodist Publishing House, 2024). https://www.umc.org/en/content/social-principles-the-natural-world (Accessed November 2025).

13. John Wesley, Sermon 51, "The Good Steward," in *The Works of John Wesley*, vol 2, Sermons II:34–70, ed. Albert C. Outler (Abingdon Press, 1985), 283.

14. Wesley, "The Good Steward," 284.

15. Joerg Rieger, *No Rising Tide: Theology, Economics, and the Future* (Fortress Press, 2009), 145.

16. In March 2000, the Interfaith Council on Environmental Stewardship published "The Cornwall Declaration on Environmental Stewardship," a statement that emerged from a 1999 consultation of approximately thirty-five scholars on environmental stewardship in West Cornwall, Connecticut, and soon endorsed by around 1,500 religious leaders and many laymen worldwide. The text is available at "The Cornwall Declaration on Environmental Stewardship," Interfaith Council on Environmental Stewardship / Cornwall Alliance, accessed November 2025, https://cornwallalliance.org/wp-content/uploads/2014/04/the-cornwalldeclaration-on-environmental-stewardship.pdf. I am grateful to my colleague Laurel Kearns for drawing my attention to this and other relevant analyses.

17. The Evangelical Climate Initiative's "Climate Change: An Evangelical Call to Action" (2006) is available at https://legacy.npr.org/documents/2006/feb/evangelical/calltoaction.pdf. Jim Ball, formerly of Evangelical Environmental Network (EEN), organized and led the Evangelical Climate Initiative and later founded Young Evangelicals for Climate Action to nurture a generation of climate leaders. He is the author of *Global Warming and the Risen Lord: Christian Discipleship and Climate Change* (Russell, 2010), and maintains a creation care-focused web presence at http://creationcare.org.

18. Wesley, Sermon 60, "The General Deliverance," I.5, in *Works*, 2:441

19. Thomas Aquinas, Summa contra Gentiles, book II, chapter 82, §8. Discussed in Greg Van Buskirk, *Iconic Dignity and NonHuman Nature Wesley and Aquinas in Constructive EcoTheological Dialogue*, https://www.academia.edu/37807797/

20. There is little ecological precedent, with however important exceptions such as Izaak Walton, *The Compleat Angler* (Dover Publications, 2003), first published in 1653.

21. Maddox, Randy, "Anticipating the New Creation: Wesleyan Foundations for Holistic Mission," *The Asbury Journal* 62, no. 1 (January 1, 2007), https://place.asburyseminary.edu/asburyjournal/vol62/iss1/4.

22. Jennie Richards, "John Wesley, Founder of Methodism, Promoted a Vegetarian Diet—Humane Decisions," April 10, 2022, https://humanedecisions.com/john-wesley-founder-of-methodism-promoted-a-vegetarian-diet/.

23. Wesley, Sermon 23, "Upon Our Lord's Sermon on the Mount, Discourse the Third," in *Works,* 1:516–17.

24. Wesley counsels to say instead "yes yes or no no." Wesley worries that this be misread as a prohibition against, say, swearing in a courtroom as required by British law. He insists it is not, and cites Matt 5. "Again you have heard that it was said to the men of old, 'You shall not swear falsely, but shall perform to the Lord what you have sworn.' But I say to you, Do not swear at all, either by heaven, for it is the throne of God, or by the earth, for it is his footstool, or by Jerusalem, for it is the city of the great King."

25. Wesley, Sermon 23, "Upon Our Lord's Sermon on the Mount, Discourse the Third," in *Works,* 1:523.

26. Catherine Keller, *Cloud of the Impossible: Negative Theology and Planetary Entanglement.* See especially Ch 3, "Enfolding and Unfolding God: Cusanic Complicatio," 87–125 (Columbia Press, 2014).

27. Plato, Timaeus 30b, *Plato in Twelve Volumes,* trans. W. R. M. Lamb, vol. 9 (Harvard University Press, 1925), 30.

28. Cons. Evang. 1.23.35)

29. Bruno Latour, *If We Lose the Earth, We Lose Our Souls,* trans. Catherine Porter (Medford, 2024), 81.

Bibliography

Aquinas, Thomas. *Summa contra Gentiles.* Book II, chapter 82, §8, trans. James F. Anderson. University of Notre Dame Press, 1975.

Ball, Jim. *Global Warming and the Risen Lord: Christian Discipleship and Climate Change.* Russell, 2010.

Cobb, John B., Jr. *Christ in a Pluralistic Age.* Westminster Press, 1975.

Cobb, John B., Jr. *Grace and Responsibility: A Wesleyan Theology for Today.* Abingdon Press, 1995.

Cobb, John B., Jr. *Is It Too Late: A Theology of Ecology.* Bruce, 1972.

Cornwall Alliance for the Stewardship of Creation. "The Cornwall Declaration on Environmental Stewardship." Interfaith Council on Environmental Stewardship. March 2000. https://cornwallalliance.org/wp-content/uploads/2014/04/the-cornwall-declaration-on-environmental-stewardship.pdf.

Delgado, Sharon. *The Cross in the Midst of Creation: Following Jesus, Engaging the Powers, Transforming the World.* Fortress Press, 2022.

Evangelical Climate Initiative. "Climate Change: An Evangelical Call to Action" (2006). https://legacy.npr.org/documents/2006/feb/evangelical/calltoaction.pdf.

Halper, Evan, and Caroline O'Donovan. "AI Is Exhausting the Power Grid. Tech Firms Are Seeking a Miracle Solution," *Washington Post*, June 21, 2024. https://www.washingtonpost.com/business/2024/06/21/artificialintelligence-nuclear-fusion-climate/.

Keller, Catherine. *Cloud of the Impossible: Negative Theology and Planetary Entanglement.* Columbia University Press, 2014.

Keller, Catherine. *Facing Apocalypse: Climate, Democracy, and Other Last Chances.* Orbis Books, 2021.

Keller, Catherine. *From a Broken Web: Separation, Sexism, and Self.* Beacon Press, 1986.

Latour, Bruno. *If We Lose the Earth, We Lose Our Souls.* Translated by Catherine Porter. Polity Press, 2024.

Maddox, Randy. "Anticipating the New Creation: Wesleyan Foundations for Holistic Mission," *The Asbury Journal* 62, no. 1 (2007). https://place.asburyseminary.edu/asburyjournal/vol62/iss1/4.

Nasr, Seyyed Hossein. *Man and Nature: The Spiritual Crisis of Modern Man.* George Allen & Unwin, 1966. 2nd ed., 1997.

Plato. *Timaeus.* Translated by W.R.M. Lamb. Vol. 9 of *Plato in Twelve Volumes.* Harvard University Press (Loeb Classical Library), 1925.

Richards, Jennie. "John Wesley, Founder of Methodism, Promoted a Vegetarian Diet." *Humane Decisions,* April 10, 2022. https://humanedecisions.com/john-wesley-founder-of-methodism-promoted-a-vegetarian-diet/.

Rieger, Joerg. *No Rising Tide: Theology, Economics, and the Future.* Fortress Press, 2009.

United Methodist Church. *Book of Discipline of the United Methodist Church 2020/2024.* United Methodist Publishing House, 2024. https://www.umc.org/en/content/social-principles-the-natural-world. Accessed November 2025.

Van Buskirk, Greg. "Iconic Dignity and Non-Human Nature: Wesley and Aquinas in Constructive Eco-Theological Dialogue." Academia.edu. https://www.

academia.edu/37807797/Iconic_Dignity_and_Non_Human_Nature_Wesley_and_Aquinas_in_Constructive_EcoTheological_Dialogue.

Walton, Izaak. *The Compleat Angler*. Dover Publications, 2003. First published 1653.

Wesley, John. "Cause of the Inefficacy of Christianity" (Sermon 116, 1789), in *The Works of John Wesley*, 3rd ed., ed. Thomas Jackson, 14 vols. Wesleyan Methodist Book Room, 1872. https://www.resourceumc.org/en/content/sermon-116-causes-of-the-inefficacy-of-christianity.

Wesley, John. "The General Deliverance" (Sermon 60), in *The Works of John Wesley*, vol. 2, *Sermons II:* 34–70, ed. Albert C. Outler. Abingdon Press, 1985.

Wesley, John. "The Good Steward" (Sermon 51), in *The Works of John Wesley*, vol. 2, *Sermons II: 34–70*, ed. Albert C. Outler. Abingdon Press, 1985.

Wesley, John. "Upon Our Lord's Sermon on the Mount, Discourse the Third" (Sermon 23), in *The Works of John Wesley*, vol. 1, *Sermons I:* 1–33, ed. Albert C. Outler. Abingdon Press, 1984.

9. COMING TO OUR SENSES

Cultivating Bloom Spaces in a Time of Global Crises

Daniel D. Shin

In an age of artificial intelligence generating responses at lightning speeds about things ranging from everyday ordinary matters to those of epic significance, the reality on the ground is that global crises related to race, class, gender and sexuality, global warming, violence, and war among others continue to confront us as formidable challenges. Given such contextual realities, no church dare think that it can single-handedly address them in a post-Christendom world, but neither should Christian communities retreat to the comfort and security of sectarian enclaves as they are called upon to co-labor with God toward the survival and flourishing of all human and nonhuman forms of life. This paper invites Wesleyan-Methodist churches in the US to reach deep into their rich heritage of pietist spirituality of sacramental/incarnational, communal practices and graced responsibility to stay with the troubled world, rather than being overwhelmed by the currents of Anthropocene and Capitalocene. This "staying with" should not be interpreted as disavowal in "business as usual" but as persistent co-laboring in the kin-dom of God through the church's presence, service, and witness.[1]

All-hands-on-deck in the perilous hour involves diverse responses that attend to personal, social, and planetary wounded-healing amidst pain and suffering. But before embarking on any well-coordinated, comprehensive response, we must recognize another crisis that has been brewing for some time now—that is, churches declining in membership and social impact. This is a critically important concern not unrelated to global crises because the state of the churches does really matter to the welfare of the world, unless they are isolated enclaves suspended in vacuum having become irrelevant to the current historical realities. Therefore, the overall task of the paper is to examine the phenomenon of the growing number of those who do not affiliate themselves with institutionalized religions and in response reimagine the nature and mission of the church as affective power assemblages of micro/macro politics in the context of multifaceted global crises. The paper begins with journalist Jill Filipovic's essay about the millennial "nones" and identifies the principal themes of the paper: the search for community, experimentation in religions and spiritualities, and embodied practices. In section two, these themes are examined through perspectives from sociology of religion, especially that of Robert Wuthnow on America's changing religious landscape. And section three provides a close reading of Donovan Schaefer's work in affect studies, which is immensely helpful in understanding "bloom spaces" of intersubjective relations—for example, small groups and Wesleyan band meetings—as affective assemblages linked to power productions that are indissociable from socioeconomic, political, and ecological realities in the world. This incarnational shift is pivotal in coming to our senses about the important role of religious affects as forces of "natureculture" that pulsate, circulate, and intertwine in "bloom spaces" to not only (re)enchant but to attune inter-corporeal collectives to protest, lament, and strategize amidst current global crises in order to create new worlds that are yet to come. The paper will conclude with some reflections on the church's responsibility in a time of global climate crisis.

Filipovic on The Millennial "Nones" and the Search for Community

In an intriguing CNN article entitled "I'm a millennial 'none,' but I still want Easter," journalist and social commentator Jill Filipovic describes the spiritual longings of many millennial "nones" who no longer claim religious belonging but still find something appealing about embodied experiences in community as well as nature.[2] Filipovic grew up as a twice-a-year church attending Christian but now considers herself a "none" who simply does not believe. However, this should not suggest that she is without meaningful ties to the Christian heritage, albeit in unconventional ways. While not formally attached to religious beliefs and practices, she says that the "nones" do care about making religious holidays meaningful by using them as anchors to stay rooted in cultures and family histories and as trampolines to jump off to what feels appropriate. The "nones" are actually on the "hunt for something fundamentally human: community, connection, and devotion. Something like church, without the church part." They may not set foot in a church, temple, or mosque, but this does not mean that they do not seek sanctuary, kinship, a holiday table, and even divine grace!

At the time of her writing, Filipovic was in transit from New York to Nairobi and was thinking about the prospects of finding communities where friends were tied together tightly like family. She says that such networks of connections were carefully built and fulfilled the needs for belonging and life together. Finding herself in a new city, Filipovic goes on a quest for friends and community, not any kind but those dedicated to physical and spiritual practices that offer grounding and meaning. One such practice is celebration of Easter. Not surprisingly, she does not subscribe to orthodox formulations of sin, penance, forgiveness, and resurrection, but the promises of newness, freedom, and revival marked annually in a common ritual are certainly attractive. The newly found friends and neighbors may not share a common understanding of Easter because they come from different religions, cultures, nationalities, and histories, but despite such differences there is one shared devotion of building the little clan, a home. Filipovic says even the "nones" need such rituals and communities outside religious houses. She then concludes saying, "We can find it even if we do not believe the divine is a single omnipotent being in the sky, but that it lives in the smell of a wet forest, the daily dedication to a solitary run or a quiet meditation, and, this weekend, in the ringing laughter of friends and family gathered around a shared table."

There is much to think about here. First of all, there is a hunger for and pursuit of community in which life is shared together.[3] Notwithstanding their exodus from institutional religions, a picture that emerges here is a journey not of solitary individuals alone in isolation but instead of friends and neighbors connected as kins who enjoy together rituals of meal sharing and embodied spiritual practices. The continuing importance of networks of relations in community is palpably present. Second, departure from institutional religions is not necessarily negative but constructive toward opening up possibilities for new and different interpretations of life's meaning, community, and participation in the broader world. Millennial disaffiliations do not suggest that they do not care. Quite the reverse! They profoundly care but on their own terms, and they seek to translate the traditional symbols in creative ways that feel right to them, not something entirely secular apart from the religious but something of a hybrid between the two, perhaps post-secular spirituality? And third, there is a clear movement of the "nones" away from doctrinal beliefs toward something experiential involving the body, feeling, materiality of everyday lived experience, and the sacred in nature.[4] What follows hereafter are investigations on the above themes: one, desire for community; two, creative experimentations in religion and spirituality; and three, embodied practices in everyday life. There are other important themes in the essay, but I will focus on the above themes with an eye toward civic and political participation for the sake of the common good in the world. Furthermore, these themes are deeply and obviously relevant to the Wesleyan/Methodist traditions given their long history in building communities through band, class, and society meetings, experimental innovations in theology and practices of ministry, and experience-oriented sacramental pietism. Given the limitations of space, connections of the themes to the Wesleyan/Methodist traditions will be touched upon, and I invite the reader to expand them further in their own contextualization.

Wuthnow on Community, Experimentation, and Embodied Practice

The phenomenon that Filipovic so captivatingly describes may feel like yesterday's news, but it is not something to be taken lightly because this seismic shift in America's religious demographic is still unfolding. Here are some relevant data about the millennial "nones."[5] According to the 2015 Pew Research Center's report "America's Changing Religious Landscape," the number of people who identified themselves as religiously unaffiliated in 2007 was 16.1 percent and by 2014 it grew to 22.8 percent, approximately fifty-six million people. This means that the "nones" were more numerous than either Roman Catholics or mainline Protestants. Recently the Pew Center has updated the number of religiously unaffiliated at 29 percent, an increase of 7 percent since 2015 and still rising.[6] The reasons for the exodus of "nones" from the church vary. David Kinnaman and Gabe Lyons identify the following reasons: perception of Christians as hypocritical, judgmental, anti-LGBTQ+, too political, and sheltered from the rest of the world. As a remedy they suggest humility, authenticity, care, and meaningful connections both internally and externally.[7] There certainly is enough blame to go around intramurally for the negative perceptions, but there also are external social factors contributing to America's changing religious demographics: increased educational attainment, economic pressures, physical mobility, delayed marriage and family religious formation, and growing interest in social justice issues rather than regular religious attendance among others.[8]

To gain critical purchase on what Filipovic describes as a widespread phenomenon in the US, we turn to recent findings in sociology of religion on America's changing religious landscape. Ever since Robert Putnam's *Bowling Alone* publication in 2020, it has garnered much attention and is helpful in addressing the question at hand.[9] Based on a mountain of data about the social engagement of Americans from the 1950s to the 1990s in various ways—such as political, civic, and religious participations; workplace and informal social connections; and altruistic voluntary and philanthropies activities—Putnam observes that there has been a significant decline.[10] For instance, with regard to political participation, voting rate has declined noticeably in the presidential elections, from 62.8 percent in the 1960s to 48.9 percent in 1996.[11] This downward spiral is seen in the broader civic disengagement, including church attendance, which has decreased by a third. Putnam considers this trend as rather disconcerting because when people engage socially, they accumulate social capital that has positive consequences for their psychological, social, and economic well-being and ultimately the overall health of America's democracy. For instance, church participation helps develop civic skills, shape communal norms and interests, and facilitate civic recruitment, all considered critical to the vitality of a democratic society.[12] Putnam views faith groups as "bulwarks" against the erosion of social capital as well as "incubators" for volunteering and local leadership skills.[13] He is not without qualified optimism and prognosis for improvement, but his overall assessment is there is an unmistakable sense of civic malaise related to decreasing social capital. The image of a lonely bowler symbolizes people becoming more isolated, deprived of social networks, and detached from civic life, a picture vastly different from Alexis de Tocqueville's observation of vibrant voluntary associations in America that were deemed critical to the health of its democracy and general well-being.[14]

The alarm Putnam sounded was timely concerning the decline in traditional forms of social and civic participation, such as the Elks and the Lions, but interestingly there was a plethora of new expressions emerging, such as small groups, social movements, and new forms of communication technology.[15] He certainly was aware of such novel developments on the horizon and even of Robert Wuthnow's work, but was focused narrowly on traditional types of organizations, for example, unions, veterans, and church groups.[16] Be that as it may, what is of interest is the ongoing significance of his work in thinking about America's religious landscape and particularly toward thinking about the difference social connections make to the overall health of persons, communities, societies, and the world. For instance, the conceptual tools he provides such as social capital, bonding and bridging, and machers and schmoozers can be useful as building blocks of new communities.[177] We will later circle back to Putnam's concepts and argument below, but what is made apparent in this discussion is the importance of communities for the common flourishing of individuals and societies.

Another major sociologist of religion who has been grappling with America's changing religious landscape is Robert Wuthnow. Since his work on the topic has been profoundly comprehensive, spanning several decades, the focus will be limited to the key themes related to the above themes. The first is his observation about the ongoing importance of community. The common perception that America is across the board becoming more and more socially disconnected may not necessarily be true. Both inside and outside the traditional religious expressions, people are in search of communal sense of belonging and support.[18] In fact, around the time when Wuthnow's *Sharing the Journey* was published in 1994, he reports that about 40 percent of all Americans claimed to be in in small groups, such as reading groups, support groups like Alcoholics Anonymous, self-help groups, or church-related groups, where the participants felt that they were seen and heard.[19] He actually considers the small group movement as a quiet revolution that redefines community as "an antidote to social disconnectedness."[20]

Wuthnow's observation is informed by his sociological analysis of the American society that takes into account the broader social context of declining traditional institutions that have provided a sense of belonging, support and purpose, continuation of individualism that places a premium on autonomy and self-expression, and the ongoing search for existential meaning in a highly secularized modern world. In response to such changes and challenges, small and intimate groups have sprouted all over America's religious/spiritual landscape. These micro-communities are often temporary or episodic, focused on individual needs for personal growth or therapeutic help, and are built around specific issues (e.g., addiction recovery or bereavement) and experiences, rather than geographical proximity, common social or religious identity, and history as in traditional communities. Wuthnow writes, "Whereas traditional communities were often defined by their stability and shared histories, support groups reflect the fluid, transitional nature of contemporary life, with members coming together for a season to deal with specific crises and then moving on."[21] These micro-communities seek to meet a wide array of spiritual, bodily-psychological, and communal needs. He is not without criticism because heavy emphasis on self-help and personal growth can lead to the neglect of wider social concerns and thereby perpetuate the problem of isolation, which is the very concern it sought to address.[22] And the fact that they often are temporary in duration also limits people from long term relationships that endure through life's vicissitudes. Wuthnow recognizes the immense value of these small groups and their staying into the foreseeable future, and suggests maintenance in tandem of both traditional forms of community and small groups to foster broader sociopolitical participation through the former as well as the intimacy, specificity, and countercultural narrative through the latter. He observes, "As society continues to grapple with issues of isolation and fragmentation, the role of support groups may become even more central, serving as important social spaces where people can reconnect with others in meaningful ways."[23]

Another major theme in Wuthnow's work that is helpful in understanding the "spiritual but not religious" phenomenon is the restructuring of the Americas' religious landscape.[24] He examines restructuring through a comparison between the era of "dwelling" or "habitation" that spans from the colonial times to the 1950s during which people attached themselves to stable institution-based religious organizations and the era of "seeking" or "negotiation" since the 1960s to the present in which traditional religious expressions are being radically challenged and people are experimenting with new expressions of spirituality and religion.[25] A major contributing factor to the fluidity of the current pluralistic religious/spiritual landscape is that people are no longer interested in traditional forms that are rigid and long-term but are drawn to loosely connected patterns of sociability, volunteer activity, and political participation, which are flexible, porous, and egalitarian.[26] Such shifts away from traditional religions to more experimental expressions with therapeutic and pragmatic ends can be seen in switching memberships, sporadic affiliations, yoga, Zen meditations, alternative Eastern healing practices, astrology, belief in angels and miracles, New Age practices, social justice movements following cultural upheavals of the 1960s, and ecumenical and interfaith dialogues.[27]

So, traditional forms of social connections are giving way to new ways of doing community through multiple networks of associations taking place in both in-person and virtual meetings that provide personal support, communal belonging, and opportunities for specific social and civic engagements. Wuthnow observes, "Successful civic organizations are ones that deliberately reconcile themselves to the porousness of their environment and capitalize on the loose connections of their participants."[28] However, he warns that loose connections and fragmented communities can neither be substitutes for the deep family ties nor antidotes to complex social problems such as poverty. While specific project-based participations are commendable, long-term civic participations that foster deep engagement of local politics and broad alliances are indispensable in bringing about substantial and lasting political reforms.[29]

To more fully appreciate Wuthnow's discussion on experimentation, it is necessary to situate it in the broader horizon of his evolutionary understanding of religion.[30] Given a wide array of generative functions of religion, such as shaping personal and communal identities, addressing existential and ethical questions, and strengthening communal bonds and civic engagement through rituals, belief systems, and structured experiences of the sacred, he explains that religions and spiritualities have remained relevant through various adaptive measures. This means that while institutional religions face a time of tumultuous challenge to their prized traditions, it is also a time of new possibilities inviting dialogue, interplay, and transformation in order to adapt to the changing milieu. Wuthnow writes, "American religion has become more complex, more internally differentiated, and thus more adaptable to a complex, differentiated society."[31] Indeed, America's religious landscape is not homogeneous but has evolved into a complex reality requiring attention to its multifaceted dimensions in openness, dialogue, and creativity. Such adaptive measures are no easy tasks but are certainly important and necessary considering how spirituality and religion are not without consequences to the overall health of the society. Wuthnow offers examples of religious movements that have advocated for human rights, economic equality, and ecological justice.[32] For example, he shares how those characterized as mystics engaged in alternative spiritualities are more likely than the general public to be socially minded, empathetic to others, and critically assessing of the American society.[33]

In his recent work *Why Religion Is Good for American Democracy*, Wuthnow explains that diverse religious representations can contribute positively toward the democratic process of America.[34] While the sheer multiplicity of religious expressions may be discomfiting for some, they have opposed tyranny, championed liberty of conscience in pacifism and conscientious objection against war, advocated for freedom of assembly, fought for human dignity and public welfare, and have been actively involved in immigration policy discussion, public health, and so forth. Religious diversity can be a source of conflict, but it also can be a catalyst to innovative, alternative expressions that can sharpen and vitalize American democracy.[35] Based on such reasons, the significance of religions for America's democracy needs to be properly recognized, especially since they are not going away anytime but will persist into the future.[36] So, somewhere between common jeremiads of pessimists and the easy panacea of optimists on the decline of civic participation, Wuthnow offers penetrating assessment of emerging adaptations in the new religious landscape with attention to complexity, detail, and their implications.

We now turn to the third theme, embodied practices. The concept of practice already appeared in Wuthnow's earlier works such as *After Heaven* where after discussing the two emergences—that is, new alternative spiritual/religious movements and traditional evangelical groups—he noted that there is a third way of practice-oriented spirituality in which people invest their time and energy in spiritual disciplines, such as prayer and meditation, in some collective body accompanied by deep reflection, narrative construction, and responsible service to others in the neighborhood and society.[37] In his recent work *What Happens When We Practice Religion?*, practice is treated in greater depth addressing recent interdisciplinary conversations on habit, improvisation, and power in religious life.[38] This theoretical reflection signals a discernible shift from the cultural turn in Clifford Geertz, Peter Berger, and Thomas Luckmann; the shift is toward the practice approach in Talal Asad, Catherine Bell, Michel de Certeau, and Pierre Bourdieu, and finally to embodied practices of ordinary people in the lived religion approach represented by Robert Orsi among others. Wuthnow's discussion about how religious/spiritual practices actually work in people's everyday situations through bodily interactions with the world serves as an unmistakable counterpoint to beliefs and worldviews-oriented approaches in religious studies.

He explains that integral to understanding embodied practices is situation, which refers to the socio-material, emergent nature of a place because of people's physical and social relations to it. In situations certain cues are processed as cognitive schemata with complex information generating certain responses, which when repeated becomes encoded in habits. Spaces are locations of significance in situations generated by appropriate practices over time. Affordances are understood as opportunities for action in situations, and they can be physical or otherwise insofar as they generate occasions for action. Power dynamics refers to the fact that a sacred space exists physically and is therefore subject to control. What is significant about this argument in terms of affect is that while Wuthnow does not consider people's subjectivities as mere products of social structures or something in their private consciousness, he stresses that often it is the situation, rather than the agent's subjective will, that explains their behavior. Then, he further extends the analysis on situation and says that feelings need to be examined in religious situations in which they are shaped and governed in distinct ways by the surrounding community through certain communal rules and conventions as appropriate in everyday realities. When understood this way, religious institutions are emotive institutions.[39] Moving on to the everyday realities of people's lives, Wuthnow addresses religious bodies in terms of their routines, rituals, and disciplines. Bodily routines, such as walking or singing, are relatively simple activities that can receive religious meaning through socialization and repetition. The key concepts identified here in Wuthnow's work concerning practice (e.g., situation, space, affordances, and power dynamics), invite further reflections about communities as affective assemblages and serve as a segue to Donovan Schaefer's work in the next section.

Of course, there are other important themes in Wuthnow's prolific work, but I have identified above three key themes that are relevant to the present study on the millennial "nones"—that is, search for community, experimentation, and embodied practices. Both Filipovic and Wuthnow have shed much needed light on the contemporary religious landscape from their distinct perspectives, the former offering an incisive social commentary at the grassroots level and the latter providing sociological research data and theoretical analysis. In the following section, I will offer a close reading of Schaefer's *Religious Affects* and seek to address the themes identified.[40]

The Affective Turn to Embodied Practices in the Everyday World

Schaefer defines affects as "the propulsive elements of experience, thought, sensation, feeling, and action that are not necessarily captured or capturable by language or self-sovereign 'consciousness.'"[41] Formed by a long and complex history of biological configurations, affects are patchworks of heterogeneous compulsions that circulate like currents through a person's body and are tethered to multivalent networks of affective economies. They are contagious, sticky, and entangle with other bodies and materials to produce a complex set of relationships, often coalescing as power assemblages, religious and otherwise.[42] Hence, affects and their complex patterns of homeodynamic interactions are highly significant for the present investigation on the search for community and its implications in the world.

With a preliminary understanding of affect in hand, we first turn to Shaefer's discussion on constitutive relationality. Affects that accumulate to form fields of force in constitutive relationality are compulsory and intractable, meaning that it is not something that the self as sovereign consciousness can switch on and off at will. Relationality with other bodies and material objects is constitutive, meaning that bodies are naturally wired with affective compulsions to crave interaction with other bodies and objects.[43] The fact that relationality is fundamental or even obligatory is demonstrated in situations where it is denied, such as solitary confinement that causes excruciating pain of deprivation. Drawing upon Edward Wilson's notion of *biophilia*, Schaefer goes on to suggest that constitutive relationality is part of the onto-phenomenological makeup of bodies that innately move toward life and lifelike processes moving toward them.[44] Such insights into the compulsory, intransigent, and even recalcitrant affective bodies of relationality inform Schaefer's animalist understanding of religion which is very helpful in coming to terms with affective economies of vital materiality in the world, such as gardens, animals, and forests, all swarming to systems of power. He writes, "The animal language of movement compelled by affect is the language in which religion is written."[45]

It is obvious that constitutive relationality is rich in significance for understanding communal connection, and this is made evident in Schaefer's discussion of Kathleen Stewart's work on bloom spaces. Stewart defines bloom space as an affectively suffused lifeworld where the transaction between bodies and worlds take place. It is a zone of a magnetic core, enticement, an allure, and even a threat, a process of interaction between bodies participating in multiple networks with systems of power that transport the body into the materiality of lifeworld. It is nurtured through refrains understood as "scratching on the surface of rhythms, sensory habits, gathering materialities, intervals, and durations."[46] Schaefer also draws upon Marcel Proust's work on religious ecology or divinity-field of places, persons, families, substances, ideas, practices, music, buildings, machines, emotions, and natural elements to explain constitutive relationality. It is the interplay of bodies with their lifeworlds that generates affective assemblages, which both represent and constitute religious worlds with their histories, symbols, narratives, and practices. As such, religious bloom spaces are not solely or primarily about technologies of information or belief transmission but reservoirs of compulsion that compel and shift the body from distance to proximity to other life forms and objects that can enliven, captivate, enchant, and create worlds.[47]

Schaefer's insights on constitutive relationality shed much light on the discussion above by Filipovic and Wuthnow on the search for community. Together they point to how we are hardwired, even obligatorily and intransigently, for connections with living creatures and material worlds. This means, at least theoretically, the future status of propulsion toward networks of communal relations is relatively secure.[48] And Schaefer's insight on constitutive relationality sheds additional light on Putnam's two major forms of social participation, the machers and schmoozers. On the one hand, there are machers who participate actively in the civic life, those who "follow current events, attend church and club meetings, volunteer, give to charity, work on community projects, give blood, read the newspaper, give speeches, follow politics, and frequent local meetings." And, on the other hand, there are schmoozers who are active socially but in informal ways, those who "give dinner parties, hang out with friends, play cards, frequent bars and night spots, hold barbecues, visit relatives, and send greeting cards."[49] This is an interesting comparison, and if the trend is leaning toward schmoozers, which is confirmed by people moving away from traditional associations to informal small communities such as affinity groups and Wesleyan band meetings, then an exploration of America's changing religious landscape through affect studies can be generative.

Turning to the second theme, experimentation, recall here Filipovic's thoughts such as wanting the church without the church and not believing traditional faith formulations, and Wuthnow's on innovation. It is rather obvious there is poetic imagination with a different kind of plausibility, or sensibility to be more exact, at work that invites, prompts, and calls for change in the search of new forms of spirituality.[50] Schaefer's meta-level discussion about the rationale for turning to affects in religious studies is apropos in addressing this question. The bone of contention in Schaefer's argument is basically that dominance of social constructionism and cognitive-linguistic approach in religious studies has held sway in much of contemporary scholarship privileging transcendence-prone discursive regimes constituted by symbols, beliefs, narratives, and cosmologies at the expense of experiences that overflow the boundaries of sovereign rational subjects into the bodily and the material.[51] He, therefore, proposes a radical departure from the "suffocating textualism" of the empire of books, including Protestant reduction into a Bookworld, toward religious ecologies of other bodies, food, community, labor, music, natural landscapes, architecture, and so forth. He asks, "What if religion is not only about language, books, or belief? In what way is religion . . . about the way things feel, the things we want, the way our bodies are guided through thickly textured, magnetized world?"[52] What Schaefer is suggesting is nothing short of a paradigm shift in religious studies in conversation with materialist phenomenology and affect studies.[53] It seeks to decenter religious studies shaped by the classical liberal model of rational subjectivity encased in the matrix of linguistic regimes and set it within an expansive transspecies understanding of religion that underscores bodies embedded in practices, images, material objects, affects, languages, and nature in continuity with nonhuman animals.[54]

Undoubtedly Schaefer's programmatic turn toward materialist phenomenology and affect comes down hard on linguistic fallacy, but it does not mean exclusion of linguistic-conceptual schemes, only their delimitation as one of many channels in the religious matrix bound with other thick embodied forces.[55] Schaefer writes, "This template of religion as a dance does not forbid the introduction of conceptual, cognitive, or textual analysis. It only points out that these forms of religious experience and expression will be, at most, one facet of a more complicated network of influences . . . both conceptual and kinesthetic."[56] At times, he seems far too critical of cognitive-linguistic operations in an attempt to swing the pendulum in religious studies in the other direction, but he does consider language as a bodily technology to talk, to think, and to question, a play within the cosmic dance, itself emerging out of an embodied experience affectively suffused.

Given the radical and generative character of Schaefer's disciplinary proposal, it is necessary to reflect on the significance of his work for Christian presence, service, and witness in the world. Most obviously, if his proposal is warranted, then the church needs to come to terms with the affective turn in alignment with incarnational understandings of God's reality in the world.[57] This involves serious attention to the interplay between sensing bodies and things in the ordinary world along with circumscribed networks of discursive regimes. Indeed, theological anthropology and ecclesiology have much to gain in grappling with how persons and communities are not insular or autonomous within cognitive-linguistic worlds but are porous and constituted by their dancelike interactions with both human and nonhuman forms of life as well as the material realities in the world. This is not to reject the proper place of discursive scaffolding of beliefs in the transmission of Christianity but to enfold them toward the creation of an atmosphere, "an affectively saturated fold or matrix to which bodies are pulled into or absorbed becoming entangled in that world."[58] Linguistic heritages in church history, as exemplified in the Reformation's cry "sola scriptura," need not be dismissed as they will remain as prophetic and regulative ideals, but revisited to maintain the dialectical tension between the Scripture and tradition in view of God's expansive revelation in the world. Or more comprehensively and methodologically stated, explore in greater depth the generative potential of the Wesleyan quadrilateral—scripture, tradition, reason, and experience—to ensure attention to bodies and materiality of everyday life entangled in socioeconomic, political, and ecological realities of the common world.[59]

Concerning the third theme of investigation—that is, embodied practices—we turn to Schaefer's thoughts on (re)configuration and concepts related to change in the transmission of affect. Reflecting on the etymology of the word *religion*, which means to bind, he reinterprets it to mean that captivating allure in bloom spaces is something like a love-talk, a process of entrainment that transforms the players in the field through body's affective channels (i.e., visual, olfactory, sonic, gustatory, and tactile senses).[60] These bodily senses have critical epistemological roles to play in learning and embracing change as they are absorbed into particular orbits of knowledge like moths to a light.[61] If this is a more accurate description of educational processes and conversion experiences, then it is important to keep an eye on where bodies go and their affective determination of what is "truthful, faithful, proven, experienced, self-verifiable."[62] Schaefer writes, "Pedagogy is about transforming the way the world feels, rather than simply absorbing knowledge: the body 'learns by *switching affections*.'"[63] He then goes on to entertain the possibility of hyperplastic reconfiguration and determines it as being too optimistic, but he nonetheless remains open to the possibility of semi-stable affective assemblages through means such as pedagogy, rituals, and everyday practices in the world.[64] Bodily practices, such as rituals, have the potential to shape affective technologies and various networks of connections, both human and nonhuman, through rewiring the circuits.

Another layer of Schaefer's thoughts concerning embodied practices is the topic of post-adaptationist theory of evolution. Contrary to the popular misunderstanding of evolution as exclusively defined by adaptation for survival, post-adaptationist theory suggests that the actors are not strictly calculating, rational beings driven by ulterior motives for survival and self-interest but instead are auto-telic and comfortable with indeterminacy. This is due to eccentric ensemble of emotions and remainders in their bodily interplay with intra-active vital materiality in entangled environment.[65] Far more than what has been granted, inefficiency, digression, and susceptibility to contingency of accidents brought forth by destabilizing traces of *differánce* in landscapes are simply accepted as part of life, rather than as causes of concern. Schaefer explains bodies do not necessarily move according to "a transcendent or global register of fitness," instead they have their own hypercomplex heterogeneous ends that can be frivolous, foolish, aleatory, and errant in excess of survival in their play.[66] Of course, bodies do adapt for the sake of survival, but they also need to be understood as exaptative, meaning that adaptation in view of some higher ends is not the sole driving force of evolution. Instead, they are known to compile semi-inert structural features that produce dynamics which are accidental and playful in character.

Then, in light of this animalist framework, Schaefer goes on to suggest that even systems of meaning, including religion, are produced not exclusively by the integrity of rational determination becoming the object of capture by economic, political, religious, or other interests, but by multivalent networks of colliding traces in and across bodies. He writes, "Rather than a regime of stable, enduring metaphysical truths, meaning, bodies, and even evolution itself are constituted through crashes."[67] Pointing to the surplus of bodily economies beyond the capitalist logic of the market, he refers to Kimerer La Mothe who suggests that religion may be best understood as a dance, a rhythmic bodily movement of discovery and response through which affects connect to religious histories, practices and beliefs, and affective technologies. When understood this way, affective bodily practices bear enormous religious significance, becoming channels of pain and pleasure, transgression and salvation. Schaefer writes, "Religions build on a body's available repertoire of affectively bodily technologies, bending them, deterritorializing them, and reconstituting them in new configurations with other technologies fixed in the same orbit."[68] So, while religions do have functional roles to play in the world, as adaptationist evolutionary theorists claim, they also exceed that framework in the great dance of poetic species.

Appropriation of Schaefer's thoughts on embodied practices in ecclesial undertakings would involve co-laboring with the grace of God, creating atmospheres of bloom spaces where affects, bodies, material objects, nature, symbols, narratives, and cognitive-linguistic constructions all come together in a dance of the universe. In terms of essential Christian practices (i.e., worship, fellowship, education, and mission), thoughtful and robust attention needs to be given to the allure of polyphonic refrains in music and arts, rituals, symbols and narratives, objects, food, architecture, and so forth. Ann Pellegrini's observation makes this point, "At the end of the day, the ability to win over converts or spark spiritual rededication does not rise and fall on fact checking of biblical hermeneutics. It is a matter rather of affective congruences. . . . The participant is invested (or reinvested) in a deeper structure of religious feeling that can tie together disparate, even contradictory, experiences, bodily sensations, feelings, and thoughts."[69]

And such bodily practices cumulatively result in different outcomes, including positive ones like moving toward healing in circumstances of despair. While mindful of post-adaptationist theory, Schaefer writes, "Healing is often a retrieval and rehabilitation of a ring of joyful affects through reencountering other bodies as well as material things in the world."[70] Moreover, he explains that bodily practices bear political significance as they are connected to a panoply of power relations that push and pull the bodies to different trajectories. There is no easy optimism here, but religions certainly can play a constructive role in the world.[71] He states, "Religion is an extraordinary powerful distribution network through the global nervous system of affect. But this distribution network should not be presupposed to cleanly align with any single snapshot of health and flourishing."[72] Schaefer's sentiments echo Eve Sedgwick's that here is no need for paranoid responses to religion as the constructive potentials and instantiations are certainly there.

So, not all is doom and gloom as there is potential for healing and politics for the common good. Though creation of affective assemblages is not in the first place about intentional gains, they do generate body's multidirectional engagement with political, religious, and cultural systems of power not as an afterthought but throughout the process from the beginning.[73] Schaefer writes, religion is "an affective economy in its complexity, as a hybrid system driven by erotic accident in conjunction with rationalized lines of force."[74] Doing due diligence in this regard means coming to terms with how religious selves as embodied histories are connected to diverse affective assemblages in global networks that bear enormous potential as power structures and economies. And considering that religious power grid can either be repressive and harmful as in toxic religions or generative toward diverse expressions of love, joy, healing, and other metamorphic possibilities, even deep compassion and pursuits of justice across religious differences, much is at stake in how such networks are construed and put into use.[75] Hence, without making instrumental functions of religions and spiritualities their exclusive goal, Christian communities can posture themselves in micro/macro politics to pursue higher ends of promoting health and flourishing of all God's creation.

In this section, I have examined Schaefer's work on religious affects exploring both theoretical and practical concerns, especially noting how the turn to affect is informed by an animalist understanding of religious studies that is critical of transcendence-prone cognitive-linguistic approaches because they eclipse bodies and the material world. What this programmatic shift brings into clear focus is the transspecies nature of the world in which all life forms and material world are interrelated and the responsibility for micro/macro political engagement in the world toward common flourishing. The natural world needs to be understood as a common environment shared by all, whether human or nonhuman forms of life, requiring collective responsibility. I will now conclude with a brief reflection on sympoietic responsibility in face of climate change in the US and elsewhere.

On February 14, 1990, the spacecraft *Voyager 1* snapped a picture of the earth from over three billion miles away, and soon thereafter Carl Sagan famously called this iconic image of our planet "The Pale Blue Dot" and offered reflections that still resonate with us today. Sagan says,

> That's here. That's home. That's us. On it everyone you love, everyone you know, everyone you ever heard of, every human being who ever was, lived out their lives. . . . The Earth is the only world known so far to harbor life. There is nowhere else, at least in the near future, to which our species could migrate. . . . Like it or not, for the moment the Earth is where we make our stand . . . /the distant image of our tiny world . . . underscores our responsibility to deal more kindly with one another, and to preserve and cherish the pale blue dot, the only home we've ever known.[76]

This beautiful and yet haunting image of the earth as a fraction of a dot in a vast cosmic arena and the penetrating words of Sagan not only remind us of the importance of letting go of vain things like petty misunderstandings, hatred, and delusions that demonstrate the folly of human deceit but also of our responsibility for the care of one another and the planet earth. For Wesleyans, the concept and practice of responsibility is not something foreign, as it is believed that God's love graciously shed abroad in our hearts renders us responsible.[77]

One of the most pressing responsibilities for us today is the colossal challenge of eco-justice around the world. According to David Korten, this means getting rid of the defective map of ego-nomics, which promotes self-centered financial gains and dehumanizing consumptions that are destructive to the earth, and instead accepting a new map of eco-nomics that promotes mutual flourishing of both human and nonhuman forms of life. To explore contemporary significance of response-ability toward healing a wounded world, we turn to Donna Haraway's *Staying with the Trouble*. Haraway, a scholar in the field of science and technology studies, proposes terrapolitics for all companion species as kins that decenters human exceptionalism in the stories of Anthropocene and Capitalocene, and invites big enough stories or third stories, such as Chthulucene, that can lure, imagine, and encompass multi-species assemblages. The story of Chthulucene is about imagining a new world in which symbio-genetic kinships made in material-semiotic relationality interweave toward survival and healing of Earthbounds. There are many facets of the storytelling, such as fact-telling and theory-telling, that engage all faculties and point to how living and dying well together in a more habitable world entails understanding that everything is connected sympoetically. Haraway explains that companion species are collectively producing systems that are not self-defined but in constant rhythm of mutual accepting and giving in agential intra-action. This involves bodily practices of ongoing detachment and attachment that are pivotal in rendering each other response-able toward sympoi-esis, but they also need to be cobbled together with stories and concepts about eco-relationality.

Therefore, Haraway repeatedly emphasizes, "we must change the story; the story must change," "it matters what ideas we use to think other ideas," and "think we must; we must think." The carrier bag of both storytelling and naturalcultural history provides seeds that can generatively resist, resignify, and repair the world, rather than giving in to despair and cynicism. However, this is not a story of salvation with unfound, cruel optimism and progress but worlding, unworlding, and reworlding of all earthlings as kins through threads of reciprocating attunement to become-with in order that at least partial healing, modest rehabilitation, and possible resurgences in hard times may happen. Haraway's proposal of sympoietic art of living and dying well together involves both embodied practices and cognitive-linguistic expressions, such as narratives and theories, and at the heart of its proposal lies responsibility for the survival and wounded-flourishing of all interconnected creatures on earth. The wisdom of *ubuntu*, "I am because we are," reverberates loud and clear, even expanding to include all kins that have breath and the material world because we are all interconnected.

Sympoietic responsibility resonates deeply with James Gustafson's theocentric piety. He writes, "The task of ethics is to discern the will of God—a will larger and more comprehensive than an intention for the salvation and well-being of our species."[78] As we grapple with the call to response-ability for the care of the earth, theocentric piety is crucial in loosening the iron grip of exclusive humanism and reconnecting us to other forms of life and the natural world. Recall here Gustafson's emphases in theocentric ethics: God is not in service of human interests but quite the reverse, human interests are situated in the larger context of God's world and purpose; salvation of human beings may not be the chief end of God; and human beings emerged at a certain point and may also vanish at some point in the history of the world.[79] These are sobering, if not fighting, words against anthropocentric forms of piety. According to Gustafson, Christian faith and life cannot be construed anthropocentrically with human interests at the center and creation in service of human needs, but understood to be about being rightly related to God and to all that which is related to God, both human and nonhuman forms of life as well as the earth's entire ecosystem. Gustafson's argument here needs to be connected to Schaefer's transspecies efforts to dethrone human exceptionalism and deepen our sense of responsibility toward interrelationality with nonhuman animals and the material world in new configurations.

How is this to be translated into theology and practice of ministry in the world? Our responsibility is informed by theocentric planetary piety that not only enchants but also attunes and mobilizes intercorporeal collectives toward new worlds that is yet to come. More specifically, one of the crucial roles of Christian communities is to create bloom spaces where the love of God and love of all human neighbors pulsate and circulate, culminating in affective assemblages as power structures that are response-able for the wounded flourishing of all God's creation. Local churches and small groups—such as band and class meetings, life groups, house churches, and Fresh Expressions gatherings—bear potential as bloom spaces where bodily practices and storytelling about God's kin-dom can come together to nurture, invent, and discover communal ways of surviving and thriving. They can be recalibrated as affective assemblages for personal, social, and planetary healing that are networked with micro and macro politics for the common good of all. This is a heavy responsibility but a journey accompanied by joy and fulfillment. Korten writes, "The most precious gift of our human experience is the opportunity to feel the joyful exhilaration that comes from fulfilling our responsibility to share in the care of life."

Conclusion

This investigation began with a conversation about the millennial "nones" in American religious landscape and explored the themes of community, experimentation, and embodied practices interdisciplinarily with social sciences, religious studies, and theology. The search for community will continue into the future and be expressed in new and unexpected ways that connect them to complex networks of embodied practices in the world. It obviously is too premature to predict how the phenomenon of the "nones" will unfold, and it would be ill-advised to make them targets of proselytizing that translates them into mere numbers in grids of calculated cost-benefit ledger, even in light of how crucial communal connections are to the health of persons and societies. Religious assemblages can certainly be coextensive with socioeconomic, political, and religious ends, but as we have seen above they are more akin to bodies in poetic dances of discovery and wonder, a play in an affectively suffused cosmos. In other words, there are no shortcuts to the wounded-flourishing we have in mind, so we acclimate ourselves to being on the way somewhere in the middle, an interlude that cannot be rushed. We inhabit a time of betwixt and between, a time of oscillation back and forth with the millennial "nones" in bloom spaces where we witness not only the passing of things we had once so cherished but also the manifold promises of things yet to come.

Notes to Chapter 8

1. For further discussion on staying with the troubled world as well as the concepts Anthropocene and Capitalocene, see Donna J. Haraway, *Staying with the Trouble: Making Kin in the Chthulucene* (Duke University Press, 2016). Haraway describes ongoingness as nurturing, inventing, discovering, or cobbling together ways for living and dying well with each other in a time when inhabitability is threatened. Haraway, *Staying with the Trouble*, 132.

2. "I'm a Millennial 'None,' but I Still Want Easter (Opinion) | CNN," accessed June 13, 2024, https://www.cnn.com/2017/04/14/opinions/nonreligious-millennials-celebrating-holidays-filipovic/index.html.

3. On individualism and the search for community, see Robert N. Bellah et al., *Habits of the Heart, With a New Preface: Individualism and Commitment in American Life* (University of California Press, 2007). Here are the relevant generation groups to the present study according to their birth years as determined by the Pew Research Center: Baby Boomers (1946–1964); Generation X (1965–1980); Millennials (1981–1996); and Generation Z (1997–2012). For further discussion on the generation groups, see Corey Seemiller and Meghan Grace, *Generation Z* (Routledge, 2018); James Emery White, *Meet Generation Z: Understanding and Reaching the New Post-Christian World* (Baker Books, 2017); Jeffrey Jensen Arnett, *Emerging Adulthood: The Winding Road from the Late Teens Through the Twenties* (Oxford University Press, 2023); Christian Smith and Patricia Snell, *Souls in Transition: The Religious and Spiritual Lives of Emerging Adults* (Oxford University Press, 2009); and National Study of Youth and Religion, https://youthandreligion.nd.edu/.

4. Charles Taylor's work on secularization is relevant here, especially concepts such as the immanent frame and cross-pressures. See Taylor, *A Secular Age* (Harvard University Press, 2018).

5. For further discussion on the "nones" and the changing religious demographics in the US, see the following: Linda Woodhead, "The Rise of 'No Religion': Towards an Explanation," *Sociology of Religion* 78 (January 1, 2017): 247–62, and Ryan P. Burge, *The Nones: Where They Came From, Who They Are, and Where They Are Going* (Fortress Press, 2023). For the latest report from the Pew Center on the "nones," see Gregory A. Smith and Patricia Tevington, Justin Nortey, Asta Kallo, "Religious 'Nones' in America: Who They Are and What They Believe," Pew Research Center (blog), January 24, 2024, https://www.pewresearch.org/religion/2024/01/24/religious-nones-in-america-who-they-are-and-what-they-believe/.

6. Gregory A. Smith, "About Three-in-Ten U.S. Adults Are Now Religiously Unaffiliated," Pew Research Center (blog), December 14, 2021, https://www.pewresearch.org/religion/2021/12/14/about-three-in-ten-u-s-adults-are-now-religiously-unaffiliated/. A recent PRRI report states that about one-third of Generation Z identified themselves as religious unaffiliated. "A Political and Cultural Glimpse into

America's Future: Generation Z's Views on Generational Change and the Challenges and Opportunities Ahead | PRRI," PRRI | At the Intersection of Religion, Values, and Public Life. (blog), January 22, 2024, https://www.prri.org/research/generation-zs-views-on-generational-change-and-the-challenges-and-opportunities-ahead-a-political-and-cultural-glimpse-into-americas-future/.

7. David Kinnaman and Gabe Lyons, *unChristian: What a New Generation Really Thinks about Christianity . . . and Why It Matters* (Baker Books, 2007); David Kinnaman and Aly Hawkins, *You Lost Me: Why Young Christians Are Leaving Church . . . and Rethinking Faith* (Baker Books, 2016).

8. Robert Wuthnow, *After the Baby Boomers: How Twenty- and Thirty-Somethings Are Shaping the Future of American Religion* (Princeton University Press, 2010), 20–50.

9. Robert D. Putnam, *Bowling Alone: The Collapse and Revival of American Community* (Simon & Schuster, 2020).

10. According to Putnam, the multiple causes of decline in social capital are the following: pressures of time and money, mobility and urban sprawl, TV ownership and viewing, and most importantly generational succession due to the decline of highly civic minded WWII generation.

11. Putnam, *Bowling Alone*, 35.

12. Putnam says, "Internally, associations and less formal networks of civic engagement instill in their members habits of cooperation and public spiritedness, as well as the practical skills necessary to partake in public life." Putnam, *Bowling Alone*, 338. In an earlier book, Putnam and his coauthors observe that democracy "is easier in a community that has inherited a substantial stock of social capital in the form of norms of reciprocity and networks of civic engagement." Robert D. Putnam, Robert Leonardi, and Raffaella Y. Nanetti, *Making Democracy Work: Civic Traditions in Modern Italy* (Princeton University Press, 1994), 167. Of related interest is Robert Bellah, *The Good Society* (Knopf, 1991).

13. This argument is well taken in light of the vital contribution of black churches in the Civil Rights Movement and beyond. Putnam, *Bowling Alone*, 66.

14. Putnam observes that in the first two-thirds of the century Americans were more active socially and politically in their communities, such as in "churches and union halls, in bowling alleys and clubrooms, around committee tables and card tables and dinner tables" but participation decreased noticeably in the years following. Putnam, *Bowling Alone*, 183–286, 183. Dated but a relevant work here is Robert Nisbet, *The Quest for Community: A Study in the Ethics of Order and Freedom* (ISI Books, 2010).

15. See Putnam, *Bowling Alone*, chapter 9.

16. Also see Nancy T. Ammerman, "Organized Religion in a Voluntaristic Society," *Sociology of Religion* 58, no. 3 (1997): 203–15. On a different note, it needs to

be mentioned that one of the criticisms against Putnam's work is that it provides inadequate engagement of the broader socioeconomic and political realities that are at work. See Carl Boggs, "Social Capital and Political Fantasy: Robert Putnam's 'Bowling Alone,'" *Theory and Society* 30, no. 2 (2001): 281–97.

17. For further discussion, see Corwin E. Smidt, *Religion as Social Capital: Producing the Common Good* (Baylor University Press, 2003), Heidi Rolland Unruh and Ronald J. Sider, *Saving Souls, Serving Society: Understanding the Faith Factor in Church-Based Social Ministry* (Oxford University Press, 2005), and Baker, C., & Skinner, H., *Faith in Action* (Manchester: William Temple Foundation, 2006). Unruh and Sider observe that participation in local congregation often extends beyond it to the wider community with capacity for relationship building and leadership ultimately leading to greater social capital for flourishing. Unruh and Sider, *Saving Souls, Serving Society*, 219. Putnam defines social capital as "connections among individuals—social networks and the norms of reciprocity and trustworthiness that arise from them" and they have value because they "can affect the productivity of individuals and groups." It is accumulated through the processes of bonding and bridging: the former refers to the social process through which internal cohesion and solidarity are achieved in inwardly focused groups, and the latter entails broader relations beyond the primary group with those who are different from themselves. He writes, "To build bridging social capital requires that we transcend our social and political and professional identities to connect with people unlike ourselves. This is why team sports provides good venues for social-capital creation." Putnam, *Bowling Alone*, 19, 411. And Putnam's own recommendations for promoting more robust networks of social connections, such as smaller schools and community inductive urban designs, are well taken as they are demonstrated in his subsequent work Better Together. Robert D. Putnam, Lewis Feldstein, and Donald J. Cohen, *Better Together: Restoring the American Community* (Simon & Schuster, 2004).

18. Robert Wuthnow, *Sharing the Journey: Support Groups and the Quest for a New Community* (Free Press, 1996).

19. Wuthnow comments, "These are not simply informal gatherings of neighbors and friends, but organized groups: secondary school classes, Bible study groups, Alcoholics Anonymous and other twelve step groups, youth groups and singles groups, book discussion clubs, sports and hobby groups, and political or civic groups." Wuthnow, *Sharing the Journey*, 45.

20. Wuthnow, *Sharing the Journey*, 158.

21. Wuthnow, *Sharing the Journey*, 24.

22. Wuthnow writes, "There is a danger, however, that support groups, by focusing so much on the individual's need for healing, may contribute to a further fragmentation of social life, as the bonds they create are often temporary and tied to specific life events." Wuthnow, *Sharing the Journey*, 73.

23. Wuthnow, *Sharing the Journey*, 179.

24. Robert Wuthnow, *The Restructuring of American Religion* (Princeton University Press, 1990).

25. Wuthnow writes, "a traditional spirituality of inhabiting sacred spaces has given way to a new spirituality of seeking . . ." Robert Wuthnow, *After Heaven: Spirituality in America Since the 1950s* (University of California Press, 2023), 3. He defines spirituality as "the beliefs and activities by which individuals attempt to relate their lives to God or to a divine being or some other conception of a transcendent reality." Wuthnow, *After Heaven*, viii.

26. Wuthnow writes, "These efforts generally do not take the same forms as they had in the past because of the increased diversity, fluidity, interdependence, and specialization of contemporary life." Robert Wuthnow, *Loose Connections: Joining Together in America's Fragmented Communities* (Harvard University Press, 2002), 202. See also Robert Wuthnow, *Creative Spirituality: The Way of the Artist* (University of California Press, 2001).

27. On spiritual practices and tinkering, see Robert Wuthnow, *After the Baby Boomers*, 112–35, and Paul Heelas et al., *The Spiritual Revolution: Why Religion Is Giving Way to Spirituality* (Wiley-Blackwell, 2005). Wuthnow cautions that such spiritualities of seeking direct peak experiences result in "a transient spiritual existence characterized more often by dabbling than by depth." Robert Wuthnow, *After Heaven*, 168.

28. Wuthnow, *Loose Connections*, 208. On experimentation in beloved communities, see Jacob L. Goodson, Brad Elliott Stone, and Philip Rudolph Kuehnert, *Building Beloved Community in a Wounded World* (Cascade Books, 2022), 86–98.

29. Wuthnow, *Loose Connections*, 96–97.

30. For further conversation on religion and evolution, see Robert N. Bellah, *Religion in Human Evolution: From the Paleolithic to the Axial Age* (Belknap Press, 2017).

31. Robert Wuthnow, *Rediscovering the Sacred: Perspectives on Religion in Contemporary Society* (Eerdmans Publishing, 1992), 305.

32. Robert Wuthnow, *Producing the Sacred: An Essay on Public Religion* (University of Illinois Press, 1994), chapter 7.

33. Wuthnow, *The Restructuring of the American Religion*, chapter 8. Also see his discussion about the Civil Rights Movement in Robert Wuthnow, *Faith Communities and the Fight for Racial Justice* (Princeton University Press, 2023). For further discussion on the mystical and political, see David Tracy, *On Naming the Present* (Orbis Books, 1995), 3-24; Johann Baptist Metz and J. Matthew Ashley, *A Passion for God: The Mystical-Political Dimension of Christianity* (Paulist Press, 1997); and John K. Downey, *Love's Strategy: The Political Theology of Johann Baptist Metz* (A&C Black, 1999).

34. See also Robert Wuthnow, *America and the Challenges of Religious Diversity* (Princeton University Press, 2005). Putnam also makes a similar argument in Robert D. Putnam and David E. Campbell, *American Grace: How Religion Divides and Unites Us* (Simon and Schuster, 2012).

35. Robert Wuthnow, *Why Religion Is Good for American Democracy* (Princeton University Press, 2021).

36. For related conversations, see Peter L. Berger, ed., *The Desecularization of the World: Resurgent Religion and World Politics* (Eerdmans Publishing Co., 1999), and Stef Aupers and Dick Houtman, "The Spiritual Turn and the Decline of Tradition: The Spread of Post-Christian Spirituality in 14 Western Countries, 1981–2000," *Journal for the Scientific Study of Religion* 46 (September 1, 2007): 305–20.

37. Robert Wuthnow, *After Heaven: Spirituality in America Since the 1950s* (University of California Press, 2023), 168.

38. Robert Wuthnow, *What Happens When We Practice Religion?: Textures of Devotion in Everyday Life* (Princeton University Press, 2020).

39. Wuthnow, *What Happens When We Practice Religion?*, 129.

40. Donovan O. Schaefer, *Religious Affects: Animality, Evolution, and Power* (Duke University Press, 2015). For a helpful introduction to affect studies, see Melissa Gregg and Gregory J. Seigworth, eds., *The Affect Theory Reader* (Duke University Press Books, 2010), especially chapter 1.

41. Schaefer, *Religious Affects*, 23. From Silvan Tomkin's nonbinary perspective, affect saturates experience, cognition, and behavior at every level. According to Kathleen Stewart, "Ordinary affect is a surging, a rubbing, a connection of some kind that has an impact. It's transpersonal or prepersonal—not about one's feelings becoming another's but bodies literally affecting one another and generating intensities: human bodies, discursive bodies, bodies of thought, bodies of water." Kathleen Stewart, *Ordinary Affects* (Duke University Press Books, 2007), 128.

42. Schaefer, *Religious Affects*, 27–28, 47. For further conversation on affects and political assemblages, see William E. Connolly, *Capitalism and Christianity, American Style* (Duke University Press Books, 2008).

43. Schaefer, *Religious Affects*, 116. On Schaefer's discussion of constitutive relationality, see chapter four.

44. Schaefer, *Religious Affects*, 194. Also, see Bruno Latour, *Reassembling the Social: An Introduction to Actor-Network-Theory* (Oxford University Press, 2007), and Sara Ahmed's discussion on affects as contagious in "Happy Objects" in *The Affect Theory Reader*, 34–39.

45. Schaefer, *Religious Affects*, 106.

46. Schaefer, *Religious Affects*, 104–06 and 186. See Kathleen Stewart, "Afterword: Worlding Refrains," in *The Affect Theory Reader*, 339–53.

47. Schaefer, *Religious Affects*, 118. For further discussion on aesthetics of affects, see Nigel Thrift, "Understanding the Material Practices of Glamour," in *The Affect Theory Reader*, 289–308.

48. The implications of this for consumption-driven global capitalism and its devastation of the earth obviously is a grave concern, a topic for another discussion, but addressed in Patricia Clough, "The Affective Turn," in *The Affect Theory Reader*, 206–25.

49. Putnam, *Bowling Alone*, 93–94.

50. Charles Taylor's work *A Secular Age* is helpful here. It is sufficient here to point out that for Taylor the critical issue in secularization is not primarily about lack of belief in God but rather the deeper issue of the conditions of belief that have changed so that there is "a move from a society where belief in God is unchallenged and indeed, unproblematic, to one in which it is understood to be one option among others, and frequently not the easiest to embrace." Charles Taylor, *A Secular Age*, 3. However, what is of interest to the present study is not only the conditions of belief but also, perhaps more importantly, the conditions of religious affects.

51. Schaefer, *Religious Affects*, 10 and 28. Schaefer's discussion about linguistic fallacy is present throughout the book as it is one of his main currents of thought. For examples, see Schaefer, *Religious Affects*, 22–23, 50–57, 106–18, 180, and 201.

52. Schaefer, Religious Affects, 3, 51, and 204–09. See also chapter 1. Later in the book, Schaefer writes, "This sense of religion is best understood not as faith or belief . . . but as an affective, radically embodied encounter with the world, our histories, our relationships, and the semistable forms of our bodies." Schaefer, *Religious Affects*, 192.

53. Manuel A. Vasquez, *More Than Belief: A Materialist Theory of Religion* (Oxford University Press, 2010).

54. Schaefer, *Religious Affects*, 22. On the implications of the affective turn, see Steven Brown and Ian Tucker, "Eff the Ineffable," in *The Affect Theory Reader*, 229–49.

55. Schaefer, *Religious Affects*, 8–11, 23, 30, and 59.

56. Schaefer, *Religious Affects*, 190. Commenting on religious beliefs, Schaefer says that they are themselves affectively driven and have their roots in landscapes of feeling. He writes, "Discourse is just one of many intransigent shapes rated into the worldwide creature of animal religion." Schaefer, *Religious Affects*, 209.

57. On the significance of incarnation, see Catherine Keller, *No Matter What: Crisis and the Spirit of Planetary Possibility* (Fordham University Press, 2024).

58. Schaefer, *Religious Affects*, 112. Schaefer cites Barbara King who says, "while something can be learned from [cognitive accounts of religion], they are sterile to the degree that they fail to grasp the significance of what matters most: people deeply and emotionally engaged with others of their kind, and eventually with the sacred." Schaefer, *Religious Affects*, 194.

59. Related to the topic of experimentation, John Wesley can be considered a bricoleur par excellence in divinity, both in theology and practice of ministry. For instance, this is demonstrated in his ecumenism that incorporated in creative ways the major contributions of Puritanism, Anglicanism, Moravian Lutheran Pietism, Roman Catholicism, and Eastern Orthodoxy. See Theodore Runyon, *The New Creation: John Wesley's Theology Today* (Abingdon Press, 1998), 207–15.

60. Schaefer, *Religious Affects*, 29 and 65–66.

61. Schaefer, *Religious Affects*, 192.

62. Schaefer, *Religious Affects*, 118.

63. Schaefer, *Religious Affects*, 67. Also relevant here is LaMothe's point that religion "is not what a person believes, nor what he has or does per se. Religion rather exists in the moment of its performances as kind of doing that embodies a person in relation to a sense of the world." Kimerer LaMothe, *Between Dancing and Writing: The Practice of Religious Studies* (Fordham University Press, 2004), 248. Quoted in Schaefer, Religious Affects, 191–92.

64. For instance, Schaefer thinks religious conversion is as much about ongoing confirmation and attunement of adherents in their commitments as it is about spreading the Good News to others because of the deep, visceral, and recalcitrant textures in our embodied animality. Schaefer, *Religious Affects*, 111. On affects as rogue intensities, see Kathleen Stewart, Ordinary Affects, 44.

65. Schaefer, *Religious Affects*, 102, 187. On intra-action, see Karen Barad, *Meeting the Universe Halfway* (Duke University Press, 2007).

66. Schaefer quotes Sara Ahmed, "Transmission of affect involves conversion points that throw curves into the straight line of sight between bodies." Schaefer, *Religious Affects*, 172. On the notion of religion as play, see Schaefer, Religious Affects, 186–205. Derrida defines destinerrance as loss of control, deviation or skidding, due to unforeseen accidents befalling an essence in the play of différance and contingence of inter-dynamic traces Schaefer, *Religious Affects*, 150–60. See also Bellah, R*eligion in Human Evolution*, chapter 1.

67. Schaefer, *Religious Affects*, 155.

68. Schaefer, *Religious Affects*, 210.

69. As cited in Schaefer, *Religious Affects*, 34.

70. Schaefer, *Religious Affects*, 116.

71. For further discussion, see Lauren Berlant, "Cruel Optimism," in *The Affect Theory Reader*, 93–116.

72. Schaefer, *Religious Affects*, 21, 175–77.

73. Schaefer, *Religious Affects*, 7, 21–23, 27–28, 53–59, 86, 124–28, and 144. Schaefer maintains the link between language and power, and agrees with Lauren Berlant who says, "affect theory is another phase in the history of ideology theory." Schaefer, *Religious Affects*, 21. He also writes, "Reframing religion as animal offers new techniques to explore religion's imbrication with the flows of power running between bodies and worlds." Schaefer, *Religious Affects*, 35. And also see Kathleen Stewart, *Ordinary Affects*, 84. For further discussion on the relation between religion and politics, see William E. Connolly, *Why I Am Not a Secularist* (University of Minnesota Press, 2000).

74. Schaefer, *Religious Affects*, 176.

75. Schaefer, *Religious Affects*, 21, 78, and 129–46.

76. Carl Sagan, *Pale Blue Dot: A Vision of the Human Future in Space* (Random House, 2011), 6–7.

77. Randy L. Maddox, *Responsible Grace: John Wesley's Practical Theology* (Kingswood Books, 1994).

78. James M. Gustafson, *Ethics from a Theocentric Perspective, Volume 1: Theology and Ethics* (University of Chicago Press, 1981), 6.

79. Gustafson, *Ethics from a Theocentric Perspective*, chapters 1 and 2.

Bibliography

Ammerman, Nancy T. "Organized Religion in a Voluntaristic Society," *Sociology of Religion* 58, no. 3 (1997): 203–15.

Arnett, Jeffrey Jensen. *Emerging Adulthood: The Winding Road from the Late Teens Through the Twenties.* Oxford University Press, 2023.

Aupers, Stef and Dick Houtman, "The Spiritual Turn and the Decline of Tradition: The Spread of Post-Christian Spirituality in 14 Western Countries, 1981–2000," *Journal for the Scientific Study of Religion* 46 (September 1, 2007).

Baker, Chris, and Hannah Skinner. *Faith in Action* (Manchester: William Temple Foundation, 2006)

Bellah, Robert N. et al. *Habits of the Heart, With a New Preface: Individualism and Commitment in American Life.* University of California Press, 2007.

———, *Religion in Human Evolution: From the Paleolithic to the Axial Age.* Belknap Press, 2017.

Berger, Peter L., ed. *The Desecularization of the World: Resurgent Religion and World Politics.* Eerdmans Publishing, 1999.

Boggs,Carl. "Social Capital and Political Fantasy: Robert Putnam's '*Bowling Alone*,'" *Theory and Society* 30, no. 2 (2001): 281–97.

Burge, Ryan P. *The Nones: Where They Came From, Who They Are, and Where They Are Going.* Fortress Press, 2023.

Connolly. William E. *Why I Am Not a Secularist.* University of Minnesota Press, 2000.

Downey, John K. *Love's Strategy: The Political Theology of Johann Baptist Metz.* A&C Black, 1999.

Filipovic, Jill. "I'm a Millennial 'None,' but I Still Want Easter (Opinion) | CNN," accessed June 13, 2024, https://www.cnn.com/2017/04/14/opinions/nonreligious-millennials-celebrating-holidays-filipovic/index.html.

Goodson, Jacob L., Brad Elliott Stone, and Philip Rudolph Kuehnert. *Building Beloved Community in a Wounded World.* Cascade Books, 2022.

Gregg, Melissa and Gregory J. Seigworth, eds. *The Affect Theory Reader.* Duke University Press Books, 2010.

Gustafson, James M. *Ethics from a Theocentric Perspective, Volume 1: Theology and Ethics.* University of Chicago Press, 1981.

Haraway, Donna J. *Staying with the Trouble: Making Kin in the Chthulucene.* Duke University Press, 2016.

Heelas, Paul, Linda Woodhead, with Benjamin Seel, Bronislaw Szerszybski, and Karin Tusting. *The Spiritual Revolution: Why Religion Is Giving Way to Spirituality.* Wiley-Blackwell, 2005.

Keller, Catherine. *No Matter What: Crisis and the Spirit of Planetary Possibility.* Fordham University Press, 2024.

Kinnaman, David and Aly Hawkins. *You Lost Me: Why Young Christians Are Leaving Church . . . and Rethinking Faith.* Baker Books, 2016.

Kinnaman, David and Gabe Lyons, *unChristian: What a New Generation Really Thinks about Christianity . . . and Why It Matters.* Baker Books, 2007.

Latour, Bruno. *Reassembling the Social: An Introduction to Actor-Network-Theory.* Oxford University Press, 2007.

Maddox, Randy L. *Responsible Grace: John Wesley's Practical Theology.* Kingswood Books, 1994.

Metz, Johann Baptist and J. Matthew Ashley. *A Passion for God: The Mystical-Political Dimension of Christianity.* Paulist Press, 1997.

National Study of Youth and Religion, https://youthandreligion.nd.edu/.

Nisbet, Robert. *The Quest for Community: A Study in the Ethics of Order and Freedom.* ISI Books, 2010.

Putnam, Robert D. *Bowling Alone: The Collapse and Revival of American Community.* Simon & Schuster, 2020.

Putnam, Robert D., Lewis Feldstein, and Donald J. Cohen. *Better Together: Restoring the American Community.* Simon & Schuster, 2004.

Runyon, Theodore, *The New Creation: John Wesley's Theology Today.* Abingdon Press, 1998.

Sagan, Carl. *Pale Blue Dot: A Vision of the Human Future in Space.* Random House, 2011.

Seemiller, Corey and Meghan Grace. *Generation Z.* Routledge, 2018.

Schaefer, Donovan O. *Religious Affects: Animality, Evolution, and Power.* Duke University Press, 2015.

Smith, Christian and Patricia Snell. *Souls in Transition: The Religious and Spiritual Lives of Emerging Adults.* Oxford University Press, 2009.

Smidt, Corwin E. *Religion as Social Capital: Producing the Common Good,* Baylor University Press, 2003.

Smith, Gregory A. "About Three-in-Ten U.S. Adults Are Now Religiously Unaffiliated," *Pew Research Center* (blog), December 14, 2021.

Smith, Gregory A. and Patricia Tevington, Justin Nortey, Asta Kallo. "Religious 'Nones' in America: Who They Are and What They Believe," *Pew Research Center* (blog), January 24, 2024, https://www.pewresearch.org/religion/2024/01/24/religious-nones-in-america-who-they-are-and-what-they-believe/.

Stewart, Kathleen. *Ordinary Affects.* Duke University Press Books, 2007.

Taylor, Charles. *A Secular Age.* Harvard University Press, 2018.

Tracy, David. *On Naming the Present.* Orbis Books, 1995.

White, James Emery. *Meet Generation Z: Understanding and Reaching the New Post-Christian World.* Baker Books, 2017.

Woodhead, Linda. "The Rise of 'No Religion': Towards an Explanation," *Sociology of Religion* 78 (January 1, 2017): 247–62.

Wuthnow, Robert. *After the Baby Boomers: How Twenty- and Thirty-Somethings Are Shaping the Future of American Religion.* Princeton University Press, 2010.

———. *After Heaven: Spirituality in America Since the 1950s.* University of California Press, 2023.

———. *America and the Challenges of Religious Diversity.* Princeton University Press, 2005.

———. *Creative Spirituality: The Way of the Artist.* University of California Press, 2001.

———, *Faith Communities and the Fight for Racial Justice.* Princeton University Press, 2023.

———. *Loose Connections: Joining Together in America's Fragmented Communities,* Cambridge, Mass: Harvard University Press, 2002.

———, *Producing the Sacred: An Essay on Public Religion.* University of Illinois Press, 1994

———. *Rediscovering the Sacred: Perspectives on Religion in Contemporary Society.* Eerdmans Publishing, 1992

———. *The Restructuring of American Religion.* Princeton University Press, 1990.

———. *Sharing the Journey: Support Groups and the Quest for a New Community.* Free Press, 1996.

———. *What Happens When We Practice Religion?: Textures of Devotion in Everyday Life.* Princeton University Press, 2020.

———. *Why Religion Is Good for American Democracy.* Princeton University Press, 2021.

Unruh, Heidi Rolland and Ronald J. Sider. *Saving Souls, Serving Society: Understanding the Faith Factor in Church-Based Social Ministry.* Oxford University Press, 2005.

Vasquez, Manuel A. *More Than Belief: A Materialist Theory of Religion.* Oxford University Press, 2010.

10. METHODIST EDUCATION AS AN ALTERNATIVE FOR THE FUTURE

Claudia Lombardo

> *We forgot that the world did not belong to us. We forgot that it had to be protected, that it was necessary to stop and take time. But the problem was not speed, not even acceleration. It was haste. We forgot that to inhabit the world one must not be in a hurry, that one must know how to delay in the present, that one must link up with those who have gone before us, that one must learn to live in provisionality, uprootedness and uncertainty. We forget that, without this delay, without this attention, the world becomes a desert.*
>
> —Joan-Carles Mèlich. The Fragility of the World. 2021. Tusquets

> *The future is a complex construction. . . . The present, that strange country that is also past and future at the same time.*
>
> —Jorge Carrión. Solaris, sound essays to be more contemporary. Podcast. Ch. 1 Accelerated time

Introduction

I am grateful for the invitation to participate in this Fifteenth Oxford Institute. This is the first time I am participating in this important event. I received the invitation to participate with enthusiasm and joy. It is a great challenge: what concepts to share as an educator at a table of political economy in an institute of Methodist theological studies.

When we talk about economics we talk about education; when we talk about politics we talk about education. Economics and politics have a full impact on education, and education also has an impact on them. Political economy has a strong impact on educational projects and the programmatic definitions of institutions.

Methodism has had a long and strong educational tradition since its beginnings with the establishment of Kingswood School founded by John Wesley on 24 June 1748. Methodist education has developed significantly and today has more than 1000 institutions in 80 countries. With teaching proposals that have a strong emphasis on the integral formation of people, attending to academic, social, and spiritual aspects, they consider that education is key to promoting peace, development, and the well-being of society.

I bring here some ideas that may help us think about this current context, and review, in this global economic panorama, what we Methodists have to say, in addition to our churches, with so many educational institutions through which many lives pass and are formed—institutions in which we have the enormous opportunity to witness that "the world is our parish and that we have good news of salvation to give."

When we look at our educational spaces and projects, it is necessary to ask ourselves: What educational institutions do we need in this contemporary world? How do we need to think about our institutions (churches and schools) so that they can be spaces of transformation for this prevailing economic system? Do we offer tools from our educational or ecclesial communities to face these times of uncertainty? Do we generate alternatives that are delayed in the present to create better and more hopeful futures?

I would then like to present some axes on which to reflect:

- the new scenarios that are being defined and in which the ways of thinking, knowing, socializing, living, and working are being reconfigured;
- the new subjectivities that are being defined in order to cross the provisionality that characterizes these scenarios; and

- the good news as an alternative for the future that allows us to build hope in the possibility of transforming the world.

The New Scenarios

I start from an initial idea: to inhabit the world we need to understand it.

We are living in a time of dizzying and constant change brought about by technological developments that modify our lives. Continuous and portable connectivity is a phenomenon that has radically transformed the way we interact with the world and with each other. Thanks to the explosion of new media and formats, such as smartphones, tablets, and IoT (Internet of Things) devices, we are constantly connected to a global network of information and communication. In this context, the portability of devices plays a crucial role. The ability to carry with us powerful communication and information access tools allows us to be present and active in multiple spheres of our lives—whether personal, professional, or social—regardless of our physical location, enabling us to access data, news, entertainment, and social networks anytime, anywhere. The dissolution of time and space as we conceived it has become a palpable reality. These developments not only transform the way we communicate but also redefine our perceptions of time and space, erasing traditional barriers and opening up a range of possibilities for human connection and social interaction.

Constant interaction through mobile devices and online platforms allows people to be present even in their physical absence, creating a sense of proximity regardless of distance. This ability to be "present in absence" is enhanced by the explosion of these new media and formats, such as virtual reality, augmented reality, and social networks, which offer immersive and personalised experiences.

Another characteristic of this era is cultural convergence, which refers precisely to the intersection and fusion of old and new media. This media convergence leads to the flow of content across multiple media platforms where the barriers between producers and consumers of content are blurred. In this context, consumers are not only passively receiving information but also actively participating in the creation and distribution of content, a participatory culture that implies a change in people's behavior. This phenomenon is driven by collective intelligence—that is, the conception that knowledge is shared and built collectively, transforming the way we interact with the media, with information, with each other, and in work and production environments. Henry Jenkins points out that this cultural convergence occurs not only in the media, in the circulation of information, and in exchanges but also in our brains. And this then also impacts the way we engage with knowledge.[1]

Cultural convergence has a complex and strong impact on contemporary society as it brings a number of benefits. The participatory culture makes consumers become producers of content, which in turn fosters creativity and innovation, as well as the democratization of voices and expressions. The convergence of media diversity, which, as we said, occurs in the integration of different platforms and formats, enriches the user experience by allowing broader and more varied access to information, knowledge, and entertainment. Collective intelligence, which through collaboration and knowledge-sharing, enhances the creation of better-quality content and more efficient problem-solving. Global access as cultural convergence facilitates the spread of ideas and cultures, promoting greater understanding and tolerance between different communities.

But it also presents us with challenges: information overload, where the abundance of content can be overwhelming, making it difficult for those of us who use it to discern relevant and truthful information. Unequal access, as not everyone has the same access to the technologies needed to participate fully, which can widen the digital divide and complicate social and labor market insertion. Ethical and legal questions about the use and abuse of information, personal data, and images due to the ease of sharing and modifying content. Loss of privacy and security as participation in multiple platforms can expose us to risks that are difficult to notice and manage.

Today's world is empty of things and filled with disturbing information, like disembodied voices, Byung-Chul Han tells us in his book *Non-*

Things, because digitalization dematerialises and disembodies the world. We move from thing to non-thing. We no longer inhabit the earth and the sky, but we inhabit Google Earth and the cloud. Nothing is solid and tangible; we consume and produce more information than things. The Industrial Revolution reinforced and expanded the sphere of things and the need to possess them, while digitalization subordinates things to information. We do not handle the things in front of us but communicate and interact with infomata, which serve as actors. This information sometimes falsifies events, it feeds on the surprise stimulus, but this stimulus does not last long, new stimuli are needed and this makes us get used to perceiving reality as a source of stimuli and we do not see, recognize or perceive those silent, discreet, habitual things, which do not stimulate us, but anchor our being.[2]

Another aspect to consider is that information is not as easy to possess as things. This may give the impression that it belongs to everyone, that we all have the possibility to possess it, but the world of information is governed by access. Links to things or places are replaced by temporary access to networks and platforms. As Han states, "Information capitalism is an intensified form of capitalism. Unlike industrial capitalism, it also turns the immaterial into a commodity. Life itself takes on the form of a commodity. Many human relationships are commercialized. Social media exploit communication to the full."[3]

The digital revolution we are going through is a process of profound and accelerating transformation. It has radically changed the way we live, communicate, and work. It has had a profound and multifaceted impact on the world of work, transforming both the nature of jobs and the way they are performed. Real structural change has taken place.

Some of the effects of digitalization on the workplace are that it has enabled the automation of repetitive and administrative tasks, which increases efficiency and reduces operating costs, in turn freeing up time and opening up the possibility of concentrating on more strategic and creative tasks. New digital skills are in demand, competencies in areas such as programming, data analysis, cybersecurity, and the use of increasingly valued tools in which we will all need to be trained. It facilitates remote and flexible working as technology makes it possible to work from anywhere with an internet connection, which changes the work dynamic and modifies the work-life balance. And it leads to the offshoring of jobs, allowing companies to hire talent from anywhere in the world. This can reduce costs and access a greater diversity of skills, but it can also generate global competition and put pressure on certain salaries or make others more precarious, generating greater possibilities of exclusion. Not everyone has the same access to technology and digital skills, which can increase inequality in the labor market.

Another consequence is that a certain paranoia about productivity has developed, and this leads to a sense of burnout in many workers. It not only affects processes but also generates a transformation of organizational culture. Companies must adapt to a more agile and collaborative environment, promoting a culture of innovation and continuous learning, training, and support to improve interpersonal skills. These changes reflect both the opportunities and challenges that the digital revolution brings to the world of work. Adapting to these changes is essential if we are not to remain on the margins of society and the workplace.

These labor changes and the development of the global economy do not expand without consequences, and these consequences include growing inequality, unemployment, displacement of populations, and the destruction of the environment.

The advanced, global capitalism of this era confronts us with new logics of exclusion, where individuals, companies, and peoples are expelled both from places and from the socioeconomic order pre-established by an increasingly extreme system of accumulation. Saskia Sassen calls these devastating effects "expulsions," and they affect people, companies, and communities all over the world. For Sassen, these expulsions are not spontaneous but require the creation of "predatory formations." These formations are a combination of complex public policies and technological, financial, and market developments that affect not only the wealthiest individuals but also large corporations and powerful governments. There are different types of expulsions that are pushing many people out of the system, out of institutions, out of social exchanges, or out of their land.

This concept helps us understand how today's global capitalism is reshaping the economy and society, and how these transformations affect people and the planet.[4]

Faced with this scenario, I ask again: How do we bring the good news? What tools do we have to design other futures? How do we recover, from our educational and ecclesial spaces, the people expelled by the system? How do we build conscious and disruptive leaderships that slow down in the present to create better futures? How do we build a new economic policy that needs time to develop in these times of immediacy of answers?

New Subjectivities

New subjectivities emerge in the new scenarios offered by the digital era that we have just described. Subjectivities are ways of being and being in the world, and these ways are elastic and change under the protection of diverse cultural traditions. They are constructed in the everyday practices of each culture. It is also in these traditions that bodies are sculpted: they are disciplined or liberated. Subjectivity is not rigid but is modulated by interaction with others and with the world. We must bear in mind that the influence of culture on what we are and what we do is fundamental. If cultural conditions change, so does subjectivity, and in these scenarios the new practices of displaying intimacy are decisive. In educational exchanges we must bear this in mind, especially if we are thinking of exchanges or encounters in which we can transmit the Gospel message.

In a highly mediatized society, there is an incitement to visibility. There is a collapse of internalized subjectivity (characteristic of another era, elaborated in classrooms, homes, factories), and new spaces emerge in which to build one's own subjectivity based on new ways of relating to others and acting in the world. Social media exposure has become an everyday practice, where people share aspects of their lives, thoughts, and emotions with a global audience. Social media filters, which function as make-up 2.0, allow us to modify and embellish images and videos, creating idealized versions in which we edit reality and edit ourselves. The mirror has been transformed into a screen.[5] These filters not only alter physical appearance but also influence the perception of identity and self-esteem, generating a new form of media subjectivity.

We speak, then, of intimacy as spectacle. Paula Sibilia analyses the exteriorization of the personality. We are users and consumers of media that stimulate performative ways of being and being in the world: acting before the gaze of others. This performativity adds a layer of theatricality and creativity to everyday communication, transforming the way we interact and relate to each other socially and economically. As we have already noted, we interact, we include, we include ourselves or we expel.

These performative modes of communication involve the creation of content, users become performers, using various tools and livestreams to express their ideas and connect with their audience. This exhibition not only redefines how we perceive ourselves but also how we present ourselves to others. A subjectivity is built into this interactive exhibition: alterdirected personalities no longer introdirected, no longer directed by one's own gaze but rather oriented to the gaze of others.[6]

In this subjectivity we move from the desire to possess things to the desire to experiment. We are immersed in the society of experimentation. The image, the brand is worth more than the use value of things, because we perceive from them above all the information they contain. We buy and consume emotions. Today, identity is essentially determined by information. We produce ourselves in social media. We act ourselves out, and we represent our identity. In a society as spectacularized as ours, the boundaries between the real and the fictional are blurred.[7]

Digital communication changes human relationships: we are all on social networks, but we are not always connected to each other. Digital communication changes the personal encounter. Moreover, if we consider what Alessandro Baricco warns us, we all reside in two worlds: the physical and the virtual, the analog and the digital, the world and the ultra-world. The habitat of the hyper digital individual is a reality system with a double driving force, in which the differentiation between the real world and the virtual world becomes a secondary frontier, because one and the other merge into a single movement that together generates reality.

The concept of "double driving force" refers to the coexistence and fusion of the two worlds: the analog and the digital, which coexist, integrate, and enhance each other. The analog world, the physical and tangible reality in which we live, has its own rules and limitations. It is characterized by direct interaction and traditional sensory experiences. Whereas the digital world is the virtual realm, in which, as we have already said, information and communication flow instantaneously and globally, offering new possibilities for interaction and experience, overcoming the limitations of the physical world.

The dual driving force refers to how these two worlds combine to generate an augmented and enriched reality. Digital technology not only complements the analog world but also transforms it, creating new ways of living, working, and relating. It is important to understand and harness the synergy between the analog and digital worlds in order to navigate and thrive in the contemporary era.

Baricco points out that this has produced a paradigm shift, a real mental revolution, because beyond the new tools and new ways of life, the way human beings think has been transformed, which generates a new idea of humanity. It is not changing something; it is simply changing everything. For Baricco, there has not been a mental revolution as a consequence of technology, but quite the opposite. First came the mental revolution and then the technological one. That is why he points out that we must stop trying to understand whether the use of the smartphone disconnects us from reality and we must try to understand what kind of connection with reality we are looking for when we create it, when we create these devices and the constant connection. Because the new individual is not the one produced by the smartphone but the one who invented it, who needed it and built it.[8]

We are subjects of a world that is no longer what it was. What we did before is not enough. We are subjects redefining our subjectivity. It is necessary to recover the meaning of words in these times of scarcity of words and anxiety for immediate response, in a society with transmedia narratives for some and linear and impoverished narratives for others.

Faced with these subjectivities, I ask myself: How do we give the good news? How do we establish spaces for dialogue in times when words are scarce? How do we generate educational and ecclesiastical projects that take time if cultural changes do not wait for us? How do we recover the value of the transcendental in life? How do we generate spaces for dialogue and slowed-down exchanges for quality encounters with people and the relationship with our world?

The Good News as an Alternative for the Future

The new scenarios and the subjectivities that develop in them are the starting point for educational projects that have to be revised in order to offer meaningful alternatives.

The world has changed so much that we must reinvent everything: a way of living together, the institutions we know, the way of being, the way of knowing.[9] We must also reinvent being a church today, to respond to and contain in these complex scenarios the new subjectivities that are taking shape and that we must shelter in order to build a better world and seek to transform the world toward other possible futures.

The future is a complex construct in which many of the ideas of human societies are structured. It is shaped by a web of interconnected factors that require deep understanding and careful management to maximize the benefits and minimize the risks, and in which the interaction of humans with each other and with technology can generate new forms of creativity and knowledge. The real challenge lies not in the use of technologies but in how people make decisions and manage those changes.

In this context, for many people the word *future* has lost its meaning. Words have lost their validity. Words, which should shape reality, which should help interpret the world, no longer designate anything.

We need more words that serve as tools that allow us to read our own time in such a way that we can correlate it with what was and with what is to come. We need tools that help us to live, to live through existence, to read the time in which we live in order to be able to rewrite it.

That is what education is: it is offering words that allow us to read and write the world. Educating to open up spaces that help us build hopeful outlooks. Educational institutions, and above all Methodist institutions, have the challenge of offering paths that our students have not yet traveled and that they may not even know exist.

We need to slow down in the present so that we can live in provisionality and uncertainty. We must overcome the accelerated and algorithmic times of this age, bringing from Methodism the good news that the Gospel offers us. To live is always to embark on a somewhat uncertain adventure in which we are learning and living in a state of fragility and vulnerability that is deepened at this time.

We should give students words and resources that allow them to construct a grammar that helps them inhabit the world in which we live. A grammar that allows us to interpret the world and generate options so that we can be builders of new worlds in which we can live in a fairer way, more careful with creation, in which we are careful not to generate expulsions.

The question we must ask ourselves then is whether we are doing so, whether we are educating our children and young people to interpret this world and imagine other possible worlds. Ate we educating them? Are we giving them the good news so that they can lead happy and dignified lives? Or is there a possibility that we are educating them against their own survival?

We can draw a parallel with our Methodist churches: are we recovering, are we giving the members of our community the words that help them to understand today's world, are we illuminating this understanding that we need, are we opening horizons or the opposite?

To ask ourselves how we want to educate is to ask ourselves how we want to live. Education is always framed in a purpose. When we are clear about where we want to go and what we want to achieve, we can make significant decisions about processes, contents, and proposals. Teachers always have to make decisions on small details or large projects, which implies taking sides, establishing positions, and that entails a risk. Education is always a political task; it is an ethical and political practice.

Education is not neutral. Institutional projects are never neutral; they always reflect an ethical and political position, which is why they cannot be reduced to a technical question and why it is especially necessary to define positions and commitments. The basis of pedagogical action is ideological and political, not technical, and this is related to the concrete way in which intentions are put into practice. One can speak of the complementarity of pedagogical and political projects in a broad sense.[10]

We do not need an objective education, adaptable to the changing demands of society. Rather we need an education that is at the service of society and that helps young people to read their world and to resist when necessary, to learn together while being aware that understanding the world does not mean adapting to it but precisely acting on it to transform it, to discuss together what needs to be changed.

We need to build better strategies and offer spaces of deceleration where there is time for reflection to think about how to build a better world. Recognize the strength of cultural and economic objects to look at them critically, it is not about repeating dogmas or thoughts in a linear way, but we need to understand the relevance of current debates, include them in our dialogues and exchanges to think differently, we cannot change things if we always do and repeat the same thing.

We have to create conditions in our schools and churches that allow us to live in the present because this is the age of the future. We must imagine other possible futures based on the idea that this future is not predetermined but that we must design it ourselves now, because the future is in our hands, in our classrooms, in our churches.

We have the choice to withdraw or to expand into more open spaces that do not exclude. Education is fundamental to activate solidarity and confront all individualisms because we are not condemned to sociological or economic fatalism. An education that proposes a transformative perspective must promote equality with respect for diversity in order to overcome educational and socioeconomic inequality and naturalized expulsions. It must start from the valuation of life experience and insert itself as much as possible in a social perspective and in future needs.

Educating today means questioning the notion of inexorable destiny. More than half of all children are marked by the prophecy of failure. To educate today is to interrupt this prophecy of failure, which is embodied above all in the popular sectors. These prophecies are made by economic theories, political theories, and sometimes, unfortunately, educational theories. We are here proposing that this prophecy should not be fulfilled.

This implies standing up to the inexorable in the search for a possible and better future for all. Human beings are marked by their circumstances, but at the same time we are makers of circumstances and these are the result of the work of people. Designing horizons of transformation with our students, in our communities of faith, so that they rebuild and in turn rebuild themselves.

The Methodist Church must present itself as an alternative to the loss of hope. There is no possibility of building a better future if we do not feel the desire and do not see a real possibility of social, cultural, and economic change. We cannot offer a liberating education, a liberating Gospel message, if we do not think that there is something from which we must free ourselves. We cannot bring about change if we are not aware that there is something that in the midst of all that is changing must be recovered as an anchor of hope. To seek the establishment of a more just and equitable society, committed to democratic proposals that seek the real inclusion of all people.

We have to work to form leaders with a broad commitment to peace, justice, freedom, solidarity, and inclusion without leaving people on the margins, in such a way that the Christian message that Methodist institutions have for humanity today becomes valid, new, and innovative. We must define positions and commitments, make our principles explicit, and recover our traditions with a view to the future.

Hosting dialogue as a pedagogical meeting that contributes to a critical vision that questions the established discourse and system that naturalizes inequalities and expulsions, building a critical participation that sees this new scenario as a place for intervention, in order to modify what this context poses.

That is to say, we must engage responsibly and critically with the cultural, social, and economic conditions, but with the reference that is based on the Gospel of the kingdom and the fundamental commitment to transform society in the utopian perspective that the Gospel offers us, establishing alliances to be able to generate these transformations. Educational projects do not bring about the changes that affect social structures on their own; they need to be open to possible commitments, partnerships, and alliances with the sectors that are on the frontiers of change.

The presence of the utopia of the kingdom of God has to act as a driving force for Methodist educational institutions to sustain a responsible dialogue with the world of work and with the managers of cultural developments. In order to build bridges with the excluded, we must leave aside paternalistic positions that nullify the dignity of life and open ourselves to real experiences of citizenship, of mutuality in the construction of democracy.

Introduce the dimension of selfless love into administrative processes, in an authentic spirit of service. Give practical value to the discourse that is supported by effective practices: by the fruits you will know us. Jesus as a social being relates to people by dialoguing with them, challenging them to follow him, inviting them to enter and interact.

Reclaim Wesleyan spirituality by living out the mercy that is expressed in acts of mercy by focusing on a transcendental spirituality. Seek the transformation of society with God's radical justice as its foundation. The school and the church in communication and relationship with the world it serves. Give the good news that expands into the world with possibilities created by the practice of love, justice, and mercy while critically and responsibly articulating the conditions of the context that we seek first the kingdom of God and God's eternal justice. The practice of mercy continues to be sought in order to survive in this competitive market world in the conviction that the seeds of justice of the kingdom can also grow in today's reality.[11]

The teachers' position is not a position of power but rather one of weakness. Their weakness is that what teachers do is risk-taking; they are not sure that what they do will turn out well. The task of the teacher is creative and creating is always a risky enterprise. Education is an encounter between human beings. It is not predictable; it is an event of openness to the unforeseen and even the impossible.[12]

Education as an ethical event and as a spiritual event is at some point an act of faith and therefore of courage. We can build a pedagogy of hope for a better, non-totalitarian world, a poetic and utopian pedagogy. To educate is to create true novelty, and that is risky. Risk has a dimension of search, of adventure, of exploration. It has a profoundly hopeful dimension in the love of God. This is the challenge that we must take up in our institutions in order to build an alternative for the future.

Notes to Chapter 10

1. Henry Jenkins, *Convergence Culture. La Cultura de la Convergencia de los Medios de Comunicación* (Paidós, 2008), 15.

2. Byung-Chul Han, *Non-Things: Bankruptcies of Today's World* (Taurus, 2021), 6–7.

3. Byung-Chul Han, *Non-Things*, 17.

4. Saskia Sassen, *Expulsions, Brutality, and Complexity in the Global Economy* (Katz Editores, 2015), 20–25.

5. Carrlón, Jorge, *Solaris*, "Chapter One: Accelerated Time," June 24, 2020, Spotify.

6. Paula Sibilia, *La Intimidad como Espectáculo* (Fondo de Cultura Económica, 2008), 28.

7. Byung-Chul Han, *Non-Things*, 14–15.

8. Alessandro Barrico, *The Game* (Anagrama, 2019), 29.

9. Michel Serres, *Pulgarcita* (Fondo de Cultura Económica, 2013), 18.

10. Claudia Lombardo, "La Educación Metodista Considerada en su Papel Transformador, Perspectiva Pedagógica" in *Revista de Educación*, 29:16.

11. Cesar. E. E. Barreto, "La Educación Metodista Considerada en su papel transformador, una perspectiva biblica" in *Revista de Educación*, 29 49, 54.

12. Fernando Bárcena and Joan-Carles Mélich, "La Educación como Acontecimiento Ético: Natalidad, narracion y hospitalidad" (Mino y Davila, 2014), 15.

Bibliography

Barricco, Alessandro. *The Game*. Anagrama, 2019.

Bárcena, Fernando and Mélich, Joan-Carles. *La educación como acontecimiento ético. Natalidad, narración y hospitalidad.* Miño y Dávila, 2014.

Barreto Cesar, E. E. "La educación metodista considerada en su papel transformador, una perspectiva bíblica" in *Revista de educación* 29 de COGEIME, Brasil, 2006.

Bates, A.W. (Tony). *Teaching in the digital age. Guidelines for Designing, Teaching and Learning.* Contact North, 2016.

Carrión, Jorge. *Solaris, sound essays to be more contemporary. Chapter 1: Accelerated time.* Spotify, 2020.

Carrión, Jorge and Taller Estampa. *Los campos electromagnéticos: teorías y prácticas de la escritura artificial.* 1st ed. Black Box, 2023.

Crawford, Kate. *Atlas de inteligencia artificial: poder, política y costos planetarios la ed.*- Ciudad Autónoma de Buenos Aires: Fondo de Cultura Económica, 2022.

Han, Byung-Chul. *Non-things. Bankruptcies of today's world.* Taurus, 2021.

Jenkins, Henry. *Convergence culture. La cultura de la convergencia de los medios de comunicación.* Barcelona. Paidós., 2008

Klein, Naomi.*Saying no is not enough: against the politics of shock for the world we want.* Paidós, Spain, 2017.

Lombardo, Claudia. "La educación metodista considerada en su papel transformador, perspectiva pedagógica" in *Revista de educación* n° 29 de COGEIME, Brasil., 2006

Manovich, Lev. *Software takes over.* UOC, Universitat Oberta de Catalunya, 2013.

Sassen, Saskia. *Expulsions. Brutality and complexity in the global economy.* BKatz Editores, 2015.

Serrés, Michel. *Pulgarcita*. Fondo de cultura Económica, 2013.

Sibilia, Paula. *La intimidad como espectáculo*. Fondo de Cultura Económica, 2008.

Further Reading

García Peñalvo, Francisco, Llorens-Largo, Faraón., & Vidal, Javier. The new reality of education in the face of advances in generative artificial intelligence. *RIED-Revista Iberoamericana de Educación a Distancia,* 27(1), 9–39, 2024. https://doi.org/10.5944/ried.27.1.37716.

Ierardo, Esteban. *Screen Society. Black Mirror and Teledependence*. Ediciones Continente, 2018.

Ipar, Ezequil, et al., *Dilemmas of the digital public sphere: discourses of hate and political-ideological articulations in Argentina*. University of Salamanca, 2021.

Maggio, Mariana. *Híbrida: enseñar en la universidad que no vimos venir.* First edition. Ciudad Autónoma de Tilde Editora, 2022. Digital book, EPUB.

Meirieu, Philippe. "The Future of Pedagogy. Teoría de la Educación." *Revista Interuniversitaria*, 34(1), 69-81, 2022. https://doi.org/10.14201/teri.27128.

Mèlich, Joan-Carles. *The wisdom of the uncertain. Reading and the human condition.* Spain, Tusquets, 2019.

Scolari, C., ed. *Ecología de los medios. Environments, evolutions and interpretations.* Gedisa, Barcelona, 2015.

Sigman, Mariano, Bilinkis, Santiago. *Artificial: The New Intelligence and the Contour of the Human*. Debate, 2023.

Sibilia, Paula. *Networks or walls? The school in times of dispersion*. Tinta Fresca, 2012.

INDEX

www.ingramcontent.com/pod-product-compliance
Lightning Source LLC
LaVergne TN
LVHW040403311026
851422LV00037B/431
9781791041915